...work and excellent *Midot* have made you such a pleasure. May Hashem help you continue to be a source of נחת to your family and all of כלל ישראל.

R' Shields

ArtScroll® Series

Rabbi Nosson Scherman / Rabbi Meir Zlotowitz

General Editors

The Chofetz Chaim Heritage Foundation

POSITIVE

Published by

Mesorah Publications, ltd

in conjunction with

THE
CHOFETZ CHAIM
HERITAGE
FOUNDATION

WORD POWER

Building a better world with the words you speak

The Torah's Wisdom on Human Interaction
Arranged for Daily Study

FIRST EDITION
Nine Impressions ... July 2009 — January 2015
Tenth Impression ... January 2018

Published and Distributed by
MESORAH PUBLICATIONS, LTD.
4401 Second Avenue / Brooklyn, N.Y 11232

Distributed in Europe by
LEHMANNS
Unit E, Viking Business Park
Rolling Mill Road
Jarow, Tyne & Wear, NE32 3DP
England

Distributed in Australia and New Zealand
by **GOLDS WORLDS OF JUDAICA**
3-13 William Street
Balaclava, Melbourne 3183
Victoria, Australia

Distributed in Israel by
SIFRIATI / A. GITLER — BOOKS
POB 2351
Bnei Brak 51122

Distributed in South Africa by
KOLLEL BOOKSHOP
Northfield Centre, 17 Northfield Avenue
Glenhazel 2192, Johannesburg, South Africa

ARTSCROLL® SERIES
POSITIVE WORD POWER
© *Copyright 2009, by* MESORAH PUBLICATIONS, Ltd.
4401 Second Avenue / Brooklyn, N.Y. 11232 / (718) 921-9000 / www.artscroll.com

A project of
THE CHOFETZ CHAIM HERITAGE FOUNDATION
361 Spook Rock Road / Suffern, N.Y. 10901 / (845) 352-3505

ISBN 10: 1-4226-0916-2 / ISBN 13: 978-1-4226-0916-3

Typography by CompuScribe at ArtScroll Studios, Ltd.
Printed in the United States of America by Noble Book Press Corp.
Bound by Sefercraft, Quality Bookbinders, Ltd., Brooklyn N.Y. 11232

מכתב עוז
ממרן ראש הישיבה שליט"א

בס"ד

הנה ידוע שבתורתינו הקדושה יש דינים בין אדם למקום וגם מה שבין אדם לחבירו, גם בעשרת הדברות יש גם דינים שלו לקונו וגם מה שאדם יזהר מלעשות רע לבריות.

ואונאת דברים מבואר בבא מציעא נ"ח ע"ב שזה יותר חמור מאונאת ממון. וזה אין חילוק בין איש לאשתו או אשה לבעלה. ובגמ' ב"מ נ"ט שם כתוב שכיון שדמעתה מצוי' אז אונאתה יותר חמור מה שמצערין אותה. וזה כולל בכל הדברים שגורם צער, ובפרט לצער אלמנה או יתומים חמור מאד. ולהיפך חסד אין לשער מה שיכולין לזכות עי"ז, ומבואר ברא"ש בריש מסכת פיאה כי הקב"ה חפץ יותר במצות שיעשה בהם גם רצון הבריות מבמצות שבין אדם לקונו.

ודברים שאנשים מורים היתר לעצמם, מורה או רב חושבים שבשביל לעשות שידי' משמעת מותר לבזות בלי שיעור, ואין הדבר כן רק מה שמוכרח להוכיח אבל לא לבזות, וזה חמור מאד שמבזין ברבים. רבי או כל מחנך צריך להוכיח אבל לא להוסיף דברים הגורם בושה, ובדרך כלל זה מחמת שחושב להגיב על שפוגעין בו, וזה גורם שמשלם לו כפלים וזה ודאי מכלל אונאת דברים לא יצא, ומאד צריך ליזהר בזה.

וגם ההורים אין להם לבייש ילדיהם, וכן הראוני בספר חינוך מצוה של"ח. והנה בכמה מקומות משמע שאע"פ שבדרך כלל עיקר העונש הוא בעוה"ב ובעוה"ז לא נענשים על עבירות כ"כ, אבל על לצער אנשים נענשים גם בעוה"ז.

כל א' ישים לב על כל מה שעושה או מדבר שלא יהי' דבר המצער חבירו. והנה באמת כשנענשים בעולם הבא העונש יותר גרוע, אבל להיות שאנשים מה שלא רואים כעת לא מתפעלים כ"כ, לכן אנו מדברים מה שכל א' מבין יותר.

ועי' בספר החינוך מצוה הנ"ל בלאו של לא תונו איש את עמיתו שמסיים דאע"פ שאין בו מלקות לפי שאין בו מעשה, מ"מ, "כמה מלקיות מבלי רצועה של עגל ביד האדון המצוה על זה."

והנזהר מלפגוע באנשים יחולו על ראשו כל הברכות האמורות בתורה, ויזכה לעונג בזה ובבא.

כ"ו סיון תשס"ט
אהרן יודא לייב שטיינמן

*This letter was written by the Rosh Hayeshivah, shlita
specifically to serve as a haskamah for this book.*

בס"ד

שמואל קמנצקי
Rabbi S. Kamenetsky

Study: 215-473-1212
Home: 215-473-2798

2018 Upland Way
Philadelphia, Pa 19131

בס"ד

כי ידבר שלום אל עמו

בתורה יש איסור אונאה במכירת או קניית חפץ אבל יש איסור
נוסף שלא לצער לחברו אפילו בדברים וכן אסור לומר לחברו
זכור מעשיך הראשונים. ובספר החינוך מוסיף שאף לצער
קטנים יש איסור ובפרט שקטנים אינם בכח למחול על צערם.

במוסד הקדוש ע"ש החפץ חיים מוכנים להוציא לאור ספר
בענין אונאת דברים וכדרכם בקודש למען להטיב הנהגות בין
אדם לחברו שלא מוגבל באיסורי לשון הרע ורכילות אלא
כל ענייני בין אדם לחברו ליזהר שלא להונות ולצער איש אל
רעהו.

תקותי שיתחזק על ידם כל דרכי אדם לחברו לא רק בלשה"ר
אלא כל מהלכי בין אדם לאדם ובזכות זה נזכה לגאולה שלמה
בקרוב.

לע"נ

ר׳ דניאל רובינשטיין ז"ל
ב"ר מרדכי ומרת רבקה ע"ה

דרכו אמונה שלום ואצילות
נדיב לב רודף צדקה וחסד
ישר דרך קובע עתים לתורה
אהוב לבריות נחמד וצנוע
למשפחתו נקשר בלב ונפש

נלב"ע ביום י"ט מנחם אב תשס"ח

ת.נ.צ.ב.ה.

In loving memory of

R' Daniel Rubinstein *z"l*

*W*hose pleasant ways, dignified manner, generous
spirit, steadfast belief, and staunch commitment
to Torah illuminate the path for us to follow.

**Dedicated by his children and grandchildren
The Kohn Family,** שיחיו׳
Toronto, Canada

In Loving Memory of

יעקב משה ז״ל בן זאב אליהו הכהן יבלח״ט אינמר

Yaakov Moshe Hakohein Anemer

*Y*aakov Moshe Anemer achieved in his brief 16-and-a-half years on earth a level of *kedushah,* of *shleimus* and closeness to Hashem that many spend a lifetime pursuing. As a rising star of the Telshe Alumni Yeshiva in Riverdale, Yaakov Moshe was not only admired and respected for his incredible *hasmodah,* but beloved for his exquisite sensitivity and kindness to others.

Those who were close to him — his classmates and family — were witness to Yaakov Moshe's passionate commitment to self-examination and self-improvement. Through sheer will-power and work, he refined his speech to eliminate even a hint of *loshon hora.* His mastery over his power of speech extended to his learning *sedarim* as well, where there was never an interruption for any extraneous comments or subjects.

Yaakov Moshe's parents saw from an early age that they had been blessed with an extraordinary child. He treated his parents with the utmost respect, jumping at any opportunity to help them.

The care with which he treated both his own and others' possessions testified to the refinement of this young man's exalted soul. He understood that everything came from Hashem as a gift, and he valued whatever came into his hand. When he would borrow a *sefer* from another student, he would be careful not to lean on it so as to avoid weakening its binding. He would steadfastly refuse to use anything without the express permission of the object's owner.

Even with his gentle sweetness, Yaakov Moshe understood the importance of *tochachah,* and would do his best to prod his fellow students to strive for greater heights. Those who were on the receiving end of his words never felt diminished in the least, but rather, their friend's love and concern penetrated their hearts. It was his complete lack of self-righteousness that made his words not only acceptable, but inspiring to others.

He was a Kohein, but he bore the honors and privileges of his birthright with humility. He had no reservations about being the one to serve others, and in fact, often insisted that being a Kohein did not excuse him from the obligation to perform *chesed*. One of his fellow students recalled that every Shabbos, he would find a Chumash waiting for him at his accustomed place for *davening*. He never knew who had put it there until the Shabbos after Yaakov Moshe's passing, when he saw that he would henceforth have to obtain a Chumash on his own.

All of Yaakov Moshe's exceptional *middos* blossomed from his deep, abiding devotion to Torah. He rarely left the *Beis Medrash*, finding it difficult to separate himself from the source of his spiritual sustenance. He would be among the first to arrive for *davening* in the morning, and among the last to leave the *Beis Medrash* at night, often tiptoeing into his dorm room to avoid awakening his roommates.

Yaakov Moshe found tremendous inspiration in the stories of *Gedolim* of past generations, and in meeting and hearing the words of today's *Gedolim*. Now, his brief but extraordinary life will serve as an inspiration for all those he left behind, all those who have been blessed with the opportunity to witness the heights to which one young man, with a heart full of love for his Creator, can rise.

May his memory be a blessing, and may the *zechus* engendered by this *sefer* be a constant source of *aliyah* for his beautiful *neshamah*.

Dedicated by your dear friends,
Yosef and Miriam Muss and family

We are fortunate to have enjoyed a very special relationship
with you which we will forever cherish.
You will always be our inspiration!
From your place on high, may you be a meilitz yosher
for your entire family and may you beseech
Hashem to send us the Geulah we are all waiting for.

לזכר ולעילוי נשמות

יוסף יעקב לייב בן שלמה ז״ל

Rabbi Yaakov Deitsch z"l

נתן בן אריה דב ז״ל

ואשתו לאה בת מאיר ע״ה

**Mr. and Mrs. Nathan
and Lena Seiler z"l**

שלמה בן משה ז״ל

ואשתו פריידל בת פרץ ע״ה

**Mr. and Mrs. Samuel
and Freida Deitsch z"l**

זי״ע

ת.נ.צ.ב.ה

*In memory of
those whom we will always cherish,
and whose legacies will live on in our hearts.*

Dedicated by your loving family.

This book is dedicated
to my wonderful Eishes Chayil

Miriam Sarah
Bas Freidel שתחי׳

*M*iriam, you inspire all who know you
In your humility
In your service to Hashem
Your sincerity in your commitment to friends
Dedication to your family's well being,
physically, spiritually, and emotionally.

You are the greatest brachah I could have ever
dreamed of receiving.

Hashem should bless you with long, healthy life
and you should see the realization of your prayers.

Gratefully,
Your husband,
Nachman

Table of Contents

Acknowledgments   xxiii
Introduction   xxvii
Note to the Reader   xxxi

CHAPTER 1:
Introduction   **1**

Day 1:   **Pure Power** — *The true nature of speech*
Day 2:   **Your Creations** — *The reality of words*
Day 3:   **What Did You Say?** — *The final accounting*
Day 4:   **Speaking Volumes** — *The quantity of words*
Day 5:   **Painting Self-Portraits** — *Influencing others' self-image*
Day 6:   **A Gift-Wrapped Word** — *Positive power*
Day 7:   **What You Don't See** — *Lasting impact*
Day 8:   **Permanent Marker** — *Difficult to fix damage*
Day 9   **Toxic Cleanup** — *Awareness*

CHAPTER 2:
What Fuels Hurtful Speech   **21**

Day 10: Crash Course — *Anger*
Day 11: A Legend in Her Own Mind — *Arrogance*
Day 12: The Boss — *Desire to dominate*
Day 13: Feeling Green — *Envy*
Day 14: Basic Anatomy — *Blind to other's worth*
Day 15: Heart Surgery — *Hatred*
Day 16: A Parent's Message — *Impatience*
Day 17: Your Honor — *Honor-seeking*
Day 18: A Thin Disguise — *Disguised hostility*
Day 19: The Blame Game — *Blaming others*
Day 20: Worth a Million — *Impulsive speech*
Day 21: Getting in Gear — *Lack of thought*
Day 22: Ha-Ha — *Misdirected humor*
Day 23: Holy War — *Idealism*
Day 24: Protecting the Boundaries — *Privacy*
Day 25: Wearing Armor — *Insecurity*
Day 26: Down a Few Notches — *Knocking others to feel good*
Day 27: And the Winner Is... — *Competitiveness*
Day 28: Misconstrued — *Miscommunication*
Day 29: Under the Weather — *ill/lack of sleep*
Day 30: Fighting Phantoms — *Imagined slights*
Day 31: "Either-Or" — *Negating the positive*
Day 32: 'Well What Do You Expect?' — *Justification*

CHAPTER 3:
Hurtful Speech Category I:
Slurs On Character And Reputation   **69**

Day 33: Bursting Their Bubble — *Defaming other's character*
Day 34: Free to Travel — *Past mistakes*
Day 35: What's Hidden — *Revealing past sins*

Day 36: **Not Even Normal** — *Crude assessment of others' flaws*
Day 37: **Who You Are**— *Denigrating family origin*
Day 38: **Image Erosion** — *Hitting the Achille's heel*
Day 39: **The Motive Monitor** — *Attacking other's motivation*

CHAPTER 4:
Hurtful Speech Category II:
Offensive, Disrespectful Speech   **85**

Day 40: **A Blessing and a Curse** — *Profanities, vulgar attacks*
Day 41: **Who Is Wise** — *Physical limitations/handicaps*
Day 42: **All Grown Up** — *Intelligence, maturity*
Day 43: **Looking Good** — *Physical appearance*
Day 44: **Nothing Left to Lose** — *Humiliating criticism*
Day 45: **Showtime!** — *Caustic attacks and heckling*
Day 46: **What's in a Name?** — *Derogatory nicknames*

CHAPTER 5:
Hurtful Speech Category III:
Destructive, Demoralizing Statements   **101**

Day 47: **The Absentminded Professor** — *Impatience with forgetfulness*
DAY 48: **Creating an Undertow** — *Undermining enthusiasm*
Day 49: **Threads of Brilliance** — *Negative input*
Day 50: **Their Pride and Joy** — *Disparaging what others hold dear*
Day 51: **The Career Critic** — *Belittling a profession*
Day 52: **Recipe for Disaster** — *Criticizing the cook*
Day 53: **To Each His Own** — *Demeaning others' taste*
Day 54: **Nothing to Celebrate** — *Joy in others' misfortune*
Day 55: **"I Told You So"** — *'Rubbing it in'*
Day 56: **Loaded Questions** — *Questions that are insults*
Day 57: **Don't Ask** — *Intrusive questions*
Day 58: **Exercise Caution** — *Boasting*

Day 59: **The Happy Buyer** — *Hampering happiness*
Day 60: **Helpful Hints** — *Killing with kindness*

CHAPTER 6:
Hurtful Speech Category IV:
Manipulative, Defensive Tactics   **131**

Day 61: **The Dark Side** — *Pessimistic predictions*
Day 62: **Enough Said** — *Extreme overreaction*
Day 63: **"I Can't Say"** — *Worrisome hints*
Day 64: **Boo!** — *Creating fear*
Day 65: **The Boy Who Cried, "Wolf!"** — *Practical jokes*
Day 66: **The Badger** — *Unrelenting badgering*
Day 67: **Unreasonable Cause** — *Belittling people in need*
Day 68: **Or Else** — *Motivating others by fear*
Day 69: **While You're At It** ...— *Unnecessary comments*

CHAPTER 7:
Hurtful Speech Category V:
Counterproductive Comments
Or Nonconstructive Questions   **151**

Day 70: **How Dare You** — *Angry Retorts*
Day 71: **Seeing The Future** — *Impulsive, annoying responses*
Day 72: **No Harm Intended** — *Dealing with unwanted help*
Day 73: **Eggshell Skull Rule** — *Aggravating others' sensitivities*
Day 74: **In His Shoes** — *Specific sensitivities*
Day 75: **Spilled Milk** — *Irritation at clumsiness*
Day 76: **Amazing Praise** — *Tainted praise*
Day 77: **Just Like You** — *Unfavorable comparisons*
Day 78: **Get Over It** — *Callousness toward others' problems*
Day 79: **My Favorite Things** — *Dealing with a conversation monopolizer*
Day 80: **To Whom You Speak** — *Unwanted advice*

Day 81: The Nitpicker — *Nitpicking*
Day 82: Just Testing — *Testing relationships*

CHAPTER 8:
Hurtful Speech Category VI:
Negative Imitation   **179**

Day 83: Inimitable — *Mimicking*

CHAPTER 9:
Hurtful Speech Category VII:
Revealing Private Information   **183**

Day 84: Betrayed — *Violating trust*
Day 85: The Word's Out — *Disclosing confidential matters*

CHAPTER 10:
Hurtful Speech Category VIII:
Misinforming And Misleading People   **189**

Day 86: False Hope — *Raising false hopes*
Day 87: Chain Reaction — *Delayed impact*
Day 88: Just Browsing — *Asking prices*

CHAPTER 11:
Hurtful Speech Category IX:
Subtle Negative Statements   **197**

Day 89: Beware the Undertone — *Muttering*
Day 90: Get the Hint? — *Insulting insinuations*
Day 91: The Cutting Edge — *Sarcastic statements*
Day 92: A Day at the Zoo — *Comparisons to animals*
Day 93: Music to Their Ears — *Tone*

CHAPTER 12:
Hurtful Speech Category X:
Nonverbal Forms Of Onaas Devarim   **209**

Day 94:   In Your Face — *Non-verbal negative communication*
Day 95:   The Poison Pen — *Written insults*
Day 96:   In Your Hands — *Hand motions*
Day 97:   Not a Word — *Facial expressions*
Day 98:   The Silent Treatment — *Silence as a weapon*

CHAPTER 13:
Identifying Personal Pitfalls   **221**

Day 99:   A Gentle Awakening — *Routine challenges*
Day 100:   Hello, Goodbye — *Cell-phone etiquette*

CHAPTER 14:
Strategies   **227**

Day 101:   The Big Payoff — *Great reward*
Day 102:   Prepared for Landing — *Be prepared*
Day 103:   Defusing the Bomb — *Know your worth*
Day 104:   Image Transplant — *See good in others*
Day 105:   Human Like Me — *Think of yourself as the listener*
Day 106:   Positively Powerful — *Pass on a compliment*
Day 107:   Take 15 — *Control your anger*
Day 108:   No Offense — *Generate a positive atmosphere*
Day 109:   Fork in the Road — *Wait before you respond*
Day 110:   Under Examination — *Measure your words*
Day 111:   The Cure — *Become a source of comfort*
Day 112:   Soft Spot — *Develop resilience*
Day 113:   Reading the Signs — *Pick up non-verbal cues*
Day 114:   Be a Seer — *Focus on potential*
Day 115:   Just Like Me — *Accept differences*

Day 116: **Going Another Round** — *Avoid needless conflicts*

Day 117: **Doing the Mending** — *Teshuvah*

Day 118: **The Foolproof Cure** — *Daily learning*

Day 119: **In Other Words** — *Test your progress*

Don't Shut the Book Yet   **269**

On the Receiving End

Afterword — The Life You Save May Be Your Own

❧ Acknowledgments

*O*ur gratitude to Hashem *Yisbarach* is inexpressible for His having permitted us to produce this book and continue to spread the concept of *shmiras haloshon* in all its facets. With the publication of this book, we are forging into new territory in our effort to bring the beauty and blessing of *shmiras haloshon* to communities throughout the world. At the behest of HaRav Pam, *zt"l*, and with the enthusiastic support of HaRav Shteinman, *shlita*, we have produced a work that focuses on eradicating *onaas devarim*, hurtful words spoken, intentionally or unintentionally, to those with whom we interact. To serve as the vehicle for this vitally important task is a privilege far beyond anything to which we could have aspired, and it is only through *siyata d'Shmaya* that we were even able to approach the project. We hope that we will be worthy, through this book, of arousing the same kind of heightened awareness and sensitivity that we have been achieving, with Hashem's constant help, in the area of *loshon hora*.

This book is based on the groundbreaking work on this subject, *The Power of Words*, by **Rabbi Zelig Pliskin,** whose books and lectures have enhanced the lives of tens of thousands. We are honored to have been given the opportunity to cull from the rich content of his classic book.

We are indebted to **Mrs. Tzivia Nagelberg,** whose outline of the concepts in Rabbi Pliskin's work formed the perfect foundation upon which to structure our book.

Mrs. Chana Nestlebaum, the writer of this book, has been the voice of our organization since it began almost two decades ago. Her words have inspired and enlightened people all over the world. It is only fitting that this important new work should be penned by her. Her clarity, believable scenarios and insightful postscripts turned what might have been a cumbersome presentation into a most readable and engaging daily boost.

Mrs. Shaindy Appelbaum, editor/editorial director, is directly responsible for the carefully crafted, progressive structure of this book, creating a flow of daily lessons designed to elevate and inspire the reader step by enlightening step. In this and countless other Chofetz Chaim Heritage Foundation projects, she has used her talent, wisdom and perseverance to inspire Klal Yisrael and change the world.

Rabbi Eliyahu Lamm and **Rabbi Eliyahu Klugman** meticulously reviewed the manuscript. Their keen insights and important corrections and clarifications greatly enhanced this book.

Rabbi Henoch Moshe Levine gave readily of his time and expertise, providing invaluable help in researching sources.

The eye-catching cover bears the unique stamp of the incomparable **Ben Gasner.**

Our success flows from the Torah leaders who map out our path:

The Manchester Rosh Yeshivah, HaGaon HaRav Yehudah Zev Segal, *zt"l,* the founding Rabbinic Advisor of our organization; **HaGaon HaRav Shmuel Kamenetsky,** *shlita,* the Chairman of our Rabbinical Board; and **HaGaon HaRav Avraham Pam,** *zt"l,* **and** *yblc"t* **HaGaon HaRav Yaakov Perlow,** *shlita,* members of our Rabbinical Board of Advisors.

Rabbi Moshe Mordechai Lowy, renowned *Rav* and *Posek,* gives freely of his precious time and vast Torah knowledge, offering crucial advice and clear halachic guidance.

Rabbi Eliyahu Brog, Rabbi Mordechai Klein, Rabbi Eliyahu Lamm, and **Rabbi Hillel Litwack,** who volunteer their time to answer questions on our Shaila Hotline, provide invaluable halachic guidance to those seeking to properly fulfill the mitzvah of *shmiras haloshon.*

We are deeply grateful to the outstanding people of the Chofetz Chaim Heritage Foundation:

To our board of directors who have been a tremendous help in forging our path into the future: **Raymond Beyda, Abraham Biderman, Aba Claman, Nachman Futterman, David Lobel, Yitzchok Mashitz, Ari Parnes, George Rohr, Kurt Rothschild, David Shweky, Gedaliah Weinberger** and **Moshe Zakheim.**

To the many dynamic speakers who have inspired us with audio-visual and taped presentations over the years, we offer our sincere thanks.

If you have benefited from a *shmiras haloshon* program or publication over the past few years, it is thanks to the selfless dedication of our staff: **Dovid Kogel, Rabbi Shlomo Orenstein, Rabbi Elchonon Snyder, Dina Bernfeld, Chaya Henny Bochner, Devorah Chaim, Machla Eichenstein, Malky Fine, Leah Fischer, Blimy Friedman, Ruchy Friedman, Miriam Grossman, Bassie Gugenheim, Giti Guggenheim, Kaila Halpern, Elana Jacobs, Gitty Kalikstein, Simi Kepecs, Breindy Kertzner, Gitty Kish, Estie Koot, Shira**

Lazar, Bruchy Leiberman, Esther Leibowitz, Blimi Lesser, Chava Londinski, Shoshana Miller, Esther Mor, Gitty Neuschloss, Leah Ozeri, Blimie Paneth, Ruchy Perlstein, Chayie Schachter, Leah Sekula, Malky Silber, Chavi Twersky, Leah Twersky, Chavie Weingot, Rivky Willman and Feigy Zelcer.

We would also like to thank our staff in Eretz Yisrael: **Binyomin and Shoshana Cohen, Mrs. Rochel Orloweck, Mrs. Naomi Rottman, Mrs. Shevi Trobelsky,** and **Mrs. Esty Feigenbaum.**

The Chofetz Chaim Heritage Foundation is forever grateful to **Rabbi Mendel Kessin,** whose penetrating taped *shiurim* on *shmiras haloshon* were the catalyst that inspired us to start our organization.

Others who have played an important role in our organization are: **Shia Bernath** and **Jacob Rosenberg, Shmuel Borger, Mordechai** and **Sorolle Gelber, Hersh Mayer Leifer, Benny Marvin, Avi Shulman** and **Chaim Snow, Sara Jaskiel, Heidy Ort, Riva Pomerantz** and **Esther Israel.**

Our thanks to **Rabbi Heshy Liener, Rabbi Nochum Stilerman,** and **Rabbi Heshy Augenbraun** for their crucial advice.

Rabbi Nosson Scherman and **Rabbi Meir Zlotowitz,** general editors of ArtScroll/Mesorah, took a strong interest in this project. Their wise counsel, editing advice, and on-the-mark comments added much to the final product. A special thanks to **Avrohom Biderman,** who has been a crucial link — as always — in the production of this *sefer* and to **Mendy Herzberg** and the entire typesetting/graphics department at ArtScroll for their dedication to this project.

Our organization's success is due to friends around the world who have brought our programs to their shul, school or community. To our 450 local coordinators — the *rabbanim*, principals and lay people who have lifted the banner of *shmiras haloshon* — thank you so much.

A very special thank you to those who have supported us financially, and are directly responsible for the largest initiative for *shmiras haloshon* in history. To the major supporters, who wish to remain anonymous, the main sponsors of this book, the families who have sponsored a day in this book, and the many others who have supported us — you have truly made a difference! Surely, your investment in the mitzvah of *shmiras haloshon*, will stand as a great z'chus for you and your families. It is our z'chus to partner with you, in bringing the teachings of the Chofez Chaim to tens of thousands, and with that to uplift all of Klal Yisrael.

The Chofetz Chaim Heritage Foundation
Tammuz 5769

❧ *Introduction*

*I*n 1998, the Chofetz Chaim Heritage Foundation brought communities around the world a moving presentation on the topic of ona'as devarim — causing pain with one's words. Rav Avraham Pam, zt'l, introduced the event with an impassioned plea to Klal Yisrael to closely examine the tone and tenor of our words to one another, and honestly assess the damage harsh words can cause in our lives and our world. He called for a great, community-wide effort in correcting this corrosive force, an effort that would equal that which has been exerted against loshon hora in recent decades.

This sefer is a response to Rav Pam's plea. In its varied, lifelike scenarios, it is designed to ring bells of recognition among all of us. The reader will not find many examples of outright, purposeful cruelty in these scenarios. Rather, he will find the everyday verbal slings and arrows aroused by impatience, stress, misguided good intentions or simple lack of awareness. These are the prime ingredients of the ona'as devarim that erode trust and drive wedges between husband and wife, parent and child, teacher and student, neighbor and neighbor.

It is our hope that by shining a light on these all-too-common habits of speech, we can work together to create a climate of tolerance and sensitivity. The "In Other Words" section at the end of each day's lesson helps to put this awareness into action, offering alternative ways of handling situations that habitually give rise to ona'as devarim.

We pray that this effort will serve as an effective fulfillment of the charge given to us by Rav Pam, and that it will play a significant role in encouraging the healing of our exiled nation, bringing us in unity and dignity to the time of our Final Redemption.

Rav Avraham Pam
1998

*T*he crucial importance of guarding one's power of speech — shmiras haloshon — has become very well known as it relates to loshon hora. However, there is another prohibition in shmiras haloshon which is rarely addressed, and that is ona'as devarim — hurtful speech.

This is distinct from *loshon hora* because it is directed at the person who hears it. It is comprised of words that cut deeply and cause a great deal of pain, and is the cause of many tragedies.

The source of this prohibition is a verse in Parashas *Behar*, in *Sefer Vayikra* (25:17): "*V'lo sonu ish es amiso* — One shall not aggrieve one's fellow." Rashi defines this as *ona'as devarim*, specifying that it refers to using words to injure the people with whom we interact in our lives.

The *Sefer HaChinuch* describes *ona'as devarim* as a prohibition against "saying to another Jew words that cause pain and suffering, from which he can find no help." They are words that leave their victim defenseless.

As Shlomo HaMelech says in *Mishlei* (12:18), words can cut deeply, "like a sword," but they are an equally potent force for good, for "the language of the wise heals." This is the contrast between careless speech and the healing power and happiness that speech can bring.

Like swords, words are sometimes used as weapons, wielded in anger or outright malice. More often, *ona'as devarim* results from simple carelessness, from speaking without regard to what the consequences might be. Nevertheless, just as a sword swung carelessly can cut as deeply as one that is wielded with purpose, so can a careless word hurt as much as a deliberate insult.

Unfortunately, people say things that are absolutely brutal, often with no forethought at all: insulting remarks, demeaning expressions, derogatory statements, and name-calling are not uncommon at all, especially in families, between husbands and wives, and sometimes between parents and children. These words leave a tragic imprint on the spirit and soul of the person who is the object of such torrents of insults. Really, what we are describing here is verbal abuse.

We have today in our society — even in the *frum* society — a breakdown in marriages. I would venture to say that in most cases, the breakdown in *shalom bayis* starts with some form of verbal abuse. It doesn't matter whether it's done deliberately to hurt, or it's done out of uncontrollable anger, or out of carelessness. Sometimes the abuse comes in the form of a joke, but the joke hurts; the other party doesn't see it as funny. It leaves a scar.

The Torah's prohibition against aggrieving one another goes one step further, adding the words, "and you shall fear Hashem, your G-d." Why is this statement made at this particular point? Perhaps a person has enough self-control to avoid harsh words when he is in front of others. Perhaps, when there's company around, he is genial and polite. But what happens when the audience goes home and the door shuts behind them?

Some people feel free to use abusive language in private. To their minds, nobody is listening. Therefore the Torah reminds us that this is not so; Somebody is listening, Somebody is recording every word. If a person were able to find the strength to control his speech in front of other people, then this verse, "and you shall fear Hashem, your G-d," should help him maintain the sense of being seen and heard, even when he is in the privacy of his home.

The Vilna Gaon describes this graphically in his famous *Igerres HaGra*, which he wrote to his Rebbetzin while en route to Eretz Yisrael. Included among the advice and blessings he gives her is his urging to carefully guard against improper speech: "They [Hashem's emissaries] accompany each person regularly, and they never separate from him. Wherever he goes they go, and they record every word."

Can you imagine? A person talks in private. He makes sure that nobody is around. Yet in reality, he is surrounded by secretaries who record everything, word for word. One day it will be played back to this person, and he will find it difficult to believe that he had ever said such things.

Therefore the Torah says, "Do not aggrieve your fellow, and you shall fear your G-d, for I am Hashem, your G-d."

Once the words leave one's mouth, it is too late. I would suggest this advice. One should ask oneself: "Was I sent down from Heaven to this world to make life miserable for someone, for anyone? Is that why the Divine gift of speech was given to me? To degrade and defile this gift of G-d — speech — is an insult to the Creator, especially when the same power can be used to heal and soothe a depressed spirit.

Much more needs to be said publically about the tragedy spawned by *ona'as devarim*. This concept needs the kind of exposure that has been applied to *loshon hora* in recent years. More yeshivos and Bais Yaakovs should be teaching their students to recognize and restrain themselves from this type of speech. The result would surely be fewer marital problems, less estrangement of children from their parents and fewer dropouts from the yeshivos. Powerful words should be written about this topic and circulated widely to encourage people to use the gift of speech wisely. Certainly, everyone should understand the imperative to be extremely careful in avoiding words that inflict wounds that perhaps will never heal, or may linger on for a long, long time.

In contrast to the devastation wrought by unkind words, the Chofetz Chaim writes of the magnificent reward for one who thinks before he speaks. He writes, "One who keeps his mouth closed merits the *"or haganuz,"* the light of Creation which the *Ribono Shel Olam* set aside for the righteous to enjoy in the World to Come. This light is described as something so radiant that not even an angel can imagine its beauty or the joy of basking in it. Yet this is the reward for simply sealing one's lips at the proper time.

The *Ribono Shel Olam* should give us the *siyata d'Shmaya* to appreciate the great gift of speech, which bears such golden blessings within it, and to use it properly, so that we will be worthy to greet the *geulah*, speedily in our days.

Note to the Reader

ONA'AS DEVARIM — HURTFUL SPEECH

Ona'as devarim is verbal assault — the causing of pain to another through the use of harsh, angry or insensitive words. The Torah prohibits this type of hurtful speech in several ways. The first is the commandment, *"Lo sonu ish es amiso* — You shall not aggrieve your fellow" (*Vayikra* 25:17). Rashi explains that this prohibition is directed at the words we use in our personal relationships. And it is a total prohibition; it offers no allowance for inflicting even the slightest pain for the briefest moment, unless there is no other way to accomplish an important constructive purpose. Harsh words also violate the Torah's mandate of *"V'ahavta l'reiacha kamocha* — And you shall love your fellow as yourself" (*Vayikra* 19:18), for certainly no one would desire such treatment for themselves. Finally, the embarrassment *ona'as devarim* may cause violates the Torah's unequivocal prohibition against shaming others.

At the end of each day's lesson, the "In Other Words" section offers practical suggestions for personal growth in the specific area discussed that day. If you feel that, in following these suggestions, you are taking upon yourself a specific commitment, it is recommended that you say *bli neder*, so that your commitment does not have the force of a vow.

CHAPTER 1:
Introduction

The journey upon which we are about to embark travels through the completely familiar terrain of human interaction. The way in which we speak to each other in our era of unguarded, impulse-driven communication sounds perfectly normal to our ears, and yet often, we are leaving hurt, insult, sadness and despair in our wake. Casually strewn criticism and insults, often said in jest, do not just blow away. They take root, and what grows from them is a harvest of every form of personal misery.

The Torah bids us to understand the boundless reach and power of a spoken word. Right from its opening verses, it illustrates this power as G-d creates all of Creation with ten utterances. Thus, the first lesson the Torah teaches us is that words create worlds. Our own words continue G-d's labor, forming the atmosphere of our homes, communities and nation.

This is a journey into the familiar terrain of parent-child, teacher-student, husband-wife, boss-employee, friend-friend interaction. You will recognize words you've said and heard, situations you've experienced and people who are like some you know. But you'll view this terrain with new eyes, learning to see the ripple effect of these common conversations and comments. With siyata d'Shmaya, you'll learn how to alter this old, familiar terrain by re-planting it with beautiful words of respect, dignity and praise. In doing so, you will learn how to plant your own Gan Eden, right here on earth.

DAY 1

א תשרי
1 TISHREI / CYCLE 1

א שבט
1 SHEVAT / CYCLE 2

א סיון
1 SIVAN / CYCLE 3

❧ *Pure Power*

*I*magine. The world is brand new. It is the sixth day of Creation, and for the first time ever, living creatures tread upon the newborn earth. Birds soar through the pure blue skies and insects swarm in the soil below. Now is the moment Hashem has chosen for his crowning achievement: the creation of man. Suddenly, from a heap of dust, there he is. But this supposedly exalted creature is not larger, nor stronger, nor swifter than the other species. He is just a collection or organs and limbs.

But then, the Torah tells us, Hashem brings this creature to life. "And Hashem blew the soul of life into his nostrils, and man became a living being" (*Bereishis* 2:7). What exactly was the breath with which Hashem gave life to Adam, and through him, all of mankind?

Onkelos explains that it was a *ruach memalela* — a speaking spirit. The life force in man is his ability to speak. This is what made him the crowning achievement, for with this gift, he would be able to communicate with the Master of the World. He would be able to express his innermost thoughts and emotions. He would have the tool for learning Hashem's Torah. Just as Hashem created His world with the power of speech — the ten utterances of *Bereishis* — man continues to create his world each day with the words he speaks.

The power of speech imbues us with a G-dliness of our own. The Zohar, in describing the breath of life Hashem blew into Adam, states that "One who blows, blows from within himself." This means that in the act of bringing man to life, Hashem breathed a part of

Himself into Adam. It is precisely our ability to speak that identifies us as G-dly, spiritual creations.

The breath that Hashem put into us is what we utilize when we utter a word. Chazal (*Sefer Hakanah*) teach that each word is a tiny fragment of our Divine life force, our *neshamah*, being released into the world.

Now, it is clear why the words we speak wield such awesome power. They are the channel through which the vast, immeasurable power of the Upper Worlds is let loose in our physical world. With a few words of *tefillah*, we can open the gates of Heaven; and with a few words of loshon hora, we can stir into action the fiery angels of prosecution in the Heavenly Court.

The daily lessons contained in this *sefer* are meant to help break through the illusion that our words are just mundane tools of everyday life. We will see how these minuscule puffs of our Divine essence are not at all the ephemeral entity they seem to be, but rather a lasting, world-changing force that echoes through the centuries. Through our learning of this *sefer*, we have the opportunity to strengthen our connection to the Divine power within us, and use it to fill the world with the light of Hashem.

In Other Words:

"*If I am about to say something hurtful to someone, I will imagine that my spoken words are a permanent, concrete entity.*"

DAY 2

ב תשרי
2 TISHREI / CYCLE 1

ב שבט
2 SHEVAT /CYCLE 2

ב סיון
2 SIVAN / CYCLE 3

❧ *Your Creations*

ou walk into your local bank to make a deposit. As you step up to the teller's window, you smile and say, "Good morning, Mr. Smith. How are you today?"

Those two short sentences contain eight words. They are said so frequently that they might almost be considered meaningless. In fact, from behind the bulletproof glass, Mr. Smith probably did not even hear them. It would seem that those eight words were discharged from your mouth to simply evaporate, like a puff of steam, into the air. You spoke, but in essence, nothing happened.

However, we have already learned that this cannot be the case, because a word is a spark of a person's *neshamah*. A Divine entity such as this cannot be released into the air without creating an impact.

Those eight words become spiritual creations, created by you, the speaker. As Rav Avraham Azulai, (*Chesed L'Avraham* 2:68) grandfather of the Chida, taught, each word of kindness, each word of Torah or *tefillah*, creates a heavenly advocate for the speaker, and each hurtful word, each word of *loshon hora* or falsehood, creates a prosecuting *malach*. If your intention in greeting the bank teller was to make a *Kiddush Hashem*, even if no one heard your words, you have created something eternal and beautiful with them.

On the other hand, perhaps you are forced to wait a long time in line, and when you finally get to the teller, he makes a mistake with your deposit. "Mr. Smith, why don't you use your head!" you say irritably. This sentence also creates eight *malachim* — prosecutors — that will stand as an ugly accusation against you. You have once again created something eternal with your words.

There is a toy that fascinates young children. It is a small capsule that contains a tightly condensed sponge. The sponge is released from the capsule into water, and little by little, the sponge assumes the shape of a lion, or a bear or a horse. The children love to see something come from nothing, to see shape define itself out of a shapeless blob.

Our words may appear to us as amorphous, undefined "blobs" as well. But if we could observe them from Heaven's view, we would see that as they are released into the world, they take on a very definitive shape. Also, like the sponge, they were never really "nothing" to begin with. Each word is shaped into the creature it will show itself to be. It is our decision to release it or keep it packed inside its container.

The journey we are embarking upon with this learning is one that takes us closer to the Divine spark inside us, and to the Heavenly source of our power. To get there, the first step is to become intensely aware of the shape and form of the tiniest utterances that issue forth from our lips. Once we engage the enemy — careless speech — in battle, Hashem will send us the strength to triumph.

In Other Words:

" *I will think of five ways in which my life will benefit when I gain better mastery of my power of speech.* "

DAY 3

ג תשרי
3 TISHREI / CYCLE 1

ג שבט
3 SHEVAT / CYCLE 2

ג סיון
3 SIVAN / CYCLE 3

☙ *What Did You Say?*

*T*he angry child stormed out of the room and shouted at his brother, "I hate you!" Little did he know that his mother was standing just a few feet away.

"What did you say?" she asked him. It wasn't a question, the child well knew. It was an accusation. Now he would have to reckon with the words that had come out of his mouth: "I hate you." These were forbidden words in his family, but he had said them, and he could not pretend to himself that his words would have no consequence.

The Talmud (*Chagigah* 5b) teaches that in the Next World, each of us will have to answer this question regarding every word we spoke in our lifetimes. It proves this by citing a verse in *Amos* (4:13) which states, "*u'magid l'adam mah sicho* — He recounts to a person what were his words."

This alone is a fearsome prospect. Every word you have said — those that popped out in a moment of anger or frustration; those that you knew, even as you spoke them, should not be spoken; those that discouraged or wounded others — every word will be recounted into your ear.

The word *"mah,"* meaning "what," adds a far deeper and more disturbing dimension to this concept. Rav Chaim Volozhiner writes in *Nefesh Hachaim* that there is a particular reason why the verse states "*mah sicho* — what were his words," rather than the more common formulation of "*es sicho* — his words." The use of *"mah"* means that a person will not only hear his words, but he will see *what* his words did, what their consequences were to those who received them.

Watching our own hurtful words make their impact along the highway of life can be more horrifying than watching helplessly as an accident unfolds in front of our eyes. In life, a person may walk away from a situation thinking nothing much happened, but in the grand retrospective after 120 years, he will have to face his own words and their repercussions. He will see that the irritable word to the taxi driver caused the driver to refuse to pick up the next passenger, who had to walk a long distance, thereby missing a business appointment, which caused him to lose a customer, and so forth and so on.

Imagine, on the other hand, the impact of a pleasant word to the same driver. He is so cheerful that he takes his next passenger on a shortcut that gets him to his appointment early, enabling him to review his presentation, close the deal and come home in a happy mood that spreads to his wife and children.

"What did you say?" Someday, each of us will have to answer that question, not only regarding our words, but the ripple effect they set loose in the world. When we keep that in mind, it can inspire us to think before we speak, ensuring that the words we have said will sound sweet to our own ears.

In Other Words:

"Before I say something negative to someone, I will consider whether I would want those words tape-recorded and played for people I respect and admire."

3 Tishrei — לע״נ שולמית בת ר׳ אהרן דוד ע״ה נלב״ע ז׳ תשרי
Dedicated by the Schwartz family

3 Shevat — לע״נ העונה בת אברהם ע״ה
Dedicated by the Kamer family

3 Sivan — Shimon Spira לע״נ ר׳ שמעון אלתר בן ר׳ ישראל ארי׳ ז״ל
By his wife, children, grandchildren & great-grandchildren

DAY 4

ד תשרי
4 TISHREI / CYCLE 1

ד שבט
4 SHEVAT / CYCLE 2

ד סיון
4 SIVAN / CYCLE 3

✀ Speaking Volumes

*O*ne termite is relatively harmless. Thousands of them, however, can take down a build-ing. On the other hand, one atom bomb is far from harmless. Fortunately, however, there are not many of them in this world. Few entities are both extremely powerful and extremely plentiful. Words bear this rare trait.

There is a motivational writer in the secular mar-ket, Hal Urban, who published a book called "Positive Words, Powerful Results." As part of his research, he took the time to actually count how many words he spoke in a day. He started by counting the words of the famously nerve-racking song children sometimes sing to pass the time on long trips — "A Hundred Bottles of Beer on the Wall." Sung at a normal pace, one can sing about five stanzas of the song in a min-ute, which comes to an average of about 140 words per minute or 8,400 words in an hour. Taking away time for eating, sleeping, working and listening to others speak, the author calculated that the average person speaks about 40,000 words a day.

Applying what we have learned so far about the impact of our words, the number 40,000 is stagger-ing. What a person does with his 40,000 words a day is clearly a matter of massive impact, determining whether he has created troops of prosecuting *mala-chim* or troops of defenders in the course of his day's interactions. One who has not developed a habit of speaking with forethought can trip into a morass that will be extremely difficult to escape.

Visualize the results of an hour-long, loshon-hora-filled conversation. Employing whatever picture one creates in his mind of a prosecuting angel, with whatever frightening, fiery features one may conjure, there would be 8,400 of these creatures after that one conversation. There would be enough of them to populate a small town.

The Chofetz Chaim explains that each negative conversation is like a thread. One thread is easy to break. Two threads are more difficult, but still breakable. A mass of threads, a hundred or more, can be considered nearly indestructible, even though it is composed entirely of slim, breakable threads.

One with a lifetime history of negative, hurtful speech is tied to that habit with a thick rope of these slim threads, a rope strong enough to hold the Queen Elizabeth to her moorings. The ship is not bound to that place indefinitely, however, for as soon as the ship's captain determines that it is time to head in a different direction, someone lifts the heavy rope and sets the ship free to sail. In the same way, Hashem sets us free from our negative habits of speech, as soon as we announce to Him and to ourselves that we are ready for the journey.

In Other Words:

" *As I speak, I will remember that each word becomes another thread tying me to either good or negative habits of speech.* "

4 Tishrei — Rabbi Chaim Noah Brevda ל"ז הכהן משה אברהם בן נח חיים הרב נ"לע
Dedicated by Reb. Leah Brevda, children and grandchildren

4 Shevat — In honor of Mr. Boruch and Mrs. Gitty Rudinsky
Dedicated by their children

4 Sivan — Renee Langsner ה"ע הלוי מרדכי חיים' ר בת רייזל נ"לע
Dedicated by Mr. & Mrs. Ouriel Aryeh and family

ה תשרי
5 TISHREI / CYCLE 1

ה שבט
5 SHEVAT / CYCLE 2

ה סיון
5 SIVAN / CYCLE 3

🌊 Painting Self-Portraits

There was a young camp counselor who wanted her bunk of first-grade girls to paint pictures of themselves. She walked around to each girl, giving her a few colors with which to create her masterpiece. To the girls she favored, she gave bright primary colors and soft pastels. To the girls with whom she had difficulty relating, she provided dark, muted greens, browns and grays. With those colors, they had no choice but to paint dull, depressing pictures. Obviously, the paintings of the girls who received the pleasant colors looked much nicer to themselves and everyone else. This counselor, of course, was grossly unfair and did a terrible disservice to her campers.

With each word a person speaks to another, he is providing paint for that person's self-portrait. Throughout our lives, we collect these colors from the words others speak to us, adding them, a dab at a time, to the image we create of ourselves. Others have the power, through sarcasm and disapproval, to fill our palettes with so many dark colors that we cannot help but paint ourselves in the gloomy tones of incompetence, depression and loneliness. Likewise, we each have the terrible power to do this to others in our lives.

For a parent or teacher, this power is immeasurably potent, for a child is a work in progress. Every word spoken to him is absorbed into his developing personality, becoming part of his psychic structure. A negative word to a healthy, confident adult may sting at first, but it will usually roll off, like rain from a rooftop. For a child, however, these protective layers of self-esteem have yet to be built. Harsh words seep directly into a child's framework and weaken it. The inner structure is compromised, and the damage may not become apparent for years. By this time, an entire personality has been built out of damaged materials.

Thus, one can visualize the damage being wrought when a 4-year-old who won't pick up his toys is called a "lazy boy," or a fifth-grader who brings home a C on her Chumash test is called a "bad student." These little bits of "water damage" soak into the child's developing personality, and at a certain point, the labels become part of his permanent structure.

But even a full-grown, competent adult can find his self-image eroded by harsh words sent in his direction. In marriage, in an employer-employee relationship, between friends, in any relationship in which one person's opinion matters to the other, words have the power to alter someone's self-image.

Fortunately, this process works just as well in the opposite direction. Words of praise and support also build themselves into a child's personality. They also color the self-image of those to whom we matter. In every interaction, we can choose to give out the bright colors, the soft, pleasant hues to the people to whom we speak. In doing so, we give them the material they need to paint themselves as bright, pleasant, beautiful people.

In Other Words:

"I will try to pay attention to the 'color' of the words I speak, switching wherever possible to more pleasant hues."

5 Tishrei — Moshe Schwartz ז״ל לע״נ משה ראובן בן יוסף
Dedicated by Michoel & Shayna Jacob and family

5 Shevat — Herman Pasternak ז״ל לע״נ ר׳ יחזקא-ל יהודה בן מרדכי
Dedicated by his family, Los Angeles, CA

5 Sivan — לע״נ רייזל בת חיים מרדכי ע״ה
לע״נ זיסל בת שמואל ע״ה

❧ *A Gift-Wrapped Word*

*I*magine taking a vow to never speak a negative word about another person again. You might find yourself frightened to open your mouth. You might feel repressed, unable to let your thoughts and feelings flow. But if that were your reaction, it would be because you were focusing all your attention on half of the picture. You would be seeing each word as a potential trap that could ensnare you in sin and punishment, but failing to see each word as a potential gold mine of blessing.

Once a person moves past the human tendency to vent frustrations through negative speech, the focus shifts to the other half of the picture: *lashon tov,* positive speech. This is where speech fulfills its potential to make a person the parent, sibling, friend, teacher, son or daughter he or she is meant to be. The positive word is so powerful the Zohar teaches that one may not bypass the opportunity to speak it. Noticing something positive about someone, thinking it, but not saying it, is wrong. Speech is not a loose cannon we have to rein in before it hurts someone; it is a precision tool for growth. Even one word can have an immense positive impact, as the story below illustrates.

Rosa was from Guatemala. For four years, she had worked in the Nussbaums' home, keeping it tidy and operating smoothly. She was honest, pleasant and reliable, and the Nussbaum family appreciated her tremendously. In fact, shortly after she had started working for him, Mr. Nussbaum had thought that he would learn a few words of Spanish so he could communicate with more than gestures. However, the years went by, and all he had learned to say was "muchas gracias, senora."

One fact Rosa had managed to communicate was that she had not seen her daughter since she had left Guatemala 10 years ago, when the girl was 14. One day, Rosa arrived at the Nussbaum house with an ecstatic smile on her face. Her daughter had arrived in the U.S. with her husband. The yearned-for reunion had occurred, and this mother's heart was bursting with joy. Mr. Nussbaum wanted her to know that they shared in her joy, and so, he finally set about learning a word in Spanish: "feliz," meaning happy. The next day, when Rosa arrived, Mr. Nussbaum proudly expressed his feelings in Spanish. "Feliz," he told her. "We are feliz."

Rosa's eyes lit up. She recognized the effort to reach out to her and express a heartfelt sentiment. It was as if the single word had been carefully wrapped, adorned with a bow and placed in her hands.

This is the power of *lashon tov*. Each positive word can be given as a gift, carefully chosen, wrapped with love and handed to the recipient to savor. It has the power to lift a heart, put a light in the eyes and make the world suddenly appear to be a kinder, more welcoming place.

In Other Words:

" *I will try to add more lashon tov to my conversations, and in doing so, strengthen the positive power of my speech.* "

6 Tishrei — לזכות שלמה ומלכה ומשפחתם שיחיו

6 Shevat — Dedicated as a z'chus by Mr Michael Bernadiner

6 Sivan — לכבוד יום מתן תורתנו

לע"נ הרה"ח ישראל מאיר ז"ל בן יבלחט"א אליעזר צבי נלב"ע י"ט אדר א' תשס"ה

ז תשרי
7 TISHREI / CYCLE 1

ז שבט
7 SHEVAT / CYCLE 2

ז סיון
7 SIVAN / CYCLE 3

❧ *What You Don't See*

On February 23, 1987, Ian Shelton, a Canadian astronomer, was the first human being in more than a century to witness the explosion of a star. The light of this supernova, located in the galaxy closest to the Milky Way, had the power of 200 million suns.

But more powerful still was the shower of ghostly atomic particles called neutrinos that the dying star cast off in all directions. In just the first 10 seconds of the explosion, many trillions of trillions of these highly charged particles were emitted. But had a person been in their path, he would not have seen anything, for neutrinos are completely invisible to the eye. On earth, a special neutrino detector in Japan managed to capture 11 of the billions of neutrinos that reached earth. Another detector in Ohio caught eight.

Even if there had been no technology capable of detecting the neutrinos, however, they would still have been there in the atmosphere. Reality can be very powerful, even when it can't be seen with one's eyes.

Now, imagine that rather than a star exploding, a child's parent does. A boy's father comes home from work tired and harried. He tries to get his son to sit down with him and review his day's learning, but the child's attention wanders off in another direction.

"Got the right page?" the father asks.

"My bike chain is broken," he replies.

"We need the first *pasuk*," the father reminds him.

"So I can't ride it. Can you fix it?"

"Enough already! Can't you stay on the page for a minute? You're impossible to learn with! How will you ever make it through yeshivah?"

A few minutes later, the boy is doing as his father had asked, reciting the words of the Chumash he had learned that day. Although he is failing to remember what most of them mean, the father is content that at least the boy is on task. The angry words of a few moments ago seem to have evaporated into thin air.

They may seem to have passed out of existence, but like the neutrinos, they have not. They have been added to the earth's atmosphere, along with every other word that has ever been spoken.

As the Chofetz Chaim explains, "The birds of the heavens carry the voice." Everything a person says is absorbed into the Creation in some fashion. Some words spur growth, happiness, friendship and other sources of goodness and blessing. Others spur hurt, self-doubt and negativity.

Though they are made of nothing more tangible than air and sound waves, words are as solid as the earth's bedrock. To the extent that a person masters this concept, he enlists his own human nature to help him master his power of speech. No one needs to be reminded to handle fire or a dangerous chemical with care; it's second nature. In the same way, when a person understands the true nature of words, he will naturally handle them with great care. He is then well on his way to victory in his battle with *ona'as devarim*.

In Other Words:

"
Think of a typical situation in your home that you find challenging. Now create a strategy for handling this situation in a way that maintains a positive atmosphere.
"

7 Tishrei — May today's learning be a זכות for our family.
Dedicated by Kenneth Ephraim & Julie Pinczower

7 Shevat — לע״נ דוד בן ירמיה הלוי טויבער ז״ל

7 Sivan — לע״נ גיטל בת אליהו יצחק ע״ה

DAY 8

ח תשרי
8 TISHREI / CYCLE 1

ח שבט
8 SHEVAT / CYCLE 2

ח סיון
8 SIVAN / CYCLE 3

❧ *Permanent Marker*

ittle Mordy loved to draw, paint and color. But he was only 2. He lacked the knowledge and the self-control to keep his creations within the confines of the paper his mother gave him. Rather, he would express himself where, when and how he wanted. The result of his impulsive artistry was an occasional, impromptu "mural" scrawled upon the living-room wall.

Fortunately, Mordy's mother had the foresight to supply her budding artist with washable markers, whose imprint was easily erased with a damp sponge. As soon as the wall was washed, it was good as new. The mother cautioned her son against writing on anything but paper; however, knowing that the damage was easily undone, she did not feel impelled to overemphasize her warnings.

One day, Mordy discovered the world from a new perspective: standing on a chair. Suddenly, things that had been out of reach were there for the taking, including a fat, blue permanent marker. Delighted with his new discovery, Mordy quickly climbed off the chair and got to work on a new mural. Little did he know that this time, his masterpiece would endure for a long, long time.

The Gemara teaches that *ona'as devarim*, like a permanent marker, leaves a mark that cannot be erased. Once the painful words are spoken, they are set upon their victim's consciousness forever. Even if the precise words or sentiments are eventually forgotten, the alteration the words make to the victim's self-image will remain.

"Gadol ona'as devarim mei ona'as mammon," the Gemara (*Bava Metzia* 58b) states: "Greater is the wrongdoing of *ona'as devarim* than that of causing someone a monetary loss." The reason, it explains, is that with money, restitution is possible, but with *ona'as devarim*, it is not possible. This tells us that there is not enough money in the world to undo the damage a cruel word can do. Even if one were to offer his victim a million dollars, the victim might still suffer from the cruel word. Did the speaker really mean what he had said? Was there a grain of truth in it?

This effect is amplified immeasurably when harsh words are spoken to a child. It is not only a permanent mark upon the child's consciousness; it is a weakening of the "support beams" that frame the child's budding personality. It is as if the adult were feeding the child a food that was bad for his bones, something that would become integrated into his structure and prevent him from ever reaching his full height and strength.

In the opening scenario, the mother understood that the child lacked the self-control and understanding of consequences to stop himself from doing permanent damage. An adult, however, is expected to think ahead. In speaking to a child, a spouse, an employee, a student, or anyone upon whom we have an impact, it is vital to remember that once we have written our words upon their souls, the mark will not come off.

In Other Words:

"*I will make a list of five derogatory words that I tend to use in my personal or business relationships, and ban those words from my vocabulary.*"

לע״נ אלימלך בן ישראל יצחק ואשתו העני׳ חנה בת ברוך ע״ה — **8 Tishrei**
Dedicated by the Blumstein family

8 Shevat — Maurine Lee Ronner - Friedman לע״נ מליא לאה בת ר׳ אברהם ע״ה
Dedicated by Sheva & Dovid Avnet, Brooklyn, NY

8 Sivan — May today's learning be a זכות for our משפחה.
Dedicated by Regina Walls and family, Nashville, TN

ט תשרי
9 TISHREI / CYCLE 1

ט שבט
9 SHEVAT / CYCLE 2

ט סיון
9 SIVAN / CYCLE 3

 ## Toxic Cleanup

*A*aron's house was infested with ants. He was tired of paying the exterminator each year to walk around spraying a chemical that anyone could buy at the local home-improvement store. He decided that this year, he would do it himself. He bought the insecticide and stored it on a high shelf in the basement, next to the laundry detergent.

The next day, his little boy, Chaim, climbed on a chair, then onto the washing machine, and reached up to the shelf where the detergent was kept. There he saw a curious, red plastic bottle with a hose sticking out of it and a handy trigger device at the end. He grabbed it, climbed down and ran upstairs to his mother, who was in the kitchen preparing dinner.

"Look what I found!" he exclaimed excitedly as he worked to get the trigger moving.

What would the mother do? Would she diplomatically turn away so as not to hamper Chaim's self-expression? Would she worry that stopping him might insult him? Would she risk the family's health as he contaminated the food, as well as the countertops, table and floor?

Obviously, she would not hesitate for a moment to get the dangerous substance out of the child's hands before harm could be done.

When physical danger is present, people know what to do. Act quickly. Save yourself and others. However, when the danger is spiritual, many people have a far more difficult time defending themselves.

They worry about appearing overzealous or being rejected. Therefore, damaging situations often go unchecked.

This is true with *ona'as devarim*. Even among those who adhere to Torah and mitzvos, the tenor of normal discourse can be brusque or outright insulting. Often, insulting comments come in the guise of a joke; in some circles, this comprises the entire definition of humor. It can be extremely difficult for one person, who wishes to raise the standard of speech, to turn the situation around.

To keep the spiritual poisons of *ona'as devarim* from polluting the atmosphere of one's home, a person has to see it as something real, just as real as insecticide or carbon monoxide. He has to recognize it, call it what it is and make an assertive effort to keep it out. In many instances, people speak *ona'as devarim* simply out of habit. In those instances, a person can often succeed in effecting a change just by raising the speaker's awareness:

"You know, he probably feels a little embarrassed, even if he doesn't say so, when you call him that name."

Another well-known technique for encouraging change in others is the "I" message. When a person does not attack the other with a "you" accusation, but simply explains how "I" feel about something, the other person is often more receptive to the message:

"I feel so bad when I hear harsh words between you and your brother."

Negative words are a strong toxin, but sometimes, the cleanup is surprisingly simple. There's nothing to lose by trying.

In Other Words:

"*When I hear ona'as devarim in my home, I will try to sensitize the speaker to the impact of his words (making sure not to be guilty of ona'as devarim myself in the process).*"

9 **Tishrei** — לע״נ אברהם שרגא בן אלימלך ואשתו חוה בת יחיאל ע״ה
לע״נ בנימן בלע בן גרשון ואשתו נחמה בת משה יעקב ע״ה

9 **Shevat** — Dedicated by the Dunn, Kadar, Leiberstein and Yudin families

9 **Sivan** — Dorothy Shindler Lane ע״ה לע״נ דבורה בת יצחק הלוי ע״ה
Dedicated by the Lane and Brodman families

CHAPTER 2

What Fuels
Hurtful Speech

*V*ery few people wake up in the morning and think to themselves, "Who can I hurt today?" Rather, a person's verbal affronts to others often stem from flaws in their own character that blind them to their own real agenda, and to the harm they are inflicting on others in their lives.

י תשרי
10 TISHREI / CYCLE 1

י שבט
10 SHEVAT / CYCLE 2

י סיון
10 SIVAN / CYCLE 3

✒ Crash Course

*E*li arrived home from his late-night course in business administration. As he opened the front door, it brushed against some wooden blocks which, he had no doubt, had been lying there all day. The air smelled stale, as if the garbage needed to be taken out. There on the couch, eyes just now lifting from her novel, sat Devorah, his dear wife.

"Hi!" she said, trying to rise up from the couch to greet him. She moved slowly, listlessly. Eli felt a sharp barb of disapproval pricking his heart, nearly forcing him to scream the barely repressed words, "What have you been doing all day!"

Yet he clamped his mouth shut. He didn't want the fight and the tears, or the guilt he would end up feeling. But his anger was gnawing viciously at his self-control. He was like a train whose brakes were about to fail and send him careening downhill into an inevitable collision. He knew his wife worked hard. He knew how she treasured the few minutes she had for herself each night. Yet the sight of the mess, the smell of the garbage, the certainty that there was nothing but lukewarm macaroni and cheese awaiting him in the kitchen, blew in a thundercloud of anger that obscured everything else.

"Are you all right?" Devorah asked, noting her husband's tense features.

"I'm fine," he answered irritably. "Just tell me something, though. What did you DO all day? Why do I have to come home to this?"

Chazal teach that anger robs a person of his *daas* — wisdom. Stripped of the wisdom one acquires throughout years of life experience, one is nothing more than a child. His anger — no matter how righteous he believes it to be — is a tantrum, made all the more lethal by his adult capabilities.

The aftermath of such an outburst is almost always a sense of regret. Nevertheless, the victim has been hurt. The hurtful words have been expressed, and like molten lava, they will harden into a rocky layer upon the relationship.

But what if there were a red warning light that flashed when a person began to speak in anger? What if there was a way to derail the oncoming disaster and switch it to a more productive track?

What stands between an outburst and regained control is the element of time. Counting to 10 is a good way to slam the brakes down on runaway emotions, but to really advance one's mastery of the power of words one might take a little longer — perhaps 10 or 15 minutes — to think about how the situation should best be handled. If it is unimportant, it will probably evaporate on its own. If it is important, thinking about how to approach the other person is all the more worthwhile.

While the resulting words might not be pleasant for the other person to hear, they will reflect respect for his feelings and dignity. There will be no explosion, no victim and no regrets.

In Other Words:

" *I will choose one area in which I tend to fall into anger and commit myself to waiting 10 minutes before I react the next time the situation arises.* "

DAY 11

י"א תשרי
11 TISHREI / CYCLE 1

י"א שבט
11 SHEVAT / CYCLE 2

י"א סיון
11 SIVAN / CYCLE 3

ঝ A Legend in Her Own Mind

*D*ovid stood on a line of customers, waiting for the customer-service associate to finish helping the woman before him. The woman sat at the associate's desk, a look of scorn on her face, as the associate plucked desperately at his computer keyboard trying to find an answer to her question about her account. The customer sat upright, her fingers drumming nervously on the associate's desk. "What's wrong? Don't you know what you're doing?" she demanded.

"I'm sorry, ma'am, but there seems to be something wrong with the program."

"Look, get me someone who knows what he's doing!" the customer barked, rising to her feet in agitation. "I can't sit here all day. This is ridiculous. They should put an experienced person out here."

The employee's face reddened as he looked up from his computer and saw the line of waiting customers, some of whom were so embarrassed for him that they looked away. He walked to the back of the store to find a supervisor. He felt like a bumbling incompetent, and he was certain that his boss would see him in that light as well. The woman sat back down and crossed her legs, waiting for the satisfaction she felt she deserved. "These people," she mumbled half-aloud. "They hire fools. Doesn't anyone believe in quality service anymore?"

The woman in this story committed a horrifying act of emotional violence against another person.

24 ☐ WHAT FUELS HURTFUL SPEECH

The damage was so graphic that onlookers turned away rather than having to view the victim's shame. What could have motivated this woman to attack so viciously? When one analyzes the words and posture of the woman, there is one obvious answer: arrogance. In her view of the world, her standards and expectations are the ones that must be met. Those who fail must pay.

However, as heinous an incident as this was, it was not as unique as one might think. In fact, it reveals a relatively common aspect of *ona'as devarim:* the belief that things should be done our way. To a certain extent, most people succumb to a degree of arrogance. We trust our own judgment above that of others, especially those we believe to be beneath us in experience or intelligence. Because of this sense of superiority, we do not fear the other person's impression of us. We do not care if they think of us as tough or difficult; in fact, for some people, this is a compliment.

A person who states his points softly and gently exhibits the opposite trait: that of humility. It is clear from his demeanor that he does not consider himself superior to anyone else; he understands his advantages and assets to be gifts from Hashem, bestowed for the purpose of doing good in the world. Not only does this person accomplish as much as the hard-driving, tough-talking individual, but he accomplishes more and wields far more influence on others. His words, even when they communicate reproach, are chosen with the respect that one human being owes another.

In Other Words:

"*I will pay attention to thoughts such as "I'm not putting up with this" or other such phrases denoting entitlement; and try to replace them with thoughts reflecting humility, such as "I'll have to deal with this."*"

י"ב תשרי
12 TISHREI / CYCLE 1

י"ב שבט
12 SHEVAT / CYCLE 2

י"ב סיון
12 SIVAN / CYCLE 3

❧ *The Boss*

*W*hen Michael Grossman went home from his office each night, he felt tremendously accomplished. His business instincts were nearly flawless and his iron-fisted control over his employees ensured that everything flowed smoothly each day. They knew better than to disappoint him or make any mistakes. He had trained them well; they nearly jumped out of their seats when he entered the main office.

Sometimes, he had to admit to himself, he stepped on their feelings. Sometimes his toughness backfired, too, as it did when his most valuable assistant quit on him. But he didn't mind being known as a tyrant, if that's what it took to succeed.

People who feel the need to dominate others may wallpaper their lust for power with other, socially acceptable, coverings. The doctor who dominates his nurses and staff might believe he's doing it because patients' lives are a stake. The public official may tell himself that he is responsible for the welfare of the city. The businessman might justify his arrogance with the fact that "millions of dollars" are resting on his decisions.

However, this is not a trait reserved for those with high-powered careers. A school-bus driver may enjoy the sense of power he has over his passengers, but tell himself that his motivation is their safety. A domineering parent can convince himself that he is acting for the benefit of his children. Each justifies himself with the thought that his realm of influence is so important, so essential, that there is no time or place for contradiction or error.

In reality, however, a person who seeks to dominate others is motivated by one goal: the feeling of strength he derives from seeing others bow to his will and cower in his presence. Such individuals use verbal abuse, temper tantrums and harshness to conjure an instant semblance of honor and respect. Everyone defers to them, of course, out of fear. This is quicker, easier and less threatening than trying to earn real respect by showing one's wisdom and ability over the long term.

An individual who needs to dominate others has a fundamental lack of awareness of the dignity and feelings of others. He thinks that he has the right to "step on some toes" to accomplish his goals, and yet, no such right exists. Someone locked into this mode of thinking is most likely spewing *ona'as devarim* into every channel of endeavor in his life, and thus, polluting every channel.

If the core of the drive to dominate is to gain a sense of strength and power, then the cure for this trait lies in developing real strength and power. *Pirkei Avos* (4:1) teaches us "who is strong," and the answer is "one who controls himself." Controlling others is easy compared to facing one's own flaws and negative habits, making the effort to conquer them, persisting and winning. Recognizing the humanity and feelings of other people is the first step to real, lasting power.

In Other Words:

"

If I have the tendency to dominate others, I will monitor my interactions more carefully. I will tone down my responses and try — even if I am only play-acting at first — to speak with more humility.

"

12 Tishrei — לזכות בן-חור בן יאשי-הו ואשתו לימור רות בת אסתר יעל
Dedicated by Benhoor and Limor Hanasabzadeh family

12 Shevat — לע״נ אבי מורי קלונמיס קלמן בן צבי הירש דריבין ז״ל
לע״נ אמי מורתי אסתר בת יצחק אליעזר דריבין ע״ה

12 Sivan — לע״נ ר׳ ישראל ארי בן ר׳ אלעזר זצ״ל
Dedicated by his grandchildren

ר"ג תשרי
13 TISHREI / CYCLE 1

ר"ג שבט
13 SHEVAT / CYCLE 2

ר"ג סיון
13 SIVAN / CYCLE 3

✥ *Feeling Green*

C haim knew he should be happy for his brother. There was his nephew, David, up there at the bimah reading his bar-mitzvah parashah with perfect diction and a clear, musical voice. Chaim's own son, Moshe, was still struggling to learn the blessings said before the Torah reading – a few simple lines – and his bar mitzvah was in just three months. Why couldn't Chaim have a boy like his brother's? But then again, his brother had always had the perfect life, and Chaim had always struggled to just hold his ground.

When davening was over, Chaim rushed over to his nephew, shook his hand and gave him a hug, as any good uncle would. Then he approached his brother.

"David did great," he forced himself to say. He knew he should leave it at that, but he couldn't. His jealousy boiled up from his heart into his mouth, and spurted out in the guise of words thinly disguised as teasing: "Of course, he must have known his father wouldn't settle for less than perfect. My Moshe knows we'll be proud of him even if it's not perfect."

When a person feels a sense of inferiority to others, he may find himself searching eagerly for their flaws just to prove to himself that "he's not so great." Reassured that everyone has their areas of weakness, the jealous person feels momentarily assuaged. A person who is insecure in his level of religious observance might look at others who he assumes are more religious and conclude that they are not as kind as he is, or as happy. Someone who envies others' financial security might deride them for being ostentatious or stingy with charity.

These jealous thoughts become *ona'as devarim* when they seep, as inevitably they do, into one's interactions with the other person. What is lacking in these situations is an accurate understanding of G-d's supervision of the world. When a person understands that each individual receives that which G-d has apportioned to him, and that this portion is precisely what the person needs to accomplish his purpose in this world, there can be no jealousy. One would then look at another person's lot as if it was the other person's shoe: comfortable and fitting for him, but totally unsuitable for anyone else.

Once someone has mastered this attitude, other people's good fortune no longer impinges upon his own sense of self-esteem. It's no longer a contest of "him or me." One can then be happy that the other person has achieved or acquired something that is good for *him*, and understand that this in no way diminishes his own portion.

For many people, it is easier to cry over a friend's sorrow than rejoice over a friend's good fortune. This can only be because one is never jealous of someone else's sorrow. In reality, however, we would spend many more happy hours in this world if we could make others' happiness a source of our own.

In Other Words:

"*I will stop and think about situations that evoke my feelings of jealousy. The next time I am in such a situation, I will try to steer my thoughts in a different direction: to enjoy the other person's happiness.*"

13 Tishrei — Dedicated as a z'chus by Mr Michael Bernadiner

13 Shevat — May today's learning be a z'chus for all of Klal Yisroel.
Dedicated by Jay & Ruchie Frechter and family

13 Sivan — May today's learning be a z'chus for our family and Klal Yisroel.
Dedicated by Nechemia and Miriam Baver

י״ד תשרי
14 TISHREI / CYCLE 1

י״ד שבט
14 SHEVAT / CYCLE 2

י״ד סיון
14 SIVAN / CYCLE 3

 *Basic Anatomy*

*W*here are your eyes?" the mother asks her toddler, and he places his chubby little hands over his eyes. "And where's your mouth?" she urges. He clamps his hand over his mouth, his eyes smiling with delight.

Identifying the parts of the human body is a task manageable by even the youngest children. However, the Chofetz Chaim teaches that there is much more involved in this process than we may think, for every physical trait has its spiritual counterpart in our *neshamos*. As we nourish or starve, strengthen or weaken, use or abuse these parts of our physical being, we are affecting the health of their spiritual counterparts and influencing their ability to function in the World to Come.

Therefore, says the Chofetz Chaim, when a person does a mitzvah with his mouth, he strengthens his soul's power of speech. In the World to Come, where Torah and praises to Hashem are the "conversation," one whose mouth has remained pure in this world will be endowed with magnificent power. Conversely, one who sins with his mouth may find himself eternally "mute" in the World to Come.

The heart, too, must be maintained in good health for its spiritual purpose. The Chofetz Chaim teaches that the mitzvah of "Love your fellow as you love yourself" is the key to nourishing one's eternal heart. One who indulges in hatred of others, on the other hand, guarantees that he will bring this draining, depressing spirit with him into the World to Come.

Hatred, at its root, denotes a certain level of blindness on the part of the hater. What he fails to see is the intrinsic value of the other person, a value that is certain to be there because every person is created in Hashem's image.

From where do these blinders originate? Often, they come from a person's own lack of regard for himself. He needs to feel more important, more powerful, and the strategy he pursues is the illusion of superiority. To the extent that he can lower the other person, he feels comparatively higher.

By taking off the blinders of hatred and seeking to see deeper into the value of each person, one protects the spiritual "body" with which he will spend eternity. Both his heart and his mouth are strengthened for their mission in the Next World when he resists the urge to turn against another person and spew a hurtful remark at him. Likewise, he reaps benefits by actively turning his heart and mouth into tools for good. By cultivating love of another person, building another up with words, the "health" he will enjoy for eternity is everlastingly enhanced.

In Other Words:

"If I find myself in a mind-set in which I am critical of others, I will try to imagine that these feelings do physical harm to my heart."

DAY 15

ט״ו תשרי
15 TISHREI / CYCLE 1

ט״ו שבט
15 SHEVAT / CYCLE 2

ט״ו סיון
15 SIVAN / CYCLE 3

⚓ *Heart Surgery*

*M*ordechai spent the final 45 years of his life hating his brother, Leibel. It was something Leibel had said – a thoughtless, hurtful remark — that caused his brother to declare that he would never speak to him again, and indeed, he was as good as his word. When Mordechai lost his wife and Leibel came to comfort him, Mordechai sat silently, staring past him as if he were not there.

Finally, his hatred pushed its way out of his heart, into his throat and out into the world. "Who needs you here?" he told Leibel. "Get out of my house." Leibel rose up in miserable silence and left, at last accepting that for all intents and purposes, he had no brother.

In the final analysis, however, it was Mordechai, not Leibel, who suffered from the hatred. Early on, Leibel had decided that he would simply act as if nothing had happened. He apologized many times, and then, seeing it was of no avail, he went on with his life.

Mordechai, on the other hand, lived with his hatred clinging to his soul. Ultimately, it ruled him, forcing him to destroy what should have been a source of love and comfort in his life.

Once a person understands what hatred is doing to him, he often wishes he could be rid of it, and there are strategies that can help a person accomplish that goal:

Understanding oneself is the first step. Sometimes, a person discovers that his own insecurity is engendering the negative feelings:

Reuven, a yeshivah student, doubts his own ability to learn. He feels a burning resentment against Avraham, his parents' neighbor, who always asks him, "So, what are you learning these days?" To Reuven, it seems that Avraham is trying to expose him as something less than he should be. In truth, however, Avraham is simply trying to make conversation in an area he assumes would be appropriate.

Realizing that everyone has flaws is another powerful step to ridding oneself of hatred. Once a person acknowledges this fact, he can adjust his attitude toward the other person so it no longer arouses hatred:

Sara is a hard-working teacher and mother of a financially strained, large family. Her neighbor, Esther, is a full-time mother who has ample household help, a nice new car and seemingly endless reserves of money and leisure time. When Esther tells Sara of a new purchase or any other detail of her high-budget life, Sara seethes in her resentment of Esther's insensitivity. In fact, Esther is a rather self-centered person. She has a flaw, but Sara, too, has flaws. By simply facing that fact, Sara can dispel her anger.

Taking the time to consider the situation from the other person's perspective shifts the ground underneath one's emotions. Even without finding a merit for the other person, one has at least acknowledged that he *is* another person. That alone should incline one in the direction of respecting the self-esteem, self-image and G-dliness inherent within us all.

In Other Words:

"
In thinking about people toward whom I harbor negative feelings, I will apply the suggestions above and try to change my perspective.
"

15 Tishrei — May today's learning be a z'chus for all of Klal Yisroel.
Dedicated by Dr. Gail Brenner

15 Shevat — לזכות דוד בן ברוך
Dedicated by Boris & Anna Gulko

15 Sivan — Frieda Simpson לע״נ פריידא בת בנימין אליהו ע״ה
By her children: Simpson, Rosenberg, Berger and Haberman families

ט"ז תשרי
16 TISHREI / CYCLE 1

ט"ז שבט
16 SHEVAT / CYCLE 2

ט"ז סיון
16 SIVAN / CYCLE 3

◈ *A Parent's Message*

When a diamond polisher approaches a valuable stone to cleave away its impurity, he doesn't dare attempt the job with a blunt instrument. He marks exactly where the imperfection lies, and uses precision tools to ensure that no part of the stone is unnecessarily harmed.

The diamond polisher does what a parent — one who truly appreciates the value of the *neshamah* entrusted to him — must do when helping his child overcome his own imperfections. The words he uses must be precisely aimed at their purpose. If he uses the blunt instruments of condemnation, insult and anger, he destroys a part of what is precious in the child.

Ona'as devarim, causing pain with words, is prohibited whether a person is talking to a child or an adult. But with children — especially our own — the challenge is all the greater, and the harm is all the more devastating. The challenge comes from our constant interaction with our children. They can defy us, slow us down, frustrate our best efforts and act in ways that seem utterly irrational. And when they do behave badly, we have an obligation to correct them. The combination of our own waning patience and the need to set the child straight can result in an explosion that makes the child feel terribly diminished. After all, the tirade came from an adult, a giant in the child's eyes.

Many people have had the experience of returning to a childhood home or vacation spot many years later. Inevitably, everything looks so much smaller than it was remembered to be. Of course, nothing has really changed; only the vantage point of the observer.

To a child, the adult world is larger than life, and nowhere is that perspective more pronounced than in the child's view of his parents. They are everything in his world, and whatever they say bears a mighty impact. If they tell him that he will not grow if he doesn't eat his vegetables, he will imagine himself remaining 2'2" for life. If they tell him he is lazy or a poor learner, he will accept that as the truth. The parent's messages to his child become integrated into his structure, just as the calcium he drinks in his milk becomes part of his bones.

The story is told of a father who saw his child picking up a crayon on Shabbos, thereby violating the laws of *muktzeh.* He berated the child until the little boy burst into tears. In doing so, the father enforced a rabbinic ordinance — *muktzeh* — while violating a Torah transgression — *ona'as devarim.*

A warm and loving relationship is the connecting cable that carries to the child everything — values, perspectives, information, emotion — that a parent wants to convey. Nothing is more important than guarding this connection from damage, and nothing is more likely to damage it than *ona'as devarim.*

In Other Words:

" *When I feel impatience beginning to build up in an interaction with a child, I will, bli neder, slow down, relax, prepare myself to take additional time to get through the situation, and thereby avoid ona'as devarim.* "

DAY
17

י"ח תשרי
17 TISHREI / CYCLE 1

י"ז שבט
17 SHEVAT / CYCLE 2

י"ז סיון
17 SIVAN / CYCLE 3

✎ *Your Honor*

*D*avid was gearing up. Every eye was on him as he began explaining his brilliant plan for getting the yeshivah out of its financial morass. He would be hailed as a hero, no doubt, when everyone realized how brilliant he was, and equally, how foolish they had all been in their manner of funding the school's recent expansion.

"Now, I'm afraid I'm not going to be a tzaddik like Meir here, who wants to give every other kid a full scholarship," David began.

Meir sat to David's right, looking uncomfortable with the designation "tzaddik," and even more uncomfortable with the impractical way he had run his scholarship committee.

"And I'm not going to build the greatest building in the Western world, either, like Sholom here wants to do," David continued, smiling smugly in Sholom's direction. Sholom's plan for a library and a gym looked at this point like the musings of a wild-eyed dreamer.

"Here's what I'm going to suggest ..." David continued. He purposefully unveiled his grand scheme, knowing that each of the 10 men around the table — the school's administration and building committee — would simply have to agree that no one was as astute as he.

For a person like David, honor is everything. So precious is it, in fact, that he is willing to ridicule and deride others' honest efforts in order to shore up his own reputation. *Pirkei Avos,* however, teaches that David's strategy is sure to backfire. In fact, he is achieving the opposite of what he believes himself to be achieving, for honor flees from the one who pursues it.

"Who is honored?" *Pirkei Avos* (4:1) asks, and it answers, "He who honors others." It would have been a simple matter for David to have paid tribute to the efforts of all those who had applied their time, ideas and talent to the project at hand. Even if their ideas were not all practicable, these individuals did not deserve pain and embarrassment as payment.

David could have said, "Meir, I know you feel for the families that are straining to pay tuition, and I hope that eventually, we'll be able to help them out to the extent that you want. But right now, I believe we should consider cutting back on scholarships ...." Why did he not present his point in that manner? The answer is simply that his only goal was to amass the credit and honor for himself, and avoid sharing it with anyone else.

Over the course of time, a person who operates in this mode insults myriad individuals and develops a reputation as an arrogant, self-centered person. Such a person might eventually have his day, sitting on the dais of a big fund-raising dinner, accepting an award for his efforts, but the honor will be reserved for this world alone. In the view of Heaven, the casualties of his credit-grabbing may well speak louder than his achievements.

In Other Words:

" *I will, bli neder, make a point of giving honor and credit to others whenever possible.* "

י"ח תשרי
18 TISHREI / CYCLE 1

י"ח שבט
18 SHEVAT / CYCLE 2

י"ח סיון
18 SIVAN / CYCLE 3

 *A Thin Disguise*

*S*weet" *was the word everyone used to describe Leah, the school secretary. The children especially loved her, for she dispensed Band-Aids, Tylenol and sympathy with a gentle manner and warm smile. Teachers, principals, parents — no one could find a negative word to say about this genuinely kind and caring woman.*

No one, that is, except for Mrs. Kleinman, the history teacher. For her, Leah had no smiles, and only the minimum of words.

"Can you make 25 copies of this test for me for tomorrow?" Mrs. Kleinman asked Leah one day.

"It's probably too late. I'm very busy tomorrow. You should have asked me yesterday," Leah said brusquely. "Whatever ... I'll see what I can do. But don't count on it."

When Mrs. Kleinman left the office, a younger secretary asked Leah, "Why did you give Mrs. Kleinman such a hard time? What's the big deal with making the copies?

"I don't know," said Leah. "She rubs me the wrong way. I'm always saying these nasty things to her, and then feeling guilty."

If Leah would look a little deeper into her interactions with Mrs. Kleinman, she would see that there really is no mystery in her reaction. Leah dislikes the teacher's manner of speaking to her. It seems condescending, as if Leah is her personal secretary. The feeling arose the first time Mrs. Kleinman asked her to collate a booklet, declaring, "I don't have time to do the mindless stuff." Leah thought she could let the teacher's attitude "roll off her back," and in fact, congratulated herself on not responding to it. However, she now could see that her grievance had taken root in her heart and was tainting every word she spoke to Mrs. Kleinman.

Like Leah, many people harbor a negative feeling toward someone that they may not be able to express directly. The feelings might come from envy, hurt over a past incident or some other cause. There might be many reasons why they do not express the feelings directly, but the repressed anger doesn't always just go away. If it is deeply enough rooted, it can be a constant source of *ona'as devarim*, instigating sarcasm, curtness or even rudeness in one's interactions with the other person.

The way to repair the situation is to acknowledge the sources of one's negative feelings and try to deal with them in a more forthright way. If possible, one should express the feelings directly to the other person in a calm, nonconfrontational way. If there is a dispute, perhaps it can be worked out. If there is a hurt, it can be forgiven. Even if direct expression isn't possible, or doesn't change anything, there is value in just realizing that the hostile feelings are present. With that awareness, one can sometimes find the strength to avoid *ona'as devarim,* knowing that he is allowing his anger, not his best judgment, to do the talking.

In Other Words:

"*Is there someone who rubs me the wrong way, who seems to evoke ona'as devarim from me? If so, I will try to get to the root of my hostility and deal with it productively.*"

DAY 19

י"ט תשרי
19 TISHREI / CYCLE 1

י"ט שבט
19 SHEVAT / CYCLE 2

י"ט סיון
19 SIVAN / CYCLE 3

 **The Blame Game**

*T*o Yitzchak, the problem at work was that people simply did not like to hear the harsh truth about themselves. They wanted him to paste a phony smile on his face and act like everything was just fine, when in fact, everything was in major need of rectification. The office was disorganized, the staff was incompetent, and here he was, just a junior associate, having to compensate for everyone else's laziness and sloppiness.

The situation was all the more irritating because he had endured the same problems in yeshivah and then at the school where he had taken his accounting course. Even his wife and family seemed to often fail to do what he needed them to do. It seemed that incompetence was a worldwide epidemic and he was the only one immune. How could he ever achieve success against these odds?

When a person is always right and everyone else is always wrong, there are two certain conclusions that may be made: This person is not succeeding in his life, and he does not accept any responsibility for his failures. Such a person sees himself as a victim of other people's deficiencies and imagines that all his difficulties are the result of what others do and say. His response to this situation, which he experiences as tremendously frustrating, is often to lash out with *ona'as devarim* at those supposedly responsible for his troubles.

Yitzchak in the story above is an extreme example of this kind of thinking, and someone like him would probably be faltering in many areas of life. Most people, however, engage in this type of response at least sometimes. There are two motivations for this attitude:

- It relieves the person of having to face his own mistake or flaw that contributed to the problem.
- People often respond most strongly to traits in others that they dislike in themselves. One may find it far easier to disapprove of a trait in someone else than to recognize it and disapprove of it in oneself.

Even in the event that the other person really does deserve blame for something he has said or done, the only constructive purpose to pointing that out would be to ensure that he learns from his mistake. Most often, this benefit will not be derived from harsh words of blame. Rather, the lesson will be derived from calmly suggesting or modeling a better approach to the situation in question.

Ona'as devarim, by definition, is rarely a problem when people do what we expect and act as we wish. By virtue of the fact that people are different from one another, see things differently, judge things differently and have different strengths and weaknesses, the likelihood is that most people will *not* speak or behave in complete conformance to our wishes. To master this mitzvah, therefore, one needs an arsenal of positive perceptions and responses to tap into when we discover, inevitably, that the people in our lives are only human.

In Other Words:

"*I will make a list of five common complaints I have against people in my life, and come up with a positive way to approach each of these complaints, such as a changed perspective or positive response.*"

19 Tishrei — Richard Geller לע״נ מרדכי בן אריה לייב ז״ל
Dedicated by Deborah Geller & Marc Lustig

19 Shevat — Abraham Baker לע״נ אברהם יצחק בן יוסף ז״ל
Jeanette Jarashow לע״נ שיינא בת שמואל צבי ע״ה

19 Sivan — לע״נ משה אהרון בן ישראל יהודה הלוי ז״ל
Dedicated by Tzivia Fisher (Holtz)

DAY 20

כ תשרי
20 TISHREI / CYCLE 1

כ שבט
20 SHEVAT / CYCLE 2

כ סיון
20 SIVAN / CYCLE 3

ᔥ *Worth a Million*

*A*s Tzippora lay in bed reviewing the evening's events, she found that her heart was still beating hard. The anguish aroused by the latest battle with her daughter was slow to fade. How had she gotten caught up in such a pitched battle? How had it devolved into screaming and recriminations? She thought back to the early part of the evening, when her daughter Dina had just come home from school.

She hadn't greeted her mother. She just dropped her books in the corner near the front door and threw her coat over the back of a living-room chair.

"Can't you say hello?" Tzippora had demanded.

"I had a bad day," Dina had responded. "I'm going up to my room. Don't make me supper. I'll take my own later."

"And leave me a sink full of dishes? Uh-uh, Dina. You come eat with everyone else, please."

Her daughter had turned on her with eyes that seemed cold and wild. "Stop it! Stop trying to run my life! Leave me alone!" she screamed at her mother, as if she were some evil stranger intruding into her life. Tzippora felt her adrenalin rushing through her veins. Such ingratitude from her own child!

"You little fool!" she cried. "Who do you think you are? You're an angry, difficult, immature little fool and some day you're going to be sorry for how you treat people!"

Dina hadn't emerged from her room since then. Tzippora quaked at the thought of what her troubled daughter might do next. Why had she let loose as she did, adding kerosene to the fire?

Since no one really wants to be unhappy, one would think that everyone would avoid hurtful words as much as possible. One would think that people would analyze the situations that lead them into conflict, and realize that the battle often begins with a harsh criticism or a cruel label. The victim defends himself using the same weapon, and soon, so much pain has been inflicted on both sides that forgiveness is all but impossible.

Why, then, do people set foot on that path? The answer is impulsiveness; the *yetzer hara* functions best when people react before they think about the long-term consequences. As long as their only goal is the momentary satisfaction of a little revenge, of a sharp word aimed precisely at the person with whom they are angry, *ona'as devarim* seems to make perfect sense.

But if one takes just a few moments to consider how important relationships are to a person's happiness, one would hold his fire and seek another way to deal with the irritation of the moment. A person who realizes that his angry impulses will always lead him in the wrong direction learns to turn a deaf ear to what those impulses are telling him.

In Other Words:

" *Think about someone with whom you often fall into conflict. Review the usual way in which the situation unfolds and rehearse other options you can exercise the next time the situation arises.* "

לע״נ גיטעל בת ר׳ יעקב ע״ה — **20 Tishrei**
Dedicated by Dovid & Esti Scharf

20 Shevat — Eileen Kempler לע״נ עטא אסתר בת משה לייב ע״ה
Dedicated in loving memory by the Blitzstein family

20 Sivan — לע״נ מרת ציפרל בראבכפעלד ע״ה בת ר׳ ישראל אברהם מאשקאוויטש נ״י

כ"א תשרי
21 TISHREI / CYCLE 1

כ"א שבט
21 SHEVAT / CYCLE 2

כ"א סיון
21 SIVAN / CYCLE 3

↬ *Getting in Gear*

itty always puts her cup right at the edge of the table. If her mother notices, she will remind the child to move it back to a safer spot. If not, she will clean up yet another spill. Why doesn't Gitty ever learn, her mother wonders.

Gitty's mother is exhausted from a long day of work, and when dinner is punctuated by yet another spill, she loses her temper. "You're so careless, Gitty!" she exclaims. "Why don't you ever watch what you're doing? How many times do I have to tell you to keep your cup away from the edge?"

It so happens that Gitty's mother frequently finds herself regretting something she has said. She tends to be critical and short tempered, and is therefore quick to express her firm opinion of what is wrong with other people. Every time she guiltily recognizes the pain she has caused, she tells herself that she will think before she speaks. Little does she realize that she, just like her daughter, is making the same mistake over and over again. However, hers is a mistake that cannot be fixed with a quick mop-up.

To understand why it seems so difficult for people to stop themselves before they say something they will soon regret, one must examine the process of speech.

Much of what passes through a person's lips in the course of a day comes under the category of impulsive speech. In other words, the mouth and the brain are operating nearly simultaneously, like a fountain that just keeps gushing forth. Under certain circumstances, such as when one desires to impress another person or avoid arousing someone's anger, the flow of words passes through a filter before it reaches the tongue.

The fact that this filter can be used when necessary disproves the belief held by many people that it is beyond the abilities of a normal human being to think before he speaks. Speech originates in the brain. Before the word comes the thought; by definition, speech requires thinking. The only question is whether one relies entirely on this involuntary process, or one works toward developing a conscious thought process that remains in gear at all times.

To avoid *ona'as devarim*, a person must dedicate his brain to filtering its output to a finer degree. Motivation is the key.

Someone who comes to the realization that *ona'as devarim* is a negative factor in his life must then look for a different way, a means to ensure that impulsive, damaging words do not spill out of his mouth. Even something as simple as posting a "Think before you speak" sign at the desk or on the kitchen counter can help. Turning on the word filter and using it every time one speaks is ultimately nothing more than a habit which, like all habits, can be developed through repetition. Where human effort leaves off, Divine Assistance will surely come into play to help all who devote themselves to protecting the dignity of their fellow Jew.

In Other Words:

" *I will give serious thought to the ways in which my ona'as devarim damages my life, and try to build a strong motivation to overcome it.* "

כ"ב תשרי
22 TISHREI / CYCLE 1

כ"ב שבט
22 SHEVAT / CYCLE 2

כ"ב סיון
22 SIVAN / CYCLE 3

❧ Ha-Ha

he Mendelson family had a quirky sense of humor. They loved to tease one another and were masterful mimics who could quickly capture other people's mannerisms and speech patterns or simply launch into characters they had created themselves. These "routines" and family jokes wove their way into their conversations whenever the whole family got together.

One day, the oldest sister, Rena, became engaged. Her chassan was planning to spend Shabbos with her family, and Rena was filled with panic.

"Not ONE JOKE about him!" she instructed her siblings. "NOTHING! Not a tease, not a comment. His family has a completely different sense of humor and he's definitely not going to realize you're not insulting him, believe me!"

"What do you mean, Rena? Is he the type of guy who can't take a joke?" her younger brother asked incredulously. It seemed impossible that such a person could be joining their family.

Humor, like ice cream, is in many ways a matter of taste and sensibilities. What is marvelously satisfying to one person can be repugnant to another. Beyond questions of taste, however, humor has great potential to create pain and ill will. The funny, clever comments that cannot help but pop into some people's minds can, when allowed to emerge from their mouths, greatly humiliate the person who is the subject of the comment.

This is especially so when such a comment is made in front of others. In a private venue, the victim might be able to defend himself or express his displeasure at the comment, but in public, with a whole group of people laughing and smiling at the witticism, the victim is defenseless. To admit to being hurt would only add to his humiliation, marking him as someone who is oversensitive or lacks a sense of humor.

Nevertheless, for many people, keeping a clever comment locked inside their mind is a challenge of major proportions. They may enjoy the admiration of their audience, or, in a misguided yet altruistic vein, they may feel they are bringing joy and laughter to everyone around them. Regardless of whether the speaker intends to hurt the victim, his sharp wit at the other person's expense is pure *ona'as devarim*.

Humor carries with it another possibility of *ona'as devarim* as well; that is the pain one causes to others by letting them know that their joke or story was not funny. Covering up one's negative response with a fake laugh is not usually a good strategy, because a fake laugh is as obvious as the blunt words, "That's not funny."

How, then, can one deal with a person who persistently tells jokes that one finds dull or offensive? The best way to deal with such a situation is honestly but delicately trying to inform the other person of one's taste in humor without implying criticism or insult.

In Other Words:

"*If I am someone others consider quick witted, I will make an attempt to slow down and examine my comments before I speak, honestly assessing the possible damage.*"

כ"ג תשרי
23 TISHREI / CYCLE 1

כ"ג שבט
23 SHEVAT / CYCLE 2

כ"ג סיון
23 SIVAN / CYCLE 3

❧ *Holy War*

*W*hen Avraham was 19, he went to Israel with a group of friends to learn in a yeshivah there. Once the school year got underway, however, Avraham and his friends seemed to part ways. Avraham fell in love with learning. He spent every spare moment in the Beis Medrash, taking on extra learning partners and staying up until the early-morning hours immersed in his Talmud.

His friends were growing and striving as well, but Avraham soared quickly past them. While Avraham eschewed every distraction that would take him from his learning, they took some time off from their studies to take yeshivah-sponsored tours of the land. They enjoyed spending their spare time exploring Jerusalem and visiting with friends in other yeshivos.

"How can you waste your time?" Avraham asked his friend Shmuel. "How many years do you think we have to learn without interruption? I can't believe you guys. You're still like high-school kids."

Little by little, Avraham's friends stopped inviting him to join them on their outings. They also stopped listening to his speeches about their misuse of their time. "He's not even human anymore," Shmuel exclaimed to another friend after one of Avraham's lectures.

As a Jew and as a human being created in Hashem's image, a person aspires to many lofty ideals. For some people, these ideals present themselves in stark black and white. These individuals are able to cast aside all distractions and strive relentlessly to live up to the standards they set for themselves. Ultimately, this focus and consistency are the ingredients of spiritual greatness.

There is, however, a downside to such clear vision. The person can fail to see the world as others see it, and therefore cannot understand what is holding others back from striving as he does. He can become judgmental and critical, constantly focusing on the failings he perceives in others. The result of thinking poorly of others is almost always speaking negatively to them, resulting in *ona'as devarim*.

Immediately, one can see the paradox. The idealist finds himself breaching the Torah prohibition of *ona'as devarim,* motivated by misguided piety. A person with high ideals must incorporate, as the Torah does, the laws of *bein adam l'chaveiro,* into his view of virtue. Truly great figures in the Torah world are renowned not only for their idealism, but for the way in which their sensitivity to others is fully a part of their idealism.

Spiritual issues are not the only ideals people can stumble upon. Ideals like health-consciousness, neatness, the work ethic and so forth can also engender intolerance toward those who miss the mark.

Practically speaking, insulting others is not a way to accomplish the idealist's goal of pushing them toward greater spiritual striving. It usually accomplishes just the opposite, pushing people away and discrediting ideals that are rightly held but wrongly expressed. On the other hand, one who strives and achieves, all the while maintaining a pleasant, warm and giving demeanor, can inspire everyone who enters into his life.

In Other Words:

"I will think about the ideals about which I feel most passionate, and work on having an extra dose of patience and respect for others who face a greater struggle in those areas."

23 Tishrei — Dedicated to Sidney W. Goldstein with love
By Jeff, Adele, David, Chana Zelda, Yosef, Rochel & Eliezer Yehuda

23 Shevat — לע״נ לאה בת ר׳ שלמה ע״ה
Dedicated by her loving grandchildren

לע״נ אפרים מרדכי הכהן ז״ל בן משה יצחק ורנה יארמוש יבלח״ט — **23 Sivan**
Dedicated by his grandparents, Ruth & Fishel Kipust

DAY 24

כ״ד תשרי
24 TISHREI / CYCLE 1

כ״ד שבט
24 SHEVAT / CYCLE 2

כ״ד סיון
24 SIVAN / CYCLE 3

❧ *Protecting the Boundaries*

ey, Dovid! I hear you're looking to switch yeshivos after Pesach! Where are you planning to go?"

Dovid bristled. The last thing in the world he wanted was for his long-thought-out decision to leave his old yeshivah to become the latest subject of the rumor mill. Inevitably, that would lead to even more gratuitous questions, opinions and suggestions. It would cause him to have to constantly be explaining himself to people who were little more than casual acquaintances. These things drove Dovid crazy.

He had his reasons to keep his business private, but he also had trouble doing so without appearing rude or unfriendly. "It's not up for public discussion," he coldly replied to his questioner, a boy named Yaakov.

"Well, O.K., O.K., I'm just asking," Yaakov said defensively.

"So don't ask. O.K.?" Dovid retorted as he turned to walk away.

"Whoa!" Yaakov muttered to himself. "What did I do, anyway?"

People's sense of privacy varies greatly. Some are open with much of their personal life and enjoy bouncing their ideas, goals and problems off others. On the other hand, some people feel intruded upon when others try to open a window into their personal

50   ☐   WHAT FUELS HURTFUL SPEECH

lives. Each person has his boundary line, however, and it is a line that should be respected.

However, one does not have to wage a verbal assault to protect his boundaries. In most cases, the unwanted question is just curiosity or a conversation-filler. The questioner is not usually in a position to force the other person to disclose anything he does not wish to disclose. There is no harm done to the unwilling recipient of the question; he is simply annoyed at what he perceives as an intrusion.

Therefore, there is no need to strike back in an angry manner. If a person knows himself to be protective of his privacy, he should preemptively think of a few firm but pleasant responses to unwanted questions so that he will not stumble into *ona'as devarim*. He could try humor: "Sorry, it's top secret." Or he could be simple and direct: "That's something I'd just rather keep to myself," or whatever type of comment fits his personality and suits the occasion.

To the person who feels his privacy is being invaded, it may be difficult to perceive that in some cases, the questions stem from sincere care and interest. If a person gives others the benefit of the doubt on this count, he can actually come to feel a sense of warmth toward the other person. *He cares about my life*, a person can tell himself. With that thought in mind, he can deliver a response that is free of thorns.

In Other Words:

"*I will develop some responses to questions that I consider too personal, and remember to use these responses when the situation arises.*"

24 Tishrei — Dedicated as a z'chus by Ms. Deborah Campoz

24 Shevat — Josef Diller לע״נ משה יוסף בן יהושע ז״ל
Dedicated by the Diller, Berman, Cohen, Elbaz & Tropper families

24 Sivan — Jacob Kirschenbaum לע״נ יעקב בן אפרים הלוי ז״ל
Dedicated in loving memory by his sister, Chana Leah

DAY 25

25 TISHREI / CYCLE 1

25 SHEVAT / CYCLE 2

כ"ה סיון
25 SIVAN / CYCLE 3

✦ *Wearing Armor*

*I*n days of old, soldiers went into battle wearing armor. The hard exterior protected the vulnerable flesh-and-blood being inside. Hoping not to be wounded, the soldier was willing to march miles in heat and rain, bearing what must have been a phenomenally uncomfortable outer garment.

Although it doesn't clank and glisten in the sun, armor is still worn by many people today. They fear emotional injury, and they wear emotional armor to protect themselves. Their covering hides their lack of confidence in themselves; they believe that if they were to be insulted, embarrassed or even contradicted, their self-image would crumble. To survive, they feel that they must be seen as right and strong and perfect at all times.

Of course, this is not the way of the world. People will point out others' mistakes and criticize others' failings. The insecure person thinks he can protect himself from these inevitabilities by trying to instill fear in everyone around him. That way, he will enjoy the illusion of having the upper hand, and no one will dare to expose him for the imperfect person he really is. Such people wear toughness and aggression like a suit of armor. It deflects all criticism and contradiction, allowing them to maintain their image of invulnerability.

Sadly, however, the traits people employ to hide their weaknesses usually turn others against them even more. No one believes their bluster for long. No one mistakes their hostility and aggressiveness for true valor, or their disregard for others as real individualism. "I don't care what anyone thinks," can be quickly decoded into "If I allowed myself to care what others thought, I'd be devastated by the results."

A person who tries to cover his insecurity with a tough outer layer is guaranteed to speak in hurtful ways to others. He prides himself on telling others off, saying just what is on his mind without regard to the consequences. Little by little, he digs himself deeper into the rut of insecurity as all the potential sources for real, lasting self-esteem evaporate from his life.

The only way to dig out of this rut is to see it for what it is, and then actively begin doing things that build true self-esteem. This can be done by working patiently toward worthy goals, helping others, learning to accept advice and criticism and most of all, by valuing oneself as a unique creation of Hashem, who has a vital, singular role to play in this world. As a person embarks upon this path, he finds that his abusiveness is no longer necessary. He can survive news of his own imperfection, and even use it as a springboard to tremendous personal growth.

In Other Words:

"If I have a tendency to react angrily to criticism, I will stop and ask myself, 'What am I afraid of?'"

DAY 26

כ"ו תשרי
26 TISHREI / CYCLE 1

כ"ו שבט
26 SHEVAT / CYCLE 2

כ"ו סיון
26 SIVAN / CYCLE 3

≈ *Down a Few Notches*

*A*vi labored long and hard in yeshivah. He was a slow student, but he treasured the time he spent learning, and he had found a yeshivah that was just the right speed for him. He loved being part of the high-school Beis Medrash, and despite the challenges learning posed for him, he sat there diligently for long hours each day.

Sholom also struggled with learning throughout his childhood. Unlike Avi, however, he couldn't stand being anything less than the class star. Eventually, he lost his desire to learn and in 10th grade, he dropped out of yeshivah. Better to quit the game, he thought, than to be the perpetual low scorer.

One Shabbos, Avi and Sholom found themselves sitting next to each other at a kiddush. Sholom overheard Avi's friend praising him. "You know, Avi, I wish I could sit and learn like you do. You're really great. I never saw a guy with so much focus. I think you're the best guy in the yeshivah!"

"Anyone can be the best guy in that yeshivah," Sholom interjected. "It's like an eighth-grade class, just with bigger kids. Now, if you were the best guy in a great yeshivah, like my cousin is, then it's something to talk about."

"Yeah, well, I've never been the sharpest pencil in the box," Avi concurred, his momentary sense of accomplishment now thoroughly deflated. He realized that it was probably true that in another yeshivah, he would be nothing special.

The fact that Sholom wasn't learning anywhere at all, on any level at all, did not prevent him from pass-

54   ☐   WHAT FUELS HURTFUL SPEECH

ing judgment on Avi's accomplishments. In fact, simple human psychology would indicate that Sholom's inadequacy made it all the more likely that he would knock Avi down. The fastest and easiest way for a person to feel taller is to shrink everything around him.

Cutting remarks are often the result of this phenomenon. In areas in which a person feels inadequate, he is bound to resent the achievements of others. The brighter his friend shines, the further into the darkness he feels himself drifting. Thus, he casts a little darkness on the other person as well, reducing the contrast and the discomfort it arouses.

In reality, of course, cutting the other person down to size is no accomplishment whatsoever. It brings nothing new or good into the world. Sholom in the story would have been no more satisfied with his own failures after having insulted Avi. He would still be left with his sense of inadequacy.

The true route toward salving one's feelings of inadequacy is to work toward real achievements. Once a person discovers the thrill of trying and succeeding, even in small, incremental steps, he will no longer feel the need to deny others their due. Rather, he will find in others' accomplishments and efforts the inspiration to continue on his own personal path toward success.

In Other Words:

"*If I am about to cast a shadow on someone else's achievements, I will ask myself first what purpose my comment would serve.*"

✌ *And the Winner Is ...*

Y *ou think you got a bargain? You should see what I got," said the woman to her friend. "The same exact paper towels as yours, for half the price!"*

"You got a 98 on the spelling test?" the girl asked her classmate. "Well, guess what. I got 100 plus 5 extra credit points!"

"Your son got into Yeshivah Tov Meod?" one father said to the other. "That's nice. Did I tell you that my son got into Yeshivah Mitzuyan?"

There are people who just have to compete. They see everything in reference to themselves and fail to think about what any given fact or situation means to the other person. It could be a great cause of celebration that the son in the above example got into the middle-level yeshivah. It might be far more of an achievement than the other father's son getting into a top school. However, the competitive father isn't really listening to his friend. He isn't really sharing that person's news with him. He is simply using it as a backdrop against which to present his own news.

Sometimes, competitive people will even compete over bad news. One mother complains that her baby kept her up half the night, and the other mother counters that her baby kept her up the entire night. In other words, she seems to be saying, "I don't care about your tiredness, because it's nothing compared to mine." However, in reality, the second mother's situation has nothing to do with that of the first mother. The first mother is simply looking for some sympathy because she is really feeling tired. She is not less tired simply because the other mother is also tired. She should not have to prove herself to be the most tired person in the world before she merits some sympathy from her friends.

Some people are competitive because they are insecure and need to feel that they are better than others. Some are just so self-involved that everything refers back to them. If someone tells them, "I got a parking ticket," their first response will be to tell the story of when *they* got a parking ticket. If someone tells them that their child is engaged to be married, they will immediately launch into a discussion of how *they* felt when *their* child got married. "It's all about me" is the message of the competitive person.

The result of competitiveness is an invalidation of the other person's statement. Rather than comparing oneself constantly to others, a person can take their statements at face value and respond to them on those terms. If one teaches himself to feel sincere happiness for another person, he will not be so eager to dampen that happiness by attempting to belittle it in comparison with himself. It will be enough for him to know that his friend is happy, and that is good.

In Other Words:

"*When I am about to bring myself and my achievements or experiences into someone else's story, I will make an effort to hold off and give the other person my full attention.*"

DAY 28

28 TISHREI / CYCLE 1

28 SHEVAT / CYCLE 2

כ"ח סיון

28 SIVAN / CYCLE 3

✺ *Misconstrued*

*D*ov didn't know what had hit him. He was having what seemed to be a normal conversation with his wife, Leah, when all of a sudden she became furious at him. Her eyes filled with tears and she stalked out of the room saying, "If that's what you think of me, I don't need to stay here and listen to any more."

And there he stood, alone in the living room. He re-ran the conversation again.

Dov: Today was such an unproductive day. Everything I was working on got stalled for one reason or another.

Leah: That must have been frustrating. I had a similar kind of day. Every time I started something, the baby got cranky and needed me to hold him. I got pretty much nothing done.

Dov: Well, yeah. What else is new?

Leah: Oh, really? That's what you think? How can a husband be so ungrateful?

Meanwhile, in the corner of the kitchen to which she had retreated, Leah rehearsed the grievous wound. Her husband apparently thought she accomplished nothing all day. Imagine that! Who did he think kept the whole house running?

Dov thought he had communicated sympathy to his wife, recognizing that she often had to deal with the kind of frustration he had only encountered sporadically. Leah, on the other hand, thought he was criticizing her as an ineffectual, do-nothing housewife.

Miscommunication or misinterpretation of someone's words is often at the heart of an argument, and often supplies the motivation for *ona'as devarim*. The person who mistakenly believes he has been insulted responds with a return insult, thus inflicting pain on someone who didn't even know there was a dispute.

There are several ways to avoid going to war over a mistaken understanding of someone else's words. First of all, we have to **listen to each other carefully**. Often, people begin framing their responses to other people's words before the other person has a chance to finish what he is saying. In that case, the listener is not really listening. He is thinking his own thoughts. He is therefore bound to misunderstand.

The second point is to **become familiar with people's styles of speech**. Some speak bluntly or gruffly, but their intent is not to offend. It is simply the way they express themselves.

And finally, one should **always clarify the other person's intentions**. Ask, in a calm, conversational tone, if they mean what you think they mean.

Through these three methods, a person will avoid jumping to a mistaken conclusion and acting upon it. In the course of listening, thinking and clarifying, even if the words were somewhat offensive, the listener's anger will probably lose some steam and the end result will be a calmer, more reasonable response.

In Other Words:

" The next time I feel someone has insulted me, I will think carefully about what was said and whether it could be interpreted in an inoffensive way. "

<table>
<tr><td>

DAY 29

כ"ט תשרי
29 TISHREI / CYCLE 1

כ"ט שבט
29 SHEVAT / CYCLE 2

כ"ט סיון
29 SIVAN / CYCLE 3

</td></tr>
</table>

 *Under the Weather*

*T*he tickle in Yaakov's throat grew more and more pronounced with each passing minute. Where was his water? Why was his son so slow in bringing it to him? Didn't he realize how painful it was for his father to cough after his surgery?

Yaakov could hear his son's voice. He was speaking to someone who had come to the front door — perhaps a delivery man or a neighbor. How could he just stand there and schmooze when his father was suffering such torment? A few minutes later, Yaakov's son finally arrived by his father's bedside bearing a tall glass of ice water.

"What were you doing down there for so long?" Yaakov asked irritably. "If you knew how it hurts me every time I cough, you wouldn't be standing at the door schmoozing with the neighbors."

The son understood his father's irritability. Yaakov was an active, take-charge person who was obviously finding it miserable to be forced to lie in bed and wait for others to help him. Nevertheless, his father's ill temper made the job of caring for him into a thankless task. The son had come from out of town to help out for these few days, motivated by nothing more than love and a desire to help. His father's constant complaining, while not unexpected, still hurt.

There is just a microsecond between losing one's cool and speaking *ona'as devarim*. Slamming on the verbal brakes just at that moment takes focus, awareness and self-control. None of these are readily available to someone who is not feeling well. When a person is in pain or drained of energy from illness or lack of sleep, his emotional defenses are weakened. Everything is an annoyance: noise, bright light, being too warm, being too cold, a long wait. All the person really longs for is to rest, and everything else simply stands in the way.

Despite all that, the Torah provides no special dispensation for cruel, hurtful words spoken by someone who is ill or exhausted. Therefore, this situation can present a difficult *ona'as devarim* challenge for some individuals. While there are those "perfect patients" who have a smile, a joke and a good word for every visitor, doctor and nurse, there are also many people who find the situation untenable. In their state of vulnerability, they take to bossing people around and complaining bitterly when things are not done to their satisfaction.

The first result of such attacks is the infliction of pain upon people who are trying to help. To avoid that possibility, a person needs to recognize the help being given to him. As he looks at those who come to keep him company, those who treat him and those who care for him, he would do well to realize that much is being done for him even if it is not perfect. This good should not be rewarded with remonstrations and disapproval. If, instead, one learns to strengthen his patience and appreciation, it will be an asset for him even when he is in the best of health.

In Other Words:

"When I am exhausted or ill, I will be especially attentive to the manner in which I speak to people."

לע״נ גיטל בת ר׳ ישראל חיים ע״ה — **29 Tishrei**

29 Shevat — Rabbi William B. Gold לע״נ הרב זאב בן ר׳ חיים יצחק זצ״ל
Dedicated by Rabbi Yehuda Tzvi & Sara Rivka Garsek

29 Sivan — Moshe Reisman לע״נ משה פתחי׳ בן אברהם הלוי ז״ל
Dedicated by Mr. & Mrs. Larry Fixler

ל תשרי
30 TISHREI / CYCLE 1

ל שבט
30 SHEVAT / CYCLE 2

ל סיון
30 SIVAN / CYCLE 3

❧ *Fighting Phantoms*

Ilana transferred to a new high school in 10th grade. Many of the families in this school were quite wealthy. Only a few, like Ilana, attended on a scholarship and went home each night to a simple home and a simple life. While Ilana loved the school, she often felt that others must see her as "the poor kid." She had nothing to offer in their conversations about summers in Israel and Manhattan clothes-shopping expeditions. She had no new electronic gizmos with which to impress anyone. She still listened to music on a CD player.

Because there were a handful of other girls like Ilana, she had a group of friends and did not feel lonely. Nevertheless, there was a girl named Tamar, from a very wealthy family, who sought Ilana's friendship.

"I'm her chesed case," Ilana told herself. "She wants to be the one to make friends with the poor kids, just to show how great she is. Well, I'm not going to be her project."

All Tamar's overtures to Ilana were rebuffed. When Tamar invited Ilana to study with her for an exam, Ilana claimed to already have a study partner. When Tamar tried to strike up a conversation, Ilana pretended to have something pressing to do. One day, Tamar asked Ilana outright, "Why are you always avoiding me? Can't we be friends?"

"I'm not interested in being your 'case,' " Ilana replied hotly. "You don't have to prove to me how nice you are."

The reply came down upon Tamar's heart with

crushing weight. What had she said or done to deserve this reply? It was the final thrust of a battle she was not even fighting, and yet, she was the casualty.

Fighting imaginary fights is a phenomenon that is more common than one would imagine. People tend to impute certain feelings and attitudes to others without knowing if they are real. From there, they build a case against the other person, which ultimately results in speaking to that person or treating him in a manner that reflects this undeserved hostility.

Preconceptions about others are often the basis of this kind of *ona'as devarim*. Just as Ilana in the above story prejudged her wealthy classmates, assuming that they felt superior to her, many people harbor stereotypes that feed the "phantom fight." Sometimes hostility arises on the assumption that someone will deny a favor, even when the request is never actually made; or that one will be denied permission for something.

Awareness of this tendency is important for preventing the *ona'as devarim* it can produce. The hostile thoughts keep one's mental temperature at a near-boil, so that the slightest added increment of anger will cause the molten emotion to overflow its container. Keeping one's thoughts peaceful and pleasant, rather than full of ruminations about slights that have never actually happened, is an effective way to keep one's cool.

In Other Words:

"*If I find myself 'picking a fight' with someone in my thoughts, I will examine the reality of the situation and see if my hostility is based on the other person's actual words or deeds.*"

30 Tishrei — לע"נ משה יהושע בן ר' אלעזר ז"ל
Dedicated by his daughter, Bruchy

30 Shevat — As a z'chus for our dear niece, Dvora Brocha Creighton for continued success
Dedicated by Saul and Vanessa Creighton

30 Sivan — Charlotte S. Garfunkel לע"נ זיסל בת ארי' דוב ע"ה
Dedicated by Charles, Amy, Grace, Benji and Caroline Garfunkel

א חשון
1 CHESHVAN / CYCLE 1

א אדר*
*1 ADAR / CYCLE 2

א תמוז
1 TAMMUZ / CYCLE 3

✎ *"Either-Or"*

*H*ow can you say you are a religious Jew when you eat without making a brachah?" Simcha asked his teenage brother, Moshe, who was hungrily attacking a plate of French fries.

Moshe had just come back from six months at a special yeshivah for "kids at risk." He had conquered his demons, and even though he was not ready to conform to the standards of his parents' very conservative community, he felt confident in saying he was now completely religious. He put on his tefillin each day. He covered his head. But most importantly, he felt Hashem loved him, and he wanted to grow closer to Him.

Simcha, on the other hand, was blessed with a straightforward, idealistic nature. He could not understand the twists and turns of his brother's mind.

"Either you're religious and you do what the Torah says, or you're not religious and you do what you want," he told Moshe. The painful message to Moshe was that his claim to being religious was very much in doubt.

* *During Hebrew leap years, a thirteenth month called Adar Sheni is added to the calendar. During those years, the lessons for the days of Adar should be studied during each of the Adars.*

"Either-or" is a false premise that identifies a person with his flaws. If someone is "either kindhearted or selfish," then their one act of selfishness is enough to overturn dozens of kind acts. If he is "either calm or temperamental," then the one time he lashes out in frustration belies the hours and hours he maintained his composure.

That is not, however, an accurate portrayal of the human personality. In truth, every person is a composite of every trait Hashem invested in mankind. Different personalities arise from the varying proportions of these traits within any given individual. By judging people on an "either-or" basis, one strips them of their positive traits and their potential to grow. Rather than spotting and cultivating the seedlings of greatness in a person, the "either-or" evaluator lets the seedlings wither and cultivates the weeds instead.

Breaking free of this perspective is essentially an exercise in positive thinking. The child who rejects the mother's request to help with the dishes can be told, "You're lazy!" thus erasing with one word all the child's previous efforts to be helpful. Or the same child can be told, "But you really are such a big help. I'd really appreciate if you could help me now too. I count on you!" The latter response recognizes the spark of helpfulness in the child — even if it is now quite small — and helps her identify herself with this trait.

Perhaps the best way to break out of "either-or" thinking is to look within oneself. How many times does one fight the urge to say "no" to a favor? To skip or speed through a mitzvah? To say something cruel or insulting? Those urges prove that even if one is the most helpful, zealous and soft-spoken person in the world, the other side exists within him as well. No one is "either-or." All of us are "this and that."

In Other Words:

" When someone says or does something of which I disapprove, I will try to counter the impulse to judge him according to that trait by thinking of something he has done that reflects a positive trait. "

ב חשון
2 CHESHVAN / CYCLE 1

ב אדר*
*2 ADAR / CYCLE 2

ב תמוז
2 TAMMUZ / CYCLE 3

❧ *"Well, What Do You Expect?"*

*A*t 10:30 p.m., just a few moments after Aviva Gross had gratefully settled into her bed for a night's sleep, the telephone rang.

"Why do people call so late?" she complained to her husband as she grabbed the phone on her night table.

"Hello? Yes, this is Aviva," she confirmed wearily to the voice on the other end of the line. The other woman was the class mother for Aviva's daughter's class. She was looking for a chaperone for tomorrow's trip to the park.

"You can't just call people at the last minute, and I've asked a million times not to be called past 10," Aviva responded irritably. "Even if I had the time, I wouldn't do it now," she concluded. "Next time, call me earlier."

The class mother on the other end of the phone mentally noted that next time she should not call Aviva Gross at all. She made a few more calls and finally, having found a willing volunteer, went to bed still smarting from Aviva's hostile response.

Aviva, however, went to bed with a peaceful heart. If people did not want to abide by her simple request, they got what they deserved, she told herself.

Few people make hurtful remarks to be cruel. Most often, there is some rationale behind the words they speak: they are just being honest, protecting their

* During Hebrew leap years, a thirteenth month called Adar Sheni is added to the calendar. During those years, the lessons for the days of Adar should be studied during each of the Adars.

own interests, teaching someone a necessary lesson, or responding to some provocation that the other person knew would arouse a negative response.

When someone has what he considers a valid reason to criticize another person, there is still another step to take before speaking the words. That is, to find a way to say one's piece without hostile, angry words. This is especially true when one can pinpoint a particular person or situation that tends to provoke one's anger. Knowing in advance that a certain situation is likely to arouse a negative response, a person can prepare a different response. He should even rehearse that response in his mind, imagining that the irritating situation has arisen, and that instead of lashing out, he responds in his new way.

For instance, if Aviva in the above story is frequently bothered by late phone calls, she can think of firm but nonconfrontational ways to convey her feeling to those who persist in calling late. "I realize that most people are still up at this time of night, but I am really serious about not getting calls after 10. This is very important to me."

When a doctor must treat a disease, he starts with the weakest appropriate medicine and only progresses to stronger medications if he sees that the weaker formula doesn't work. This is a valid paradigm for choosing one's words as well: the kindest, softest words that will do the job are the ones we are obligated to try first, no matter what the provocation, no matter what the rationale.

In Other Words:

"If I am about to speak harshly in the belief that I am justified, I will pause a moment until I can think of a kinder way to make my point."

CHAPTER 3

HURTFUL SPEECH CATEGORY I:

Slurs On Character And Reputation

L ittle is as precious to a person as his good name and reputation. It's something people work a lifetime to build. Words that cast a shadow over someone's reputation can cause far-reaching damage, even when no harm is intended.

DAY 33

ג חשון
3 CHESHVAN / CYCLE 1

ג אדר*
*3 ADAR / CYCLE 2

ג תמוז
3 TAMMUZ / CYCLE 3

* During Hebrew leap years, a thirteenth month called Adar Sheni is added to the calendar. During those years, the lessons for the days of Adar should be studied during each of the Adars.

ג אדר ב
3 ADAR SHEINI

❧ *Bursting Their Bubble*

*T*he kids were practically climbing the walls," Rabbi Abramson told his colleague, Rabbi Steinmetz. "You could tell in a second that it was the day before Pesach vacation. So I knew I had to do something radical to get things under control. All of a sudden, this story popped into my mind about a Pesach miracle that happened in Prague in the days of the Maharal. I just shut off the lights and started telling the story in a low voice … practically a whisper. In seconds, the room was dead silent. We ended up having one of the most productive days we've had all month," the rebbi proudly concluded.

"You shouldn't have to do tricks to get your kids under control," Rabbi Steinmetz responded. "You're probably too loose with them in the first place. Maybe you're a little too desperate for them to like you. You know a rebbi isn't a friend, he's a rebbi."

Instantly, Rabbi Abramson in the above story went from feeling like teacher of the year to feeling like a total incompetent. In just a few words, his colleague imparted a lack of confidence in his abilities, implied that he had a desperate need for his students' approval and was most likely an ineffectual teacher who inspired little respect.

There are many ways to deflate another person's pride. Sometimes a person can do this with one sarcastic comment or a needless reference to a past mistake. For instance, a teenage boy proudly proclaims,

70   ☐   SLURS ON CHARACTER AND REPUTATION

"I passed my driver's test!" and his friend responds, "Oh, well, I guess the third time's the charm!" Now, instead of reveling for just a few moments in his success, the boy is thrust back in time to his two previous failures.

People who do this have various motivations. Envy may be one of them. For instance, Rabbi Steinmetz in the opening story may be envious of his colleague's closer, friendlier relationship with his students. In the case of a sarcastic comment, the motivation may simply be an inability to pass up the chance to demonstrate one's sharpness. One may even have a somewhat altruistic motivation, believing that by bringing up past errors, he is putting the current success into its proper perspective. Sometimes, in one's self-absorbed state, one does not even realize that the other person is trying to share his proud moment.

In all cases, however, the comments reveal a deficit in the person making them, and that is in the ability to sincerely share another's happiness. If someone else's triumph is your triumph too, you would never want to dampen it, for you would only be dampening the joy for yourself as well. At the moment when someone is offering to share a taste of his success, one's best response is to graciously take a taste and appreciate its sweetness.

In Other Words:

"*I will try to recognize when someone is enjoying a moment of pride and actively seek to enhance, rather than deflate it.*"

3 Cheshvan — לזכות יעקב בן פייגל
Dedicated by Isak Boruchin

3 Adar — Ezra Polen לע״נ עזרא בן הרב דוד שמעון ז״ל
Dedicated by Shalom J. and Naomi Polen, Baltimore, Maryland

3 Tammuz — לע״נ יוסף בן אלטר איסר ז״ל
Dedicated by his wife, Adele Gittleman, children & grandchildren

ד חשון
4 CHESHVAN / CYCLE 1

ד אדר*
*4 ADAR / CYCLE 2

ד תמוז
4 TAMMUZ / CYCLE 3

❧ *Free to Travel*

I *think if we take a left at that light, we'll find the entrance to the highway," the lost husband tells his skeptical wife.*

He makes the turn, travels a few miles, follows a sign to the highway, travels another few miles and, seeing no more signs to the highway, finally stops at a red light.

"Look where we are," his wife says. "That's the same supermarket we were at a half-hour ago."

"No, it's not," the husband assures her. "It's just the same chain. It's a different ... oh, no, you're right. I give up! We're right back where we started."

The sense of trying hard and getting nowhere is the definition of despair, which arouses the universal response of "I give up!" Therefore, *ona'as devarim* that forces a person to revisit "lost" times in his life is a particularly painful, deflating type of hurtful speech.

Sometimes, the motivation for this type of *ona'as devarim* is jealousy or frustration. When a person sees the growth and change the other person has been able to accomplish, he feels inferior. For instance, a man meets up with an old acquaintance from high school who has now, 15 years later, become the head of a new yeshivah in the community. "Some Rosh Yeshivah," the man says, half-jokingly. "I remember you when you couldn't even wake up for *minyan* on Shabbos morning."

Reminding someone of past errors is also misconstrued by some people as a method of reproof. A father wants his son, a struggling C student, to spend

* During Hebrew leap years, a thirteenth month called Adar Sheni is added to the calendar. During those years, the lessons for the days of Adar should be studied during each of the Adars.

ד אדר ב
4 ADAR SHEINI

more time reviewing his learning. The son makes a commitment to do so, and keeps to it for several weeks. His grades begin to improve. Then, one fine spring day, all the boys in the neighborhood are outside after school, enjoying the last hour of sunlight. The boy joins them, and that night, his review is late, tired and rushed.

"You can barely keep your eyes open!" his father exclaims. "You're going to go right back to being a C student!" He believes that by reawakening the child's shame in his past behavior, he will inspire him to stay far from it.

For the boy, however, it is as if all the rungs he had climbed since he made his commitment collapsed under his feet. He sees himself as a person who tried to improve and failed. Eventually, he begins to feel that trying is not worth the effort.

Nobody is born perfect. Our Sages teach (*Sefer HaBris* 2:4:18) that man is constantly in motion and his mission in life is to keep moving forward. Therefore, there will always be habits, places and mistaken ideas people leave behind as they follow their forward path in life. When one reminds another person of the things they are trying to leave behind, one forces the person to continue carrying them, thereby increasing rather than lightening the burden of a fellow Jew.

In Other Words:

"*Instead of reminding a person of what he once was, I will encourage him with admiration for what he has become.*"

4 Cheshvan — לע״נ זלאטא בת יוסף ע״ה
Dedicated by Rabbi and Mrs Gershon Brafman

4 Adar — In honor of our נ״י בכור, צבי יעקב בן ישראל עמנואל רפאל
May this learning be a זכות for him. Devorah & Emmanuel Rosner

4 Tammuz — Milo Bat Jemila Sankary לע״נ מזל בת ג׳מלה ע״ה
Dedicated in loving memory by her children and grandchildren

✑ *What's Hidden*

*T*he Maharal teaches that every organ is designed to reflect its function. For instance, the eye is the only organ into which one can peer directly. One can see inside the eye because the eye's purpose is to see. The speaking organs, on the other hand, are partly hidden and partly revealed. The lips are on the outside, but the teeth and tongue are hidden behind them. This expresses the fact that speech is the body's way of revealing to the world the hidden thoughts generated by our minds, hearts and souls.

But not every word formulated inside one's brain should be verbalized. The mouth is capable of opening, but it is capable of sealing itself shut as well. One of the types of speech that is not meant to be brought out into the world is that which hurts another person. Specifically, one is not permitted to reveal another person's past sins, even if the person has become a complete *baal teshuvah* and renounced the sin.

In some ways, this seems perplexing. What greater praise could there be for someone than to tell others about the challenges he has successfully overcome? This is born out by the well-known declaration of Chazal that not even a righteous man can stand in the place of a *baal teshuvah*.

However, if one were to consider the situation from a personal perspective, the wisdom of this prohibition becomes obvious. A person who has remade himself does not want to be reminded of what he used to be. Moreover, he certainly doesn't want others to know him for the person he used to be. He may find this revelation embarrassing, and may worry that his image

* During Hebrew leap years, a thirteenth month called Adar Sheni is added to the calendar. During those years, the lessons for the days of Adar should be studied during each of the Adars.

ה אדר ב
5 ADAR SHEINI

is lowered in other people's eyes. In any case, bring-ing up the past forces the person to reconnect with it, even though he may have left it far behind.

A person could imagine the situation this way: What if there were a journal, sitting on the bookshelf in shul, that detailed all the sins of each member of the community? Even if those sins were long ago atoned for and forgiven, who would want others perusing the pages of his life, mulling over the fool-ish mistakes he had made? This is essentially what a person must endure when others mention his unflat-tering past.

There are, of course, many *baalei teshuvah* who are open about their past and even use it to help inspire others to change. However, the material of their life's story belongs to them alone. It is their prerogative to reveal it where and when they feel it is appropriate.

The words that our mouths reveal should be those that cast light on other people's good qualities, their potential and their achievements. That which is dark and casts shadows on their image should be kept in the spot Hashem provided, well hidden behind the lips, the teeth and the tongue.

In Other Words:

"*Before I speak the thoughts that occur in my mind, I will consider whether revealing them serves a positive purpose.*"

לזכות אסתר חינקא ברכה בת שולמית — **5 Cheshvan**

5 Adar — לזכות לנו ולכל ישראל לבוב״ב עוסקים בתוי״ש ומקדשים שם שמים

לע״נ לאה בת משה ע״ה — **5 Tammuz**
Dedicated by Todd and Terry Miller and family

DAY 36

6 CHESHVAN / CYCLE 1

*6 ADAR / CYCLE 2

6 TAMMUZ / CYCLE 3

✒ *Not Even Normal*

*L*et's go on the new roller coaster, The Cataclysm!" one boy suggests to the group. They are visiting an amusement park on Chol Hamoed and everyone is wildly in favor of his idea. Only David, the boy who fears heights, hangs back as they all make a dash to The Cataclysm's long line of restless ticket-holders.

"What's the matter, David?" one of the boys calls over his shoulder.

"Oh, you know, I don't like going up that high," David answers, trying to sound casual. The friends have all known each other — and each other's quirks — for years.

"Man, you're 14 years old already!" his friend exclaims. "It's not even normal! You better get help." He laughs and runs to catch up with the other boys, thinking nothing more of his comment.

David is athletic, bright, funny and a good-looking boy as well. But at this moment, he feels like a pathetic specimen who bears an indelible flaw that all can see: He's not normal. He glances around the periphery of The Cataclysm, hoping to see one or two other young men lingering on the sidelines. All he sees are mothers with their young children. Ladies, babies and David. "Why can't I just get over it?" he chides himself.

The term "normal" is a brick wall against which many individuals' self-esteem has been haphazardly dashed. People dearly want to be within the realm of normal: not too tall, not too short; not too smart,

* During Hebrew leap years, a thirteenth month called Adar Sheni is added to the calendar. During those years, the lessons for the days of Adar should be studied during each of the Adars.

6 ADAR SHEINI

not too simple; not too nice, not too selfish. Because even the most average, normal people have feelings of self-doubt, they can be extremely sensitive to comments that confirm their doubts.

The label of "not normal" comes in many forms: "You should speak to someone about that [habit, fear, problem, etc.]," "What are you *doing?*" "What's wrong with you?" "How could you think such a thing?" are all phrases that deliver the same verdict: that of strangeness.

These are terms that can throw a "normal" person with "normal" insecurities into a state of distress. Imagine, then, what they can do to someone who really does suffer from emotional or social issues. There are, of course, times when one faces a situation in which he must convey to another person that the person needs help. In that case, one still has to choose his terms very carefully and refrain from causing any needless pain.

Children, in particular, are prone to teasing others who are different from them. "Retarded" and "crazy" are unfortunately often-heard childish insults. Adults can, by example and instruction, train children away from this destructive habit. Except in a clinical setting in which determinations of normalcy have a constructive purpose, there is rarely, if ever, a useful purpose in labeling someone "not normal." Obviously, if Hashem created each individual with unique attributes and flaws, our task is to appreciate, not to deride, the distinct personalities that populate our world.

In Other Words:

"

When another person's actions or words strike me as outside the realm of "normal," I will consider a) whether there is any constructive purpose to commenting upon it; b) how to phrase my comments to maintain the person's self-worth.

"

ז חשון
7 CHESHVAN / CYCLE 1

ז אדר*
*7 ADAR / CYCLE 2

ז תמוז
7 TAMMUZ / CYCLE 3

✒ *Who You Are*

Z ev and Noach had been business partners for nearly 20 years. Their small wholesale operation had grown into a major regional supplier of imported fabric. But now, Zev felt the time had come to wind down his career and spend more time learning. The partnership was dissolved, but there were many controversies along the way. Little by little, rancor grew between the two lifelong friends and partners, until during one particularly heated telephone discussion, Noach exploded, "What else would I expect from you? You're the son of the world's most famous tax evader!"

Zev countered with his own vicious attacks on Noach's family and his wife's expensive tastes. "Maybe if you hadn't grown up like a pauper you'd know how to handle money," he concluded with fury, slamming the phone and pausing to notice that his pounding heart was audible to his own ears.

Whatever complaints Zev might have had about *Noach* or *Noach* about Zev, each other's family background was probably the least relevant, least valid of them all. People may be able to change how they act, what they think and what they do, but they can never change who they are. Their lineage, their native origins, customs and language are under the purview of Heaven alone. To criticize these factors in another person is not only a waste of effort, for there is nothing they can do about it, but it is also an attack of the most personal kind. One is not insulting what the other person has done, but rather, who the other person is.

* During Hebrew leap years, a thirteenth month called Adar Sheni is added to the calendar. During those years, the lessons for the days of Adar should be studied during each of the Adars.

Calling to the fore the misdeeds of someone's ancestors or family members also inflicts deep pain on most people. If they are ashamed of their family member, one's mention of the misdeed only fans the flames of that shame and makes one guilty of the terrible sin of embarrassing a fellow Jew. If they feel loyalty and love toward the family member, despite his guilt, they will be wounded by the comment.

Criticizing another person's spouse is a particularly dangerous area upon which to tread. The Talmud *(Bava Metzia* 87a) warns that negative comments about a spouse can sow seeds of much strife. Whether the couple is just engaged or married for many years, anything that will turn a husband's affections away from his wife, or vice versa, can only serve to upset the balance of a delicate, yet crucial relationship. No one would wish to be responsible, even indirectly, for the terrible fallout from a troubled or failed marriage.

Professional boxers and wrestlers know that there are forms of attack that are illegal under the rules of their sports. In real life, the consequences are far more serious and far reaching than those of a game, and therefore, it is all the more important to refrain from unfair attacks. Sometimes, conflict cannot be avoided, but insulting a person's family, lineage or background is quite simply an illegal move whose only purpose is to cause pain. Such a purpose can never be justified.

In Other Words:

" Starting today, if I find myself about to insult someone's ancestry or family, I will see a 'stop sign' before my eyes. This is a road I will not go down. "

<table>
<tr><td>

**DAY
38**

</td><td rowspan="2">

❧ *Image Erosion*

</td></tr>
</table>

ח חשון
8 CHESHVAN / CYCLE 1

ח אדר*
***8 ADAR / CYCLE 2**

ח תמוז
8 TAMMUZ / CYCLE 3

t was 9:25 a.m. and Aaron Schwartz had not yet appeared at his office. Moshe Weiss slouched on a plush armchair, waiting for Mr. Schwartz, his lawyer, to arrive.

"I'm sure he'll be here any second," the secretary said soothingly. Moments later, the elevator door opened and in walked Mr. Schwartz. He strode over to Mr. Weiss and extended his hand.

"I hope I didn't keep you waiting too long," Mr. Schwartz said breezily. "The traffic was terrible today."

"The traffic is terrible every day," Mr. Weiss retorted irritably. "A responsible person leaves himself enough time."

Mr. Schwartz was a sharp-minded, aggressive litigator, never afraid to ruffle feathers. But suddenly, hearing Mr. Weiss's assessment of him, his heart sunk. Was he irresponsible? Maybe he really was.

A verbal assault may seem like nothing but hot air. In reality, however, it is a powerful acid that dissolves bits of its victim's self-image. Even a confident person bases much of his self-image on the cues he gets from those around him. When people treat him as competent, likeable and intelligent, he incorporates that message into his picture of himself. But what others have the power to build, they have the power to destroy as well.

The closer to one's source of self-esteem the unkind comment hits, the more damage it does. For instance, one would hardly expect a slightly built

* During Hebrew leap years, a thirteenth month called Adar Sheni is added to the calendar. During those years, the lessons for the days of Adar should be studied during each of the Adars.

ח אדר ב
8 ADAR SHEINI

young mother's self-esteem to be wounded by someone telling her she's not strong enough to lift a heavy
load. Physical strength is not part of her image of
herself. However, if someone were to say that she
did not know how to raise her children, she would be
deeply hurt.

Rabbi Yisrael Salanter told the story of a poor
shoemaker in Vilna whose fortunes suddenly turned.
He began dressing and living in accordance with his
new stature, but his old friends could not bear to see
it. "Who was *he* to dress like that and act like that?"
they murmured.

In due course, the former shoemaker's daughter
was engaged. As her proud father stood with her
under the *chuppah*, an old "friend" approached carrying a worn-out pair of shoes. He thrust them into the
former shoemaker's face and said, "Here, can you fix
these for me?"

The wealthy father-of-the-bride was suddenly jetti-
soned back into his old identity as a poor shoemaker.
His pride in the moment at hand collapsed like a
popped balloon, and he wished he could disappear
into thin air to escape his embarrassment. With one
simple sentence — which did not even contain any
intrinsically cruel words — the "friend" had committed an act of *ona'as devarim* that did violence to
another person's self-image.

It is possible that, had the shoemaker been born
wealthy instead, his self-image could not have been
attacked on this front. However, such was not the
case. His attacker knew exactly where to strike. There
was nothing left for the father to do but stand there in
front of all his guests, disgraced at his own *simchah*.

In Other Words:

"*Before I 'take someone down a few notches,' I will first imagine the expression of the father in the above story as the shoes were thrust in his face. Then, I will reassess the words I am about to speak.*"

ט חשון
9 CHESHVAN / CYCLE 1

ט אדר*
*9 ADAR / CYCLE 2

ט תמוז
9 TAMMUZ / CYCLE 3

❧ The Motive Monitor

*F*ourteen-year-old Yaakov loved children. He also had a vivid imagination and was an expert at weaving intricate tales that could keep children spellbound for hours.

One day, his younger brother had a birthday party. Soon, there were 18 first graders dashing around his house, so rambunctious that they could not be organized into any of the games that had been prepared.

Observing the mayhem and his mother's frayed nerves, Yaakov stepped in. "Who wants to hear the scariest story in the world?" Suddenly, the ruckus stopped and 18 little boys turned to him with unanimous glee. "Me! Me!" they shouted.

Yaakov led them into a darkened playroom, sat them down on the floor and began a riveting story that neatly climaxed just as the parents were arriving to pick up their children.

"Boy, you'll do anything to get an audience," Yaakov's older brother scoffed as Yaakov emerged from the playroom. The pride Yaakov had felt at saving the day suddenly chafed against his heart. Maybe he was such a loser that he needed a bunch of little kids around him to make him feel big.

The older brother's words were clearly *ona'as devarim*, possibly brought about by feelings of rivalry or guilt that he, himself, had not bothered to help rein in the wild children. Often, when one doubts other people's motives for doing a good deed, it is a

* During Hebrew leap years, a thirteenth month called Adar Sheni is added to the calendar. During those years, the lessons for the days of Adar should be studied during each of the Adars.

ט אדר ב
9 ADAR SHEINI

means of assuaging one's own guilt for not having done similarly. For instance, if a person donates a large sum of money, one might assume he is doing it for recognition or status. If someone adopts a stricter level of Torah observance, one might infer that he is trying to appear more pious than he is.

When someone casts doubt on the person's motives, he makes the person feel hurt and humiliated, "caught in the act" of doing something good with less than perfect altruism. The person may even abandon his good deed, a result which benefits no one.

There are certainly circumstances in life when it might be appropriate to encourage someone to examine his motives. Spouses, parents, close friends, teachers or rebbeim might face such a situation, but if their concern arises out of love for the other person and desire to help him improve, they will be extremely careful in how they approach the subject

A final caveat in ascribing ulterior motives to others is that one might be completely wrong. The person who gives a lot of money might accept honor as a way of encouraging his own children to follow in his giving ways. The person who adopts stringencies in Torah observance may sincerely hope that these practices will lead him to a higher spiritual level.

A good way to avoid denigrating other people's motivations is to ask oneself, *Why do I care?* Truly, there are very few reasons why someone's positive actions should be attacked. On the other hand, recognizing their efforts and encouraging them to keep moving forward can only lead to good.

In Other Words:

"*If I find myself doubting someone's motivation in doing something good, I will think instead, 'He's doing a good thing, and it will only lead to good.'*"

CHAPTER 4

HURTFUL SPEECH CATEGORY II:

Offensive, Disrespectful Speech

*C*ertain crude words hit another person with the force of a physical blow. A person who has accustomed himself to using coarse words sows far more pain, shame and embarrassment than he may ever realize.

י חשון
10 CHESHVAN / CYCLE 1

י אדר*
*10 ADAR / CYCLE 2

י תמוז
10 TAMMUZ / CYCLE 3

✄ A Blessing and a Curse

*T*ranslated into English, the irate wife's Yiddish letter to her merchant husband, off on a long business trip, was a comedy of paradox. "My dear husband — you should live to 120 — you left me without money to pay the rent, and our landlord, who should remain healthy and strong, has been haranguing me mercilessly for days, may Hashem have mercy on him ....."

And so it went, complaints peppered with blessings, sharp criticisms countered by constant pleas to the Almighty for health, strength and good fortune for all those who embittered her life. That was the way of communication at the turn of the century.

Today, the model of communication is the Special Forces operative who goes in there and guns down everyone in the way of his mission. People who cut in front of a person in line, outbid him on a business deal, or cause any irritation whatsoever, are bound to find themselves on the wrong end of a verbal barrage filled with curses, and sometimes even profanity. This is certainly the way in the secular world, and therefore, impatience and the need for immediate gratification stand to threaten the Jewish world as well.

During Hebrew leap years, a thirteenth month called Adar Sheni is added to the calendar. During those years, the lessons for the days of Adar should be studied during each of the Adars.

י אדר ב
10 ADAR SHEINI

When anger or impatience roil inside a person, it is difficult to stop long enough to edit the words heading from brain to tongue at the speed of light. But the words that emerge have impact. Curses are real. That is why the Torah forbids cursing (*Vayikra* 19:14), even when Hashem's Name is not used.

From the perspective of a person who has been cursed, the words are potent and hurtful. They can even be shocking. To those who are close — spouses, friends, children — they are an instant betrayal of the love in which they trusted. To strangers, curses are like an unexpected slap across the face.

Profanity is another form of *ona'as devarim* that sometimes flows from uncontrolled anger.

Not only does it demean the person at whom it is aimed, it also sullies the speaker. The Talmud (*Pesachim*, 3a,b) stresses that a person must strive to keep his language clean.

The irate housewife in the letter quoted above illustrates a better way to deal with frustration. When an outburst is inevitable, one can burst out with a blessing instead of a curse. *"Zei gezunt! — be well!"* is a phrase that has a long history of use in *Klal Yisrael* as a frustration-buster. There are many blessings to offer, and one should be prepared with them so that they will be waiting in the wings when one feels the overwhelming need to shout something.

Blessing others — even out of frustration — is a powerful way to bring blessing into one's own life as well, for Hashem promises that He will bless those who bless His children (*Bereishis*12:3). Certainly, wishing good and happiness to those who have caused us frustration can only help them and us, sending more blessing into circulation and uplifting us all.

In Other Words:

"*If I am in the habit of occasionally cursing others, I will prepare a short list of blessings I can use instead. The next time the situation arises, I will employ one of these blessings.*"

ᘒ *Who Is Wise?*

*T*he young mother, out on a shopping trip, noticed a plastic baseball bat that she was sure her 4-year-old son would adore. It was just the right size and weight for him, and would satisfy his yearning to play ball like his older brothers did. She couldn't wait to see the smile on his face when she presented it to him.

On arriving home, she called her little boy into the kitchen where she was unpacking her bundles. "Shmuelly, look what Mommy bought for you. Your own baseball bat!" The little boy grabbed it gleefully and screamed, "Thanks, Mommy!" as he ran out to the backyard to test it out. Only minutes later, Shmuelly's 3-year-old sister, who had been playing quietly in the sandbox, arrived at the door in tears.

"Shmuelly hit me with the baseball bat!" she sobbed.

"That's what you do with the gift I gave you?" the mother scolded her son. "Do you think I gave you a bat so you could hurt people with it?"

A person's intelligence, physical and mental capacities are gifts from Hashem. Nonetheless, like the little boy, people sometimes use these gifts to assert their superiority over others, forgetting that if it were not for Hashem's kindness, they would be just as clumsy or forgetful or bad at spelling or math as the person they are chiding. Furthermore, no matter how brilliant a person is, there is always someone more brilliant still.

Goodness and righteousness do not depend on

* During Hebrew leap years, a thirteenth month called Adar Sheni is added to the calendar. During those years, the lessons for the days of Adar should be studied during each of the Adars.

intelligence; they depend on the use to which a person puts the intelligence Hashem has given him. Neither does happiness depend on intelligence. The world is filled with people who live positive, productive lives, who are spiritually, financially and emotionally successful despite average or even below-average academic ability.

A person who taunts someone for his intellectual deficits can shake that person's equilibrium, making him feel ashamed of his perceived lack. He may not have even thought previously that there was anything of which to be ashamed. Such simple statements as "Where's your *seichel?*" or "Where have you been?" can create fissures in a person's self-esteem, weakening his fundamental idea of himself.

The same is true of physical handicaps. Children, especially, tend to stare, tease or ostracize other children who appear "abnormal" to them. They might have a physical handicap or deformity, be mentally retarded or simply very short or skinny or fat or clumsy. It is up to parents to train their children to see past other children's unusual features and understand that the other person is also a human being who wants love and acceptance.

In denigrating someone else's mental or physical abilities, a person is actually asserting his own sense of superiority. It may be true that he is superior in that particular area, however, the correct response is not that of the little boy with the new baseball bat, to "hit someone over the head" with the gift Hashem has graciously given him.

In Other Words:

"If someone makes a mistake, indicating a lack of intelligence or competence, I will help him fix the mistake without commenting on his innate abilities."

DAY 42

י״ב חשון
12 CHESHVAN / CYCLE 1

י״ב אדר*
*12 ADAR / CYCLE 2

י״ב תמוז
12 TAMMUZ / CYCLE 3

During Hebrew leap years, a thirteenth month called Adar Sheni is added to the calendar. During those years, the lessons for the days of Adar should be studied during each of the Adars.

י״ב אדר ב
12 ADAR SHEINI

❧ *All Grown Up*

*M*eatballs *and pasketti. Bunny wabbit. Eighteen, nineteen, ten-teen.*

Learning is a process of making mistakes. Children, who are new to everything, tend to make a lot of mistakes, and many of them sound adorably funny to the adults who dote on their every word. It pays, however, to be sensitive to the reactions one has to children's mispronunciations and mistakes. Right from the beginning, children can tell when they are being ridiculed, even when there is no harm intended at all.

"What's so funny?" a child might ask when his unintentional error is greeted with smiles, smirks or even an outright laugh. Not only are his feelings hurt, but he is made to feel incompetent and foolish. He becomes afraid to try again, lest he make another mistake. Eventually, if he is often ridiculed for his mistakes, his capacity to try new things, ask questions or expose his lack of knowledge in any area shrivels. As the Mishnah (*Pirkei Avos* 2:5) teaches, "A person who is ashamed cannot learn." One who is afraid to show that he does not know will never know, because he will never ask.

If even a kindhearted laugh at a child's expense can hurt him, one can only imagine the impact when the ridicule comes with condemnation. Some common expressions parents use can fall into this category: "You sound like a baby!" "When are you going to act your age?" "You can't be serious." Children treated to such exclamations of disapproval soon learn that their instincts are not to be trusted.

That does not mean, of course, that parents and teachers should refrain from correcting mistakes out of fear of wounding a child's feelings. Children rely upon the adults in their lives to set them straight on the road to maturity. There are many positive ways to do this in language that recognizes the child's effort to do something that is difficult for him, to try something new or understand something a little above his level of ability. "That's a very good word you just used. Here's the right way to pronounce it," conveys an entirely different message than, "Can't you speak English?"

The same sensitivity one applies to children is equally applicable to adults who, like children, are trying something new or something that comes hard to them. A *baal teshuvah* or convert who is just learning Hebrew needs help, not ridicule, when he mispronounces something. A person who emigrates from another country is also in need of patience and help. Although his English vocabulary and pronunciation may make him sound childish, he is an adult, perhaps even a brilliant adult who is highly articulate in his own language.

Everyone needs to feel competent and respected. While it is true, as many parents say, "If I don't correct him, he'll never learn!" it is also true that shame and despair have never motivated anyone to strive for success.

In Other Words:

"*Rather than making a joke of someone else's mistake — especially that of a child — I will offer a gentle, respectful correction.*"

DAY 43

13 CHESHVAN / CYCLE 1

*13 ADAR / CYCLE 2

י"ג תמוז
13 TAMMUZ / CYCLE 3

* *During Hebrew leap years, a thirteenth month called Adar Sheni is added to the calendar. During those years, the lessons for the days of Adar should be studied during each of the Adars.*

13 ADAR SHEINI

❧ *Looking Good*

alk down the health and beauty aisle of your local department store. Arrayed on the shelves are hundreds of products, each promising to make the user look, feel and smell attractive. Move along to the cosmetics counter, and you'll find out, if you don't already know, that an ounce of lipstick, a small cake of eye shadow or a tiny vial of makeup foundation can cost as much as lunch for two at your local kosher restaurant.

One might believe that only women are willing to spend top dollar to look their best. That theory falls apart, however, when one checks the racks of the average suit shop and finds a vast selection of European imports featuring the latest cuts and fabrics. Then there are the hats, the shoes, the shirts; a man might easily spend on one new set of Yom Tov clothing what a poor family would spend on two week's worth of groceries.

But these points are not meant to illustrate that people are vain or materialistic. They are meant to prove that to most people, the image they project is vitally important. It is so important that they are willing to spend large amounts of money to maintain their appearance. Even people who spend far-greater amounts supporting Torah and giving to *tzedakah*, even those who clearly have correct priorities, put great stock in how they appear to others.

For some people, the concern goes beyond the normal desire to project a positive image, all the way to an unhealthy sense of insecurity. Such a person is

92   ☐   OFFENSIVE, DISRESPECTFUL SPEECH

certain beyond a doubt that everyone notices her big nose or his bald spot or some other feature that is, in reality, nothing remarkable.

Because people are so sensitive in this area, one must exercise extra care in any statement made about someone's appearance. To criticize someone's facial features or physical stature can be devastating to the person, especially since those are aspects of the person that he cannot change. Even insulting someone's clothing — and thereby insulting his taste or budget — can cut deeply into his self-esteem. Such comments definitely fall within the definition of *ona'as devarim*.

The damage, however, goes beyond insult to the person. The Gemara (*Taanis* 20b) explains that if one calls another person "ugly," one is actually criticizing Hashem, the Designer of that person's features. While some types of features may be more pleasing or less pleasing to individual tastes, none are deserving of reproach, since Hashem created them all.

The old saying, "a face only a mother could love," is instructive here. Because of the love a mother feels for her child, she sees the beauty in him. Hashem invested each facet of His creation with its own beauty, and when we extend our love toward others, that beauty becomes apparent to our eyes.

In Other Words:

"When I see someone who strikes me at first as unattractive, I will look for something appealing about him or her."

13 **Cheshvan** — Annonymous

13 **Adar** — לע״נ פייבל בן חנינה ז״ל
Dedicated by Yosef and Rivka Gesser

13 **Tammuz** — לע״נ חי׳ בת אהרן ע״ה נלב״ע חשוכת בנים י״ח תמוז תשס״ו

י"ד חשון
14 CHESHVAN / CYCLE 1

י"ד אדר*
*14 ADAR / CYCLE 2

י"ד תמוז
14 TAMMUZ / CYCLE 3

During Hebrew leap years, a thirteenth month called Adar Sheni is added to the calendar. During those years, the lessons for the days of Adar should be studied during each of the Adars.

י"ד אדר ב
14 ADAR SHEINI

❧ *Nothing Left to Lose*

I'm a bum," the boy told his little brother. "I got kicked out of yeshivah, I smoke and I curse. If I were you, I'd stay away from me."

In fact, only a few months before, the boy had been in yeshivah. He was far from a star student, but he came to class. His language was indeed occasionally coarse, but that was not so unusual among his group of friends. It had been a quick descent from those days to the dismal present.

What initiated his descent? It was a conversation with the school's new dean, who had overheard the boy discussing a rebbi with his friend. The language the boy was using burned in the dean's ears. He could not let such behavior go unnoticed.

"Look at you!" the dean scolded, an expression of disgust on his face. "You talk like a bum off the streets! You're heading straight down the tubes. You'd better shape up if you want to keep your seat in this yeshivah!"

The truth was, the boy didn't want his seat. Learning was too hard. Sitting still for so many hours drove him crazy. He never would amount to anything, he was now sure, because he didn't have it in him to shape up. He might as well just be the bum he was destined to be. Stop fighting it and let it happen.

No doubt, the dean thought he was motivating the boy to make a radical change in his ways. His tough talk was calculated to let the boy know that his infraction was serious and his behavior would not be tolerated. Instead, the rebuke knocked the last vestige of self-esteem out of the boy.

An all-out tongue-lashing might seem like an appropriate tool in some cases. However, one can never achieve something positive if one does not leave the other person with his dignity intact. If he only absorbs the message that he is worthless, he will see as futile any effort to improve. The only path from that point is downward.

If one really wishes to awaken someone to the error of his ways and inspire him to improve, it is essential to build that person's sense of dignity. This was the strategy of Aaron HaKohen, who would befriend a sinner knowing that the sinner would think, *If Aaron HaKohen thinks so much of me, how can I keep committing this sin?* The act was no longer befitting the person, once he identified himself as someone of dignity and importance.

In disciplining others, criticizing them or teaching them, whether they are employees, students or our own children, one must approach not with a chain saw, but with delicate pruning shears. The goal is not to destroy, but to cut back that which is unproductive in order to channel all the person's energy into healthy, purposeful growth.

In Other Words:

" *If I must criticize or correct someone, I will make sure to always leave him with the feeling that he is respected and valued.* "

14 Cheshvan — Dovid Zomberg לע״נ דוד אליעזר בן חיים דוב זצ״ל
By Bubby Rose Karmel and Segal, Karmel and Kanarfogel families

14 Adar — Jakob Jakubowicz לע״נ יעקב בן אליהו שרגא יעקובוביץ ז״ל
Dedicated in loving memory by his family

14 Tammuz — May today's learning be a z'chus for our family and כלל ישראל
Dedicated by Rabbi Shimon & Mrs Leah Weiner

ט"ו חשון
15 CHESHVAN / CYCLE 1

ט"ו אדר*
***15 ADAR / CYCLE 2**

ט"ו תמוז
15 TAMMUZ / CYCLE 3

❧ *Showtime!*

*T*he boys in the senior division of Camp Torah-in-the-Pines grumbled audibly when the director announced at dinnertime that tonight's special guest would be the famous children's singer, Big Berel Berger.

"Now, I know some of you senior boys think Big Berel is just for young kids," the director announced, "but you've just never seen the show he puts on for older kids. He's amazing! So I expect to see every bunk at the show tonight. No exceptions!"

That night, the senior division came, dressed in their pajamas. When Big Berel began singing, that was the cue for them to launch into an act of their own. They all put their thumbs in their mouths. Then, one by one, they began whining like small children, "I wanna go home! I wanna go sleepy!"

Berel tried to ignore the protest. The counselors meanwhile tried to herd the unruly seniors out of the gym where the show was taking place. The disruption ruined the show even for the younger kids. Berel finished up as quickly as he could and left Torah-in-the-Pines angry and humiliated.

Heckling and disrupting performers, lecturers, teachers, or anyone appearing in public, can seem like a fairly harmless prank to those whose senses of humor are inclined in that direction. Surely, they imagine, the public person is a professional and he doesn't take it seriously. The hecklers manage to create some excitement and fun for themselves in a situation that apparently doesn't hold much real interest for them. In their view, no real harm is done.

* During Hebrew leap years, a thirteenth month called Adar Sheni is added to the calendar. During those years, the lessons for the days of Adar should be studied during each of the Adars.

ט"ו אדר ב
15 ADAR SHEINI

If we take a closer look, however, we see that heckling is nothing less than holding a person up to embarrassment of the most public kind. The person is on stage, standing before an audience of strangers, being ridiculed or criticized. All the strong prohibitions against embarrassing a person in public apply to this situation, multiplied by the number of people who witness the insults. No matter how amusing or creative the heckler's routine may be, there is no erasing the pain it inflicts on the person being attacked.

Furthermore, hecklers take the joy and satisfaction out of the performance for those who can and will enjoy it. In the above story, senior boys who might have been willing to give Berel a chance would have felt babyish admitting it. The younger children who had no objection to seeing Berel perform were assaulted by a negative atmosphere that took the fun out of the performance for them as well. A small group of people managed to negate the preparation, planning and hopes of all those who wanted the evening to go well.

All of these side effects are even more pronounced when the person being heckled is a teacher or Torah lecturer. The hecklers will cast doubt and ridicule upon what might be a relevant message that could benefit people greatly.

No one is obligated to like a performance or agree with a lecture. However, no one has the right to take away from someone the opportunity to reach out and give his best to those who have come to see him.

In Other Words:

"*When I am watching a performance or attending a lecture I do not enjoy, I will imagine that I am on the stage noticing that people are displeased with me, which will surely change my perspective.*"

15 Cheshvan — In memory of Robert Cable לע״נ ראובן בן יצחק ז״ל נלב״ע כ״ה חשון
In memory of Paula Cable לע״נ פשה בת אלעזר ע״ה נלב״ע א׳ כסלו

15 Adar — Esther Rabinowitz לע״נ אסתר בת פנחס יוסף ע״ה
Dedicated by Yosef & Sarah Tribuch

15 Tammuz — לע״נ מאיר בן זלמן ז״ל
By his children Yehuda Reuven & Tamara Rochel Gilden and family

ט"ז חשון
16 CHESHVAN / CYCLE 1

ט"ז אדר*
*16 ADAR / CYCLE 2

ט"ז תמוז
16 TAMMUZ / CYCLE 3

❧ *What's in a Name?*

*T*he Blob is on the phone," the boy tells his older brother. "He wants to talk to you."

"The Blob?" asks the boys' father, overhearing the conversation. "You call your friend The Blob?"

"Blobstrum's his last name," the older boy informs his father. "And he's kind of a big, blobby guy. The Blob's his nickname."

"Does he mind?" the father asks.

"He doesn't say he minds. He's used to it."

"That doesn't mean he likes it," the father replies.

Like a caricature that reduces a person's facial features to a few overexaggerated broad strokes, a nickname often reduces a person's entire personality down to a few overexaggerated strokes. All the strengths and weaknesses, likes and dislikes, talents and goals embodied in his given name fade behind the one trait brought to the fore by his nickname.

Sometimes a person acquires a nickname in childhood, and wants to shed it as he or she gets older. The person feels "stuck" in an infantile identity when people persist in using the childhood name. It often takes a long time to get people to change their habits and start using the new name, even with everyone's cooperation.

A nickname can be a benign, friendly name that causes the person no pain, in which case the nickname is not considered *ona'as devarim*. However, if he does not like the name, (for instance, there may be a man named Shimon who does *not* want to be called Shimmy), the Sages (*Taanis* 20b with *Tosafos*) teach

* During Hebrew leap years, a thirteenth month called Adar Sheni is added to the calendar. During those years, the lessons for the days of Adar should be studied during each of the Adars.

that a person should not call him by that name. Simply because the person does not want to identify himself with that nickname, it causes him pain to hear it. The pain might be minimal, but it is unnecessary, preventable and therefore prohibited. Certainly, a nickname that does have negative connotations is prohibited. The damage done by such a name can be far reaching, as it can become a self-fulfilling prophecy.

Besides nicknames, there are names people may call each other on the spur of the moment, out of frustration or anger. Some of these words are akin to curses or profanity, while others are simply negative and undignified. In either case, they are *ona'as devarim* (*Bava Metzia* 58b). Like a negative nickname, these names can take root in a person's identity. They can become the "label" by which the person sees himself and believes others see him.

Since there is a wide range of words that might qualify as negative names, a person might try to justify his use of a particular word with the rationale that "it's not so bad." One objective way a person can judge whether a name is inappropriate is to honestly assess whether he would use such a word in front of a rabbi or someone else he respects. If the answer is "no," then the name is most likely one that should not be used.

In Other Words:

"*If there are people I call by a nickname, I will ask whether they really want to be called by that name, and if they do not, I will be sure to call them by the name they prefer.*"

CHAPTER 5

HURTFUL SPEECH CATEGORY III:

Destructive, Demoralizing Statements

All people gauge at least part of their sense of self-worth by the assessments they receive from other people. One who belittles and undermines others can erode their confidence and self-esteem in ways that will cripple their ability to live a productive, successful life.

DAY 47

י"ז חשון
17 CHESHVAN / CYCLE 1

י"ז אדר*
*17 ADAR / CYCLE 2

י"ז תמוז
17 TAMMUZ / CYCLE 3

* During Hebrew leap years, a thirteenth month called Adar Sheni is added to the calendar. During those years, the lessons for the days of Adar should be studied during each of the Adars.

י"ז אדר ב
17 ADAR SHEINI

❧ *The Absentminded Professor*

*M*eir felt the tension building up inside. How could he tell his wife that he lost his passport? They were to leave for the airport in just 20 minutes to go back to New York. Where did he have it last? Oh, yes, in Tiberius! Three hours away!

"You're like a little kid," she would chide him. "You can't remember anything! You need a baby-sitter!"

It was true that Meir had a rather poor memory for the details of life. Not only did he seem to forget about objects, he tended to forget appointments and social engagements. Names would sometimes slip his memory too. It wasn't a lack of intelligence or even a lack of caring. It was just the way his mind worked; he had complete mastery of the complex field of software design in which he worked, but apparently had little available space in his own personal hard drive.

Like Meir, many people find that the myriad commitments, activities and worries of life overpower their ability to stay focused. Then there are those who just were not blessed with good memories, or suffer from Attention Deficit Disorder or, in the case of elderly people, "senior moments" or actual dementia.

And like Meir's wife, there are many people who are impatient with other peoples' lapses. They fume while the child searches for his lost homework sheet and misses his bus: "You'd lose your head if it weren't tied on!" Or they jump into the middle of their elderly parent's sentence, supplying the simple word he can't seem to come up with. Granted, these lapses do often inconvenience others, sometimes substantially. However, insulting the person who has caused the inconvenience or loss by his forgetfulness does nothing to mitigate the damage.

Rather, condemning another person for memory lapses is a guaranteed way to make him feel unintelligent, irresponsible and childish. In the case of elderly people, it sometimes contributes to their withdrawal from social interaction; they would rather sit silently than be embarrassed. For a child, it undermines his confidence in his ability to learn. He may panic when called on in class or freeze during tests, reconfirming his belief that he can't remember things. Those who are stung by such condemnation can, and should, gently let the other person know that they are hurt.

Rather than issuing insults, a person who notices that someone has difficulty remembering things might offer some advice. There are numerous electronic devices available today that can alert people to important dates and appointments. There are simple routines that can be instituted to help children remember their belongings and homework. An elderly person might require someone to help him keep his papers and bills in order. In some cases, patience and acceptance are the only viable responses.

In any case, the key is to realize that forgetfulness is not an evil trait. It is not something to deride and zealously uproot. It is a deficit for which people can learn to compensate.

In Other Words:

"*When someone inconveniences me or hurts my feelings through their forgetfulness, I will express empathy and if possible, suggest a way to avoid a similar problem in the future.*"

---

17 Cheshvan — In honor of Herman and Sarah Siegel, my beloved parents

לע"נ מרדכי יצחק בן יוסף לייב ז"ל — **17 Adar**
Dedicated by his wife Ellen and children

לע"נ חיה הדס בת ר' יחיאל מיכל ע"ה **17 Tammuz** — Hudy Amsel
By the Berman, Borenstein and Zicherman families

The Absentminded Professor □ 103

DAY 48

י״ח חשון
18 CHESHVAN / CYCLE 1

י״ח אדר*
*18 ADAR / CYCLE 2

י״ח תמוז
18 TAMMUZ / CYCLE 3

❧ *Creating an Undertow*

sk any accomplished individual about his path to success. How did he choose that path? How did he overcome the challenges along the way? What you are likely to hear is a list of names: all the people who supported him, gave him sound advice and urged him not to give up. Every award-acceptance speech ends with "I couldn't have reached this point without ..." It is the most basic concept in human psychology that people absorb messages about themselves from those they love and admire.

The mirror image of this incredible potential to motivate others with positive input is the ability to deflate them with negativity. Many people believe they are doing a service for another person when they rip apart his plans and challenge his ability to achieve the goals he has set for himself. They are applying "critical analysis" that they believe will prevent the person from wasting his time and money on something that will, in their view, never work out.

Take, for instance, the case of a young woman who has set her sights on a particular seminary. "Even if you could get in, I don't think you could keep up with the classes there," her mother says, believing she is merely applying a mature perspective to her daughter's pipe dreams. The mother's point might be well taken, but her message is, "You can't do it." Its immediate affect is to undermine her daughter's self-confidence and place a tight lid on her aspirations.

* During Hebrew leap years, a thirteenth month called Adar Sheni is added to the calendar. During those years, the lessons for the days of Adar should be studied during each of the Adars.

י״ח אדר ב
18 ADAR SHEINI

Words that erode a person's confidence are insidious. They can remain in his mind and direct his choices throughout life, causing him to shy away from opportunities that would bring him fulfillment. This type of *ona'as devarim* pulls on its victim like a dangerous undertow, impeding his progress as he makes his way through life.

Indeed, it would be wonderful if everyone could always support everyone else's ideas, but sometimes an idea is truly impractical, dangerous, wasteful, or has some other downside that must be addressed. Even so, one must think carefully before speaking and be sure that in the effort to protect the other person from a mistake, one doesn't cripple him in a way that will keep him from ever trying again. In the scenario above, the mother could have told her daughter, "I'm glad you're aiming high! Let's ask someone who went there what it takes to get in. And do you think it would be wise to apply to one or two other schools too? There are so many good ones."

Unfortunately, the more a person's opinion means to someone, the more potential that person has to undermine the other's confidence. Parents, spouses, siblings, teachers, close friends — they are the ones on whom people count to tell them the truth. Therefore, these important people must be sure to deliver the *real* truth: that limitations can be overcome and that each person comes into the world equipped with assets meant to bring him fulfillment in life.

In Other Words:

"*If I see a need to challenge another person's unrealistic goals, I will offer suggestions that might make the idea more practical, without conveying the sense that the person isn't as capable as he believes himself to be.*"

י"ט חשון
19 CHESHVAN / CYCLE 1

י"ט אדר*
*19 ADAR / CYCLE 2

י"ט תמוז
19 TAMMUZ / CYCLE 3

❧ *Threads of Brilliance*

*A*kiva, are you crazy? You're 40 years old and you've never learned a word of Torah in your life. What on earth makes you think you can pick it up now? You don't even have the skills of a second grader!"

Had that been the attitude of Rabbi Akiva's wife, the Jewish people would be missing one of their most important links in the chain of the Oral Torah.

Fortunately, however, Rabbi Akiva's wife believed in him with all her heart. As a result, he was able to throw himself into his mission and access the intellectual and spiritual gifts that had until then remained hidden inside him.

This was not a miracle. It was the natural outgrowth of an environment that nurtured his confidence and self-esteem. Anyone rooted in such an environment will achieve the same result; he may not become a Torah giant of the ages, but he will become all that his own Divine allotment of talents and abilities will permit him to be.

One who lacks faith in his own potential can feel like a failure even in the face of success. A person who believes in himself, however, can see success even in the midst of failure. One of today's most successful real-estate investors started his career in bankruptcy court. To him, the experience was not the death knell of his career, but a chance to learn what mistakes to avoid the next time.

Calling someone a failure is one of the cruelest expressions of *ona'as devarim*. A person's self-image

* *During Hebrew leap years, a thirteenth month called Adar Sheni is added to the calendar. During those years, the lessons for the days of Adar should be studied during each of the Adars.*

is a tapestry woven of thousands of threads, and each is an impression conveyed by another's words. If the threads are predominantly the bright and light colors of "good job," "thanks," "I can count on you," "I love you," and so forth, the person's self-image is light and bright as well. Unfortunately, however, there are those whose tapestry is woven of criticism and insult. It hangs, dark and somber, like a shroud over the person's life.

Even without the use of blunt, negative labels, if a person's efforts are constantly met with criticism, the cumulative message is, "You're a failure." People strive hard to please a critical person, whether it is a parent, a teacher, a boss or a friend. The critic may believe that he is actually performing a great service, driving others to reach for higher standards.

The truth, however, is just the opposite. The great leaders, teachers and parents are masters of encouragement. They seek out the smallest shred of talent in others and nurture it with encouragement. In such an environment, people are inspired to conceive of their most creative ideas, their most idealistic plans, knowing that they will never be knocked down for trying and failing.

The power to build another human being belongs to every person. In fact, this is one of the key purposes for which Hashem endowed man with the power of speech.

In Other Words:

" *I will become more aware of the underlying message in my words when I have to correct or criticize someone.* "

לע"נ ישראל אלתר בן חיים הלוי ז"ל נלב"ע כ"ג חשון — **19 Cheshvan**
Dedicated by his grandchildren: Moshe and Malka Lieberman

לזכות שמעון ישעיהו בן יפה נ"י — **19 Adar**

לע"נ ר' שמעון לב בן ר' משה הלוי ז"ל Leon Korn — **19 Tammuz**
By his grandchildren, Steven Korn and the Silverstein, Hecht and Korn Families

DAY 50

כ חשון
20 CHESHVAN / CYCLE 1

כ אדר*
*20 ADAR / CYCLE 2

כ תמוז
20 TAMMUZ / CYCLE 3

❧ *Their Pride and Joy*

*T*he young wife walked to shul with her husband feeling as if she were living a fairy tale. Not only was she a married woman dressed in her elegant new suit, but at her side was the wonderful, talented husband with whom Hashem had blessed her. This Shabbos her husband, gifted with a fine voice, was to be the baal korei.

The wife climbed the stairs to the women's balcony. She sat down next to one of her neighbors, a middle-aged woman who had belonged to the shul for decades. At last, it was time for the Torah reading. The young wife followed every word in her Chumash, marveling at the perfection of her husband's recitation.

"Do you know who the baal korei is?" her neighbor asked between aliyos.

"I do," the young woman said proudly. "That's my husband."

"Oh, how cute!" the woman commented. "With time, I'm sure his voice will mature."

One can imagine the speed with which these words tarnished the joy in this young woman's heart. Clearly, demeaning someone or something that another person holds dear is a type of *ona'as devarim.* Indeed, it is a form of verbal insult that is easy to stumble into, because the "insult" may seem rather benign. The factor that gives it so much power to wound is that it is directed at a particularly sensitive area of the other person's ego.

For instance, a person who considers himself a good pianist may be terribly wounded by a comment

* During Hebrew leap years, a thirteenth month called Adar Sheni is added to the calendar. During those years, the lessons for the days of Adar should be studied during each of the Adars.

כ אדר ב
20 ADAR SHEINI

as benign as "Your style is classical. I have to admit, I never much cared for classical music." The pianist identifies himself closely with his music, and hearing that it is displeasing to someone else produces pain and embarrassment for him.

This is also true of people's prize possessions. Telling someone that his treasured antique Gemara is just plain old and probably not worth much, or that his fabulous new car didn't rate well in Consumer Reports serves no purpose other than to detract from the joy the owner takes in his possession.

One who has children, whether they are junior *tzaddikim* or world-class troublemakers, takes innate pride in his family. General negative comments about another person's children have no positive purpose and can do real harm. Every parent wants others to see the good in his children. No matter how annoying or lacking a child might appear to someone else, to his parent he is beloved.

If we want to play the role of enhancing other people's lives, there is no sense in relating to them the negatives we see in the people, places, activities and things they love. Rather than laying a coat of tarnish upon someone's treasure, we can admire it with them. Theirs may well be the truer view.

In Other Words:

"*Before I offer my 'constructive criticism' of someone's pride and joy, I will think carefully as to whether my comments will actually accomplish anything positive. If they will not, I will remain silent or find something positive to say.*"

☙ *The Career Critic*

*O*ne Sunday afternoon in October, Yossi Rosen noticed his new neighbor, Shmuel Shapiro, raking the leaves on his front lawn. He wandered across the street and tried to strike up a friendly conversation.

"So, Mr. Shapiro, what do you do for a living?" Yossi asked.

"I'm a music teacher. I teach string instruments in the public-school system during the day, and then I have a few private students from the yeshivah in the evening."

"Teaching, really? Well, I guess it's like they say, 'Those who can, do. Those who can't do, teach." Yossi chuckled at his witticism, expecting his new neighbor to laugh along with him. After all, everyone knew that teaching was a low-paying job. And teaching music? In Yossi's mind, that was simply not a serious job for a grown man.

However, Mr. Shapiro didn't laugh. With a weak smile, he gave Yossi a quick nod and said, "I better get back to raking. See you later."

"Yeah, see you later," Yossi said, suddenly feeling the chilly autumn breeze. He walked across the street to his own house, shaking his head and wondering, "What's his problem?"

Mr. Shapiro's "problem," obviously, was that with one thoughtless joke, Yossi had completely belittled the value of his work. His Masters degree, his years of teaching experience, his own musical talent and the talent he had succeeded in developing in his students

* During Hebrew leap years, a thirteenth month called Adar Sheni is added to the calendar. During those years, the lessons for the days of Adar should be studied during each of the Adars.

were all discounted by someone who barely knew him.

For most people, their choice of profession and their standing within that profession are major components of their self-image. It is *ona'as devarim* to belittle their profession or otherwise cast aspersions on it; for instance, by saying that lawyers are dishonest, businessmen are cold hearted or other stereotypical comments. Expressing doubt about a person's competence in his chosen field is also a form of *ona'as devarim*.

However, there are sometimes legitimate reasons to discuss the negative side of someone's profession. If, for instance, the person is struggling financially and his friend has a realistic idea as to how he could advance or change careers to make more money, this is not *ona'as devarim*. In such a case, it is *chesed*.

Likewise, a person might see that someone is not as efficient or competent as he might be. It is a *chesed* to offer helpful advice, but it must be done tactfully: "You know, I saw an ad for a course that might interest you," or "Would you like to speak to my uncle about real-estate investment? He's got a lot of experience and might be able to give you good advice."

Generally, however, most people are not involved in a constructive way in their acquaintance's career choices, training, performance or other practical aspects of their work. Many negative comments about another person's profession are simply offhand remarks that serve no purpose. By avoiding such comments, we avoid inflicting needless pain on someone who is simply trying, to the best of his knowledge and ability, to earn a *parnasah*.

In Other Words:

"If I have the impulse to make a disparaging comment about someone's profession, I will instead ask him a question that shows genuine interest in his area of expertise."

❧ *Recipe for Disaster*

*M*any a new husband has discovered the minefield that exists in the kitchen. As the young wife tries her hand at cooking for her husband, she is eager to please and sensitive to every word of appreciation or criticism. For a wife and mother, feeding the family is the quintessential act of giving. Whether she throws together scrambled eggs and toast or labors over a complicated entrée, she does it to nourish and nurture the people she loves. Seeing them partake, hearing them praise the taste of their meal is all the payment she wants.

On the other side of the equation is the husband, who can expect to eat his wife's cooking more or less every day for the next 100 years. Thus, he has a strong interest in ensuring — somehow — that his wife learns to cook what he likes. The key is in the word "somehow."

A remark like, "Uch! What did you put in this soup?", is obviously not going to be received well by the cook. An alternative might be, "You know, there's some spice in here I'm not used to. Maybe next time you could try the recipe without it?"

It is always better to couch criticism in terms of one's own tastes, rather than the general quality of the cooking. "I like my food pretty salty," tells the cook that this person has a taste for salt in his food rather than telling her that the food itself is too bland.

When a person is a guest at someone else's table, there is far-less justification for saying anything negative at all about the food. If there is something he truly cannot eat, he can simply say, "I don't have much of

* During Hebrew leap years, a thirteenth month called Adar Sheni is added to the calendar. During those years, the lessons for the days of Adar should be studied during each of the Adars.

a taste for ...." or "The meat was so good that I didn't leave room for the ..." There are many tactful ways of avoiding one or two particular foods on the table.

Children should also be trained to appreciate the cook's efforts and respond sensitively when they are offered food they don't like. "No, thank you. It's not my taste," is the phrase most children are taught to use instead of the more instinctive declaration of "Yuck! This is disgusting!" They should also be instructed not to complain to a hostess, "This isn't how my mother makes it."

Another area with great potential for *ona'as devarim* is in comparing one cook's food to another. It's one thing for a husband to mention to his wife that he enjoys his sister's cheese-cake. It's quite another to bite into her laboriously prepared cheesecake and say, "My sister's is much creamier."

If one realizes that cooking is experienced by the cook as a personal gift for others, which she prepares and bestows with anticipation, it should be simple to arrive at the correct tone and attitude when voicing necessary suggestions. Appreciation is the key.

In Other Words:

"
Before I mention any criticism about food that is served to me, I will imagine that rather than a meal, I am being presented with an expensive gift that someone spent hours choosing and wrapping for me.
"

Recipe for Disaster   □   113

כ"ג חשון
23 CHESHVAN / CYCLE 1

כ"ג אדר*
*23 ADAR / CYCLE 2

כ"ג תמוז
23 TAMMUZ / CYCLE 3

❧ *To Each His Own*

*A*sher's shopping trips with his father always ended with Asher feeling depressed. Now, he was getting ready for a new year at yeshivah, and he needed a whole new wardrobe to accommodate the three inches he had grown since the previous summer.

"What do you think of this tie?" he asked his father, pulling one off the rack.

"Are you joking?" his father replied. "Are you joining a circus?"

"Yeah, I guess you're right. It's stupid looking."

Asher's lack of taste was a well-known trait of his among his family members. In fact, his sisters joked that if Asher liked something they brought home from shopping, that was a sure sign that they should return it.

His parents, on the other hand, seemed to have superlative taste in clothing and everything else. Their comments such as "Don't you have a mirror in your room?" made him feel like a bumbling fool compared to them. What was wrong with him, he wondered, that he chose so poorly?

* During Hebrew leap years, a thirteenth month called Adar Sheni is added to the calendar. During those years, the lessons for the days of Adar should be studied during each of the Adars.

כ"ג אדר ב
23 ADAR SHEINI

Clearly, Asher suffered from the comments of his family members regarding his taste.

His parents, on the other hand, thought they were the epitome of tact, guiding their color- and style-blind son with criticism coated in a thick layer of humor. They believed they were being instructive and responsible, protecting Asher from the stares and comments he would inevitably receive if he would emerge from the house wearing the clothing he chose on his own.

Indeed, Asher needed some help with his clothing choices. Also true was the fact that if his parents didn't notice and mention that his pants were too short and his tie didn't match his suit and so forth, his friends certainly would. To prevent the necessary corrections from becoming *ona'as devarim,* tact and regard for Asher's dignity are the essential ingredients.

Rather than asking "Are you joking?" when Asher showed his father the tie he had chosen, the father could have responded without sarcasm. For instance, he might have said, "That's not bad, but do you think maybe the colors are a bit too bright?"

Before one says anything at all about another person's taste, one should ask himself if there is any real purpose. If the person really would look ridiculous to others, then there is something to be gained by trying to tactfully guide the person toward more appropriate choices. However, people's tastes differ. One cannot set oneself up as the sole arbiter of good taste and condemn anyone else whose style is different. Learning to appreciate differences will go far toward eliminating the temptation to insult someone's taste.

It is especially hurtful to criticize someone's taste when he is out in public — for instance, at shul or at a *simchah* — and he has no choice but to wear what he has on. All one accomplishes by drawing attention to his "fashion *faux pas*" is to make him feel conspicuous and foolish when he most likely set out from his home feeling well dressed and confident.

In Other Words:

"*If I don't like what someone is wearing, I will first consider that perhaps this is just a matter of taste. If it is something that should be mentioned, I will find the right way to make my comments gentle and constructive.*"

23 Cheshvan — Rose Gottfried ע״ה לע״נ רייזל בת משה ע״ה
Dedicated by her children, Carol and David Gottfried and family

23 Adar — In honor of Chaim Halevi Glazer
Dedicated by his wife, Chaya and children

23 Tammuz — May today's learning be a z'chus for our family and Klal Yisrael.
Dedicated by Yaakov Dovid Titan

כ"ד חשון
24 CHESHVAN / CYCLE 1

כ"ד אדר*
*24 ADAR / CYCLE 2

כ"ד תמוז
24 TAMMUZ / CYCLE 3

➷ *Nothing to Celebrate*

*F*or years, Leah had listened to her friend Rivka boast about her excellent parenting skills. "My children know who the boss is," she would exclaim with an air of supreme confidence.

Indeed, Rivka's children seemed an exemplary lot. They were bathed and combed by 7 p.m. each night, then tucked into neat beds in neat bedrooms, where they would say the Shema and drift off to sleep by 8. Their homework was always done. They never missed a bus. They never appeared in public in clothes that were less than pristine. As they got older and the family got larger, the children seemed to become more obedient and industrious than ever.

To Leah, a disorganized and chronically exhausted mother, Rivka's flawless performance was like a constant confirmation of her own deficiencies. Thus, when she discovered that Rivka's eldest son had dropped out of yeshivah in Israel and gone to live in India, a strong sense of unholy elation filled her heart. "I knew it!" she thought silently. "I knew those kids would start to rebel against Rivka's dictatorship one day. Now she'll see how the rest of us live. Now she'll understand that it's not all in her control!"

* During Hebrew leap years, a thirteenth month called Adar Sheni is added to the calendar. During those years, the lessons for the days of Adar should be studied during each of the Adars.

כ"ד אדר ב
24 ADAR SHEINI

The thoughts running through Leah's head in the story above were shameful even to Leah herself. She knew it was wrong to feel happiness over someone else's pain. She knew that Rivka was not a cruel or evil person who deserved no sympathy. Nevertheless, her years and years of envy gave rise to elation, rather than empathy, at the first news of Rivka's troubles.

Far worse a situation would have been created had Leah then voiced these thoughts to Rivka.

If a person harbors feelings of satisfaction over someone else's troubles, the first course of action is to try to overcome those feelings with sincere empathy. Even if the person's troubles were as predictable as the end of a poorly written novel — even if his misfortune was the only logical outcome of his lifestyle, attitudes or habits — once the troubles surface, a Jew's first response is to feel the other person's pain and if possible, try to lighten his burden.

In some situations, however, it might take a lot of time or effort to arrive at this perspective. When a person does not find the strength to shake off feelings of joy at the other person's distress, his best strategy is to stay away from the other person. This is the surest way to prevent hints of one's true feelings from leaking out into the conversation, thereby causing the other person the additional, sharp pain of knowing that others are rejoicing in his misfortune.

Of course, this strategy is but an emergency measure meant to prevent the sin of *ona'as devarim*. The long-term plan for anyone who finds himself greeting other people's bad news with joy is to strengthen the foundations of *ahavas Yisrael* in his own life, activating the trait of compassion that is at the core of every child of Avraham.

In Other Words:

"If I find myself feeling somewhat satisfied by another person's misfortune, I will try to arouse empathy by imagining myself in the same situation."

24 Cheshvan — In memory of Marilyn Beckman לע״נ מזל טובה בת מאיר דן ע״ה
Dedicated by her daughter and son-in-law Cheryl and David Sykes

24 Adar — May today's learning be a זכות for our entire family.
Dedicated by Bill and Sue Berry

24 Tammuz — לע״נ שלמה בן קלונימוס יוסף ז״ל
נלב״ע כד׳ תמוז תשמ״ה ת.נ.צ.ב.ה

❧ *"I Told You So"*

*I*f there exist four words in the English language that exemplify the qualities that define *ona'as devarim,* "I told you so," would be those words. They are typically the response of someone whose good advice has been disregarded, and as a result, the person who ignored the advice is suffering. The words have no positive purpose. The person who is suffering does not need anyone to add to his suffering.

These words, or similar ones, are the classic example of "rubbing salt in the wound." They make something that already hurts hurt more. Why, then, do people so often say things like, "You should have listened to me," or "I told you this would happen"?

Parents and teachers sometimes express these thoughts because they hope that in doing so, they will create a "teaching moment" that will impress the child or student with the need to be more attentive to advice in the future. When the person is raw and hurting, he may seem to be more open to learning the lesson.

Does it work?

Showing a lack of empathy toward people very rarely sparks them into self-improvement. Instead, it gradually diminishes the list of people from whom an individual feels he can find support in his times of need. Those who respond with "I told you so" are those who appear to care nothing about his pain or difficulty. They appear to lack love or sincere regard for the person. Eventually, this serves to cut off sincere communications.

* During Hebrew leap years, a thirteenth month called Adar Sheni is added to the calendar. During those years, the lessons for the days of Adar should be studied during each of the Adars.

25 ADAR SHEINI

Between parent and child, there is little that can do more damage than disrupting lines of communication. As children come of age and move into adulthood, parents who lack an open relationship with their children lose their opportunity to influence them regarding the choices and challenges they face. This is a terribly high price to pay for the pleasure of pointing out one's "rightness" throughout the years.

On the other hand, the value of learning to listen to the advice of people who are more experienced is an inestimable asset. Instilling it in others is a worthy goal of a parent, teacher or friend. A poorly timed "I told you so" is not, however, the way to nurture this trait. Rather, one could bring out the idea in other ways. One could ask, at some time down the road, when the issue is no longer painful, "I wonder if this could have been avoided. What do you think?" Or, when a similar situation arises, one could suggest that the person try a different strategy.

The point, however, is not that a person necessarily must prepare a set script to use whenever this situation arises. If his words are spurred by a desire to help the other person avoid costly errors, and not by the desire to assert his superior knowledge, they will most likely come out right.

In Other Words:

"If I feel that an 'I told you so' is in order, I will carefully consider when and how such a message might be conveyed in a way that will be productive and not hurtful."

כ"ו חשון
26 CHESHVAN / CYCLE 1

כ"ו אדר*
*26 ADAR / CYCLE 2

כ"ו תמוז
26 TAMMUZ / CYCLE 3

❧ *Loaded Questions*

*O*ften, neutral or even positive interchanges provide a context for hurtful words to be spoken. This is a problem that can be conquered, simply by learning to identify *ona'as devarim* in common conversation, and replacing it with more positive, productive words.

Below are three instances of *ona'as devarim* disguised as "innocent questions." There is no doubt that these "questions" will leave the second party feeling foolish. By examining the questions and the underlying message contained in them, we can develop a sharper sense of where *ona'as devarim* is hidden.

> I. *"What do you think you're doing?"* the owner asked the salesman. It wasn't much of a mystery; the salesman was rearranging the showcase.

What is the underlying message? The owner is telling his salesman that he disapproves of the salesman's activity.

How could this be expressed without *ona'as devarim*? "I'd rather you fill some orders than work on the display right now." Or, "Make sure the high-ticket merchandise is up front." In other words, the owner should directly express what he wants, rather than ridicule the salesman.

⌇⌇⌇

> II. *"Oh, yes, I remember the last time you bought your wife a birthday present. How many times did you have to return it?"* Yaakov asked his brother, Yosef.

* During Hebrew leap years, a thirteenth month called Adar Sheni is added to the calendar. During those years, the lessons for the days of Adar should be studied during each of the Adars.

What was the underlying message? To Yaakov, the comment was probably just banter. But to Yosef, the message was an accusation of ineptitude.

How could Yaakov have avoided *ona'as devarim*? He might have offered some empathy: "It's hard to pick out a gift for a woman." Or he could offer help: "Want my wife to find out what she'd like for her birthday?"

~

III. "So, you're a talmid chacham, are you? Tell me, how many kings ruled over Yehudah in the course of Jewish history?" the wealthy donor asked the yeshivah student who had come to collect at his home. The young man, a diligent student of Talmud, was stumped. "Ach, they don't teach you kids anything," the donor said.

What was the underlying message? He was telling the young man that his diligence in Gemara didn't really amount to much.

How could the donor have avoided embarrassing the young man? He could not, for his only real intent was to aggrandize himself at the expense of the student.

~

Sometimes, questions are truly queries in search of information. At other times, however, they are aimed at conveying disapproval or causing embarrassment. In the above three episodes, the questions are obviously in the latter category. Were they well intentioned, they would have been stated otherwise. For instance, if the wealthy donor had asked the yeshivah boy to tell him a *dvar Torah*, the interaction would have reflected respect for the other party. The questions asked above reflected just the opposite.

In Other Words:

"Rather than asking a sarcastic or hurtful question, I will try to figure out what point I am really trying to convey, and convey it respectfully."

26 Cheshvan — May Hashem bless all of Klal Yisroel with Hatzlachah, Brachah and Shalom.

26 Adar — Julius Spiller לע״נ יוסף בן משה הערש ז״ל נלב״ע כ״ח אדר
Dedicated by Phyllis, Miles, Fern and Adina Spiller

26 Tammuz — Toni Siebzener לע״נ טויבא בת ר׳ יהודה יואל ע״ה
Dedicated by Kalmen & Faygee Siebzener

✒ *Don't Ask*

*N*ice house. What did you pay for it?" Mendy asked his new neighbor. He had never been inside the house when the previous owner lived there. She was a reclusive old woman who had nothing to do with the community. Now, he strolled around the living room, dining room and kitchen with his new neighbor Nosson at his side, appreciatively admiring the polished wood floors and freshly tiled kitchen.

Nosson didn't answer the question. He pretended not to hear. Where he grew up, people did not ask such questions. It was considered rude. Still, he understood that Mendy did not mean to be rude.

"So what did you say you paid for the house?" Mendy persisted. "Because one just like it down the block went for nearly a half-million."

"I'd rather not say," Nosson finally answered.

"You overpaid? Or maybe you don't want everyone to know what a bargain you got. Which is it?"

The conversation volleyed back and forth fruitlessly for a few more minutes until, gratefully, Nosson showed Mendy out the door.

People vary in what they consider personal information. For the majority of people, details about health, marital relations, difficulty with children, finances and uncertain future plans fall within this category. One's right to inquire in these areas depends on many factors: how close one is with the other person, how open or reserved that person tends to be, norms within one's family or community are some of them.

Being asked questions that seem to delve too deeply into one's personal matters is a source of discomfort and sometimes resentment as well. While one might be asking strictly out of concern for the other person, one still needs to be sensitive to the fact that the questions may not be welcome.

The best way to avoid upsetting another person with personal questions is to preface the questions with an acknowledgment that they might be out of line: "Don't feel you have to answer this but ..." or "If you'd rather not discuss this, I understand ..." This rule applies only if one is sufficiently close to the other person to ask a personal question. If one does not really know another person, he can never be sure what areas of life might be painful for that person to discuss, or even think about and should therefore refrain himself from asking at all.

Questions that delve into the details of truly painful areas of another person's life should not be asked unless one has concrete help to offer. Leave those discussions up to the other person, if he or she wishes to open the subject. Such situations include people who are waiting to have a child, having trouble finding a *shidduch*, undergoing treatment for a severe disease, having serious marital problems, major issues with a child or debilitating financial difficulties. In such cases, the greatest level of caring is shown not by asking probing questions, but by just being there, available, in whatever way the other person requires.

In Other Words:

"*Before I ask someone a personal question, I will first consider whether it may be improper to ask, and then consider whether there is any constructive purpose in acquiring this information.*"

DAY 58

כ״ח חשון
28 CHESHVAN / CYCLE 1

כ״ח אדר*
*28 ADAR / CYCLE 2

כ״ח תמוז
28 TAMMUZ / CYCLE 3

* During Hebrew leap years, a thirteenth month called Adar Sheni is added to the calendar. During those years, the lessons for the days of Adar should be studied during each of the Adars.

כ״ח אדר ב
28 ADAR SHEINI

❧ *Exercise Caution*

*A*t the conclusion of the yeshivah dinner, the retiring rebbi started out the door. A middle-aged man caught up with him and shouted, "Rabbi Gelbstein! I don't want to miss the chance to speak with you. Do you remember me?"

"Sure I do," Rabbi Gelbstein said. "You look exactly the same. Shua Weinstock, how are you?"

Shua was indeed much better than Rabbi Gelbstein might have expected him to be. He had been a troublesome student who came close to getting kicked out of the yeshivah many times. Rabbi Gelbstein had gone to bat for him, though, giving the principal his own personal guarantee that the wayward student would shape up.

"I just want you to know something," said Shua. "If it hadn't been for you, I don't know where I would be today. You kept me there in yeshivah, and that is what kept me from falling so far down that I might not have gotten up again. I don't know how I can ever thank you."

Shua then recounted to his former rebbi a brief outline of his life since then. He had gone on to Beis Medrash and learned full-time for several years, gotten married, started a business and brought eight children into the world. All of them were growing up on a straight path—even the boy whose personality was much like his father's.

The two parted, and the moment Rabbi Gelbstein got home, he recounted the touching story to his wife (without mentioning his name). "He said I saved him," the rebbi reported. "I actually saved the boy from destruction."

Was the rebbi boasting? He was sharing his triumph with someone who cared, who was proud and happy for his achievement. Had he instead told the story to a person who had tried teaching and quit in complete defeat, however, the same words would have been *ona'as devarim*.

What qualifies as boasting depends partly on whether or not the person being told will be happy to hear the information or hurt by it. It is *ona'as devarim* to tell a person who is struggling financially about one's great killing on the stock market; to tell a childless person about the incredible *nachas* one gets from one's child; to tell an unmarried person how wonderful it is to come home to a loving wife each evening, and so forth.

In the ideal world, one would hope that people in our lives would be happy for us even when they themselves are suffering from some lack. Being happy with one's lot is an important cornerstone of a Jewish outlook on life, but is a concept one must work on within himself, not demand from other people. Indeed, others may well be happy for us, but we should not be the ones to force-feed them the information. A diabetic might admire your birthday cake, but it would be wrong to offer him a forkful.

28 Cheshvan — In memory of Tova bas Yaakov
Dedicated by Mr. & Mrs. Moshe Gasner and family

28 Adar — Sylvia G. Ehrlich לע״נ זיסל בת אברהם יצחק ע״ה
Dedicated by Ephraim and Devorah Rich

28 Tammuz — Lola Adler לע״נ ליבע גאלדא בת נתן שמואל ע״ה
Dedicated by the Bersson Family

ᵕ᷈ *The Happy Buyer*

*I*t had been awhile since Michal had been able to buy a new outfit. She shopped around and finally found the right combination of quality and price. The next Shabbos, she wore her outfit to shul. She relished the special feeling of newness, the sharply pleated skirt and well-cut jacket.

"Good Shabbos, Michal, nice suit," said Avigail as she caught up with her neighbor on the way to shul. "It's new, isn't it?"

"Yes," Michal said proudly. "I got it at The Dress Spot on sale. I got a great price."

"The Dress Spot? Are you kidding?" Avigail said incredulously. "Value Palace has the same brands, and even without a sale they're 10 percent cheaper. And now they're having a sale. You probably paid twice what you had to. You know, why don't you bring it back and go to Value Palace?"

"I can't return it," said Michal. "I already had it tailored."

Now Michal's regal "new suit" posture was a little more slumped as she continued on her way to shul. She hadn't even considered traveling a half-hour out of town to Value Palace.

* When this month has only 29 days the lesson for the 30th day should also be studied today.

* During Hebrew leap years, a thirteenth month called Adar Sheni is added to the calendar. During those years, the lessons for the days of Adar should be studied during each of the Adars.

When someone purchases a new item, one must be careful not to unnecessarily rob him of the joy of his new purchase. Unless there is a constructive purpose in criticizing the purchase, one should find something about it to praise (*Kesubos* 17a). The more expensive the item, the more careful one must be not to comment negatively.

Even if the item does not meet one's own standards or quality or value, it is likely that the person who made the purchase is satisfied on those counts. Otherwise, he would not have made the purchase. If one cannot find something to praise, he can at least acknowledge that the item is bringing the other person satisfaction: "It must feel great to walk into the living room and see a new couch."

There may, however, be a constructive purpose to telling someone about a significantly lower price or a better quality or a defect in an item. A key factor is whether the item can be returned. If it can be, then the person has the option of acting on the advice and saving money or obtaining a better product. However, the *Pele Yoetz (Derech Eretz)* says that if the purchaser cannot return the item, one should not tell him that he overpaid.

Neither should one ascertain this fact by saying, "Can you return this, because if you can, I want to tell you something. If you can't, though, there's no point." In making such a comment, one is putting the other person on notice that he has some information that would motivate him to return the item if he could. Most of the time, all someone wants is for others to admire his purchase and share his joy. It's one of the simplest ways in the world to make another person happy; it requires no expertise, no great advice: just a generous heart and a kind word.

In Other Words:

"*My first response when someone shows me a new purchase will be to find something about it to praise and to enhance the pleasure the purchase gives him.*"

❧ *Helpful Hints*

*W*hen Mrs. Kramer came home, the baby-sitter was in the process of changing the baby's diaper. The baby was flailing around, kicking his legs and waving his arms. The baby-sitter was having trouble getting the job done.

"Move aside for a minute and I'll show you the right way to do this," Mrs. Kramer told the baby-sitter. "He's too hard for you to handle."

Ten-year-old Chaim wanted to help his father build the sukkah in his family's backyard. He climbed a ladder and began adjusting the heavy wooden beams that stabilized the walls.

"Let me do that, Chaim," his father called. "You're not strong enough to move those beams."

"But Daddy, look! I'm moving them already," the boy answered.

"Just let me do it so it comes out straight," the father reiterated.

Bubbie Cohen stood at her daughter's kitchen sink outfitted in an apron and rubber gloves. The steam rose from the hot water that poured from the spout, and she hummed a Shabbos song as she soaped and rinsed the pile of dishes.

"Mom, let me do that!" her daughter Rose insisted. "You'll wear yourself out!"

"Don't be silly," her mother replied. "You put the children to bed and I'll finish up in here."

"Mom, really, I can get it done much faster. Just let me do it, please."

On the surface, each of these scenarios presents someone who was trying to help. The mother was

*When this month has only 29 days, the lessons for the 30th day should be learned together with that of the 29th.

merely offering help to the struggling baby-sitter, help for which she would probably have been grateful. The father was trying to help the son do a job that was difficult for a child his age. The daughter was trying to relieve her mother of the burden of washing the dishes.

Under the surface, however, was a message that cast doubt on the other person's competence.

When one couches offers of help in terms that convey the other person's helplessness or incompetence, the kind offer turns into an insult. Helping someone is a *chesed* and is certainly not to be avoided. However, the wording a person uses in offering help is an important factor.

The best way to keep help helpful is to concentrate on positive instructions rather than critiques. "Steer a little more toward the center of the lane" is better than "You're way over to the left! We're going to end up in the oncoming traffic!" "Let's go over it again and you will see that you can read it perfectly" is better than "It was full of mistakes — read it again."

When a person wants to offer help — a deed of kindness — causing pain in the process is a terrible erosion of the merit his kind act should earn. To protect that priceless value of helping others, it pays to carefully measure the words that are spoken in the process.

In Other Words:

"*When instructing or helping others, I will concentrate on giving positive instructions and avoid casting doubt on their abilities.*"

לע"נ גבריאל נח ה"יד בן נחמן יבלח"ט ורבקה האלצבערג הי"ד בת שמעון יבלח"ט — **30 Cheshvan**

30 Adar — May today's learning be a זכות for the Grunfeld family.

1 Av — לע"נ מורינו הרב ר' שלמה בן מורנו הרב ר' בן ציון הלברשטם מבאבוב זצ"ל
Dedicated by Gedalia and Esther Miller

CHAPTER 6:

HURTFUL SPEECH CATEGORY IV:

Manipulative, Defensive Tactics

*T*ough verbal tactics can sometimes be used to put others on the defensive and reduce opposition to one's own agenda. In the process, the other party is often devalued, intimidated and stopped from asserting his or her own perspectives. In the end, both sides lose.

א כסלו
1 KISLEV / CYCLE 1

א ניסן
1 NISSAN / CYCLE 2

ב אב
2 AV / CYCLE 3

❧ *The Dark Side*

*Y*onason had his coat on and was digging through his pocket for his car keys.

"You're really going to the siyum?" his wife questioned doubtfully.

"Yeah, why not? This is a big milestone for Shmuel's father. To finish a mesechta for the first time in your life at the age of 75 is pretty amazing. I want to be there."

"But you know how late these things run. You'll be exhausted driving to work tomorrow. You'll have an accident, G-d forbid. I'll be worried all night."

"Rivky, don't worry. I won't stay late. I think it will be a big lift to be there," Yonason told his wife enthusiastically.

"Fine, but you know that neighborhood. There's no parking near Shmuel's house, and now it's starting to rain. You want to trudge five or six blocks in the dark and the rain?"

Yonason's resolve was beginning to dissipate. He suddenly felt the fatigue of the day catching up with him and imagined the pleasure of crawling into his nice warm bed and getting a good night's sleep. The cold rain pinging against the storm door offered another argument against going out.

"Never mind all that," he finally told his wife. *"I'm going. I told Shmuel I'd go and I'm going. Maybe I'll have some siyata d'Shmaya (Heavenly assistance) and find a parking space right in front."*

He walked out the door determined but perturbed inside. It was dark, cold, wet and late. He should never have agreed to attend.

Examining the above scenario, one gains an instant insight into the workings of pessimism. It is highly contagious. A person who sees all the negatives and problems quickly throws the proverbial "wet blanket" on other people's enthusiasm. Challenges they might have taken in stride suddenly appear bothersome, maybe even insurmountable.

The pessimist creates a reality out of potential negative outcomes that may never actually occur. He pulls other people into his grim prognosis, causing them to dwell on suffering or disappointment that might never happen. In the event that the pessimist's predictions do come true, there is usually little advantage in having worried about them in advance.

Of course, wise people do consider the consequences of their actions. They plan to the extent that planning is possible. That is not the same as dragging someone down with a dose of pessimism.

A common pessimistic statement is the one that sometimes greets newly engaged couples: "You know, after all the excitement dies down, marriage is just a lot of hard work." Rather than deflating the couple's exhilaration, one could suggest a book or a mentor that would help them through the adjustments of their first year together. But unless someone is personally involved in another person's life, even these suggestions are usually uncalled for. The best response to someone else's announcement of his plans is just plain, "*Mazal tov!* May you have a lot of success," because it's very possible that, despite other people's dark predictions, he will indeed succeed.

In Other Words:

"*Even if I am a pessimist by nature, I will assert self-control over these thoughts and try to visualize success for myself and others. If I have concerns, I will try to state them in a way that is productive.*"

1 Kislev — Sally Kaplan לע״נ שרה גיטל בת אברהם ע״ה
Dedicated by Michael and Diane Kaplan and family

1 Nissan — לע״נ יחיאל בן מענדל ז״ל
לע״נ פערל בת אברהם מענדל ע״ה

2 Av — לע״נ יעטא בת אברהם צבי הכהן ע״ה
Dedicated by her loving family

ב כסלו
2 KISLEV / CYCLE 1

ב ניסן
2 NISSAN / CYCLE 2

ג אב
3 AV / CYCLE 3

❧ *Enough Said*

*H*illel was a difficult, whiny 4-year-old who had caused countless baby-sitters to quit in despair. His mother, Devorah, was the head counselor of a girls' summer camp, and she counted on her baby-sitter to keep Hillel occupied while she fulfilled her duties. Now, another one had quit and Devorah was becoming desperate. She sat her little son down in the family bungalow and began to lecture angrily.

"Your behavior is totally unacceptable! No one can stand it!" she accused loudly. "I hate when you act like that. I hate when you kvetch and disobey and fight with other children."

The speech went on for 20 minutes. The neighbor in the next bungalow listened with disbelief. Obviously, the mother's diatribe was an expression of her own seething frustration, not a thought-out disciplinary strategy. "She's bludgeoning the child with words," the neighbor thought to herself. "The child doesn't hear, 'I hate when you ...' He hears 'I hate you.'"

Indeed, an elongated lecture or angry tongue-lashing can be more painful than a physical blow. Nevertheless, sometimes a strong rebuke is in order. Where does rebuke end and *ona'as devarim* begin? The elements that separate the two include many concepts already discussed, such as the true emotion behind the words: Are they coming from a loving desire to help someone improve, or anger and frustration; and the choice of words: Do they show respect for the other person's dignity?

Another key factor people often do not consider is the length of the rebuke. How much needs to be said to get the point across? If a simple sentence like, "I am very disappointed by what you did," will have the desired impact, then anything more than that is *ona'as devarim*. Additional words simply compound the other person's pain and embarrassment at having done wrong, and perhaps even anger him to the point where he rebels rather than reforms.

All one is required to accomplish with reproach is to awaken the other person to his mistake and try to elicit a commitment to improve. If one does not stop to take a breath and let the other party speak, he will not even be able to ascertain if he is accomplishing these goals.

How does a person know that his message has gotten through? Sometimes one must wait and see if the other person acts differently in the future. Some people do not easily admit they are wrong. However, as the message sinks in, their actions show that they have accepted the rebuke. The need to see immediate remorse and submission is not likely to produce positive, long-lasting results.

The final proof of whether one has gone too far is in the actual consequences of the rebuke. If it drives the other person further away, it has failed. If it has motivated him to improve, it has succeeded. It is better to err on the side of saying too little, for, if necessary, a person can always find a new opportunity to say more.

In Other Words:

"*The next time I find myself 'going on and on' in rebuking someone, I will stop for a moment and ask myself if going further will accomplish anything positive.*"

ג כסלו
3 KISLEV / CYCLE 1

ג ניסן
3 NISSAN / CYCLE 2

ד אב
4 AV / CYCLE 3

❧ "I Can't Say"

*S*uddenly one day, the rug was pulled out from Rivka's social life. She was 15, an age when friends are everything, and now, her best friend Ruth was no longer allowed to come to her house.

"But WHY?" Rivka asked urgently. "What did I do?"

"I don't know," her friend answered quietly, "Someone said something to my mother and me, something about your family, and I'm not allowed to say who it was. I don't even think it's true. But my mother said it was better if we got together at my house or at school, and I can't come to you anymore."

Rivka hung up the phone and told her mother the news. Both of them sat silently, pondering the possible scenarios that could have led to this.

"It's horrible!" Rivka intoned. "Someone out there is saying things about us and I don't know who it is. It could be anyone! It could be someone we think is our friend!"

In the situation above, Ruth is committing one sin in an effort to avoid a different one. Knowing that by naming the source of the negative information she would be speaking *rechilus* (words that generate hatred between two people), she instead speaks *ona'as devarim*, conveying information that shatters Rivka's entire image of herself and her place in the community. Rivka loses a measure of her trust in just about everyone, because she cannot know who has spoken about her. She loses pride in her family, realizing that her home has become off limits to one friend, and perhaps others too, as the information spreads.

What could have been done to prevent this damage? How could Ruth have handled the situation in a way that would not have caused Rivka pain? The first issue, of course, is the acceptance of the informant's words as fact. The laws of *loshon hora* and *rechilus* forbid a person from taking at face value negative words about another person. While one may accept the information as a warning of a possible need for caution, one must not accept it as true.

If it happened that for some reason, Ruth's mother was justified in keeping her daughter out of Rivka's house, the fact should have been conveyed without alarming Rivka. No mention should have been made of a rumor or an informant.

In a case such as this, where there seems to be no win-win solution, a rav should be consulted to determine what may or may not be believed, repeated and acted upon. When a person knows that others are speaking negatively about him, he feels terribly threatened, for he stands to lose the most important asset he has: his good name.

In Other Words:

"I will exercise the utmost caution before passing along information that will let someone know others are speaking negatively about him."

**DAY
64**

ד כסלו
4 KISLEV / CYCLE 1

ד ניסן
4 NISSAN / CYCLE 2

ה אב
5 AV / CYCLE 3

☙ Boo!

o you're going on a 747?" Avi asked his friend David. *"I don't know ... it seems that lately, every airplane accident has been a 747."*

David's face went pale. "That's not funny, Avi, Cut it out."

"Oh, don't worry. I think they give out parachutes nowadays. You know, just in case." Avi chuckled at his witticism. He was really getting a reaction out of David.

"You know I hate flying," David said pleadingly. "Why do you want to drive me crazy? I'm serious. Just cut it out!"

"Oh, stop it, David. Millions of people fly every day and they get where they're going," Avi scoffed. "You're not going to tell me that you lose sleep over an airplane flight. Maybe you should go get hypnotized or something." He laughed again and then finally changed the subject.

Following the conversation, David began researching current airplane crash statistics for 747s. His flight was in two days, and he was reasonably sure that he would not sleep again until he had arrived in Israel. He imagined the massive heaving of the Atlantic Ocean underneath the vulnerable plane as it skidded along on thin air. Even if he survived the crash, he'd probably die of hypothermia or a shark attack. What a terrible end! He kept trying to shake the morbid thoughts out of his head, but his heart was pounding and his stomach churning in fear.

When a person arouses fear in others, he is thrusting those people into one of the most emotionally painful states known to man. Fear is a paralyzing, overpowering emotion that quickly floods out any other thoughts or feelings.

There are some people who enjoy the attention they get when they "sound the alarm." They take pleasure in spreading the latest dire news reports: nuclear threats by maniacal dictators, cataclysmic hurricanes heading up from South America, supervirus epidemics for which there are no cures. The news is filled with frightening prospects, many of which are utterly out of the average person's control. For some people, all of this is just grist for the conversational mill. But for others, certain topics strike terror in their hearts.

Doing or saying things to scare others is forbidden by Jewish law (*Choshen Mishpat*, 420:32). Even to jokingly arouse someone's fears with the intention of telling him the truth right afterward is prohibited. Shouting "Boo!" or making a loud, sudden noise in order to startle someone are also forbidden, especially if done in a dark, deserted area in which the person's senses are already on high alert.

For many people, other's fears seem ungrounded and therefore silly. Avi cannot imagine that David is truly frightened because Avi does not have a fear of flying. He therefore feels that David is probably exaggerating. To more accurately understand the pain one inflicts on others when one arouses their fears, a person can think of something that he does indeed find frightening, and imagine causing that feeling in someone else.

In Other Words:

"When I hear or see something alarming, rather than spread the alarm, I will consider whether this is knowledge people can utilize for their benefit or protection. If not, I will keep the information to myself."

ה כסלו
5 KISLEV / CYCLE 1

ה ניסן
5 NISSAN / CYCLE 2

ו אב
6 AV / CYCLE 3

The Boy Who Cried, "Wolf!"

*T*he phone rang and Daniel picked it up. His friend Avraham was on the other end, obviously very agitated.

"Come quickly!" he told his friend, who lived on the next block. "I need your help! I'm watching my little brother and he got his toe stuck in the bathtub faucet and he's screaming and he won't let me touch him ..."

Daniel couldn't figure out why he was the one to get the call. He had no special expertise that would give him any more success than Avraham was having.

"Listen, I'll come and see what I can do, but I can't imagine it's going to be so much better than whatever you're doing. Maybe you should call Hatzolah."

"Just come, Dani!" Avraham pleaded. "Two heads are better than one!"

It was a cold, snowy night, but Daniel, an exceedingly good-natured young man, threw on his storm coat, hat and boots, and walked as quickly as he could to Avraham's house. When he got there, he was astounded to find three other friends peering out Avraham's living-room window, Avraham among them, laughing wildly at the sight of Daniel tramping urgently up to the door.

"I told you he'd come," Avraham said triumphantly. "I told you that Daniel Tzvi Rosenberg cannot say no to a favor. He just can't. If we called him at 3 a.m. in a hurricane to come kill a spider, he'd be here!"

Understandably, Daniel in the above story did not find the practical joke anywhere near as funny as did the perpetrators. In fact, he was terribly humiliated. He felt that his helpful nature was a badge of shame, a mark of gullibility that everyone could see.

Obviously, the group that organized the joke spent some time and creative energy devising a way to execute it, but sadly, all their effort achieved was ona'as devarim, causing needless pain to another person. The same talent and energy could easily have been applied to a positive goal, but this group felt that the laugh was worth the price.

While the Torah extols the virtue of *simchah*, it abhors mockery. Practical jokes, false alarms and other such pranks are aimed at arousing a response of alarm in someone for other people's amusement. These clearly fall within the definition of *ona'as devarim*.

One might think that the harm is minimal, since it is short lived and the victim quickly finds out that the emergency was nothing but a prank. However, the harm extends to the humiliation a person feels at having been manipulated and at the thought that others have set him up for ridicule. This hurt does not go away when the prank is disclosed. It festers and may even grow more acute over time.

How can a person be sure not to fall into causing this type of *ona'as devarim?* He can ask himself, as he imagines how funny a certain prank will be, Who will be laughing?

In Other Words:

"*If I am asked to participate in a practical joke at someone else's expense, I will decline, and inform others that their plan constitutes ona'as devarim.*"

The Boy Who Cried, "Wolf!" ☐ 141

ו כסלו
6 KISLEV / CYCLE 1

ו בניסן
6 NISSAN / CYCLE 2

ז אב
7 AV / CYCLE 3

❧ *The Badger*

*G*et upstairs right this minute and clean your room," the irate mother told her 13-year-old daughter, Tali. "It looks like a barn. Don't you have any respect for the things we buy you? Your clothes are in piles all over the place. You're not going anywhere until you get that room cleaned up."

"But Mom, I promised the Rosens I would baby-sit for them tonight. They're coming in five minutes to pick me up," Tali replied. The state of her room was the subject of a never-ending battle with her mother. O.K., it was a bit of a mess, but Tali claimed to know exactly where every item was.

Her mother, on the other hand, knew that consistent, good habits were important for her daughter to develop. She realized, even if Tali didn't admit it, how much time was lost each day trying to locate buried items and iron clothing found at the bottom of the heap.

"How are you ever going to run a household? I don't think we should buy you one more item of clothing until you learn how to take care of things properly ...."

A car horn sounded in the driveway and Tali gratefully ran out the door.

"Bye, Mom," she called out over her shoulder. "I'll see you later."

"The second you get home tonight, I expect you to get that room straightened out!" the mother shouted after her daughter.

In the above scenario, one can see immediately that the mother's approach to addressing her complaint was ineffective. That her daughter's housekeeping habits were an ongoing source of friction proves that the mother's harangues were unproductive.

That is because badgering just doesn't work. It is an irritant against which people develop emotional calluses. "There she goes again, yelling about my room" is a much more likely thought in this daughter's head than, "I see that my mother is very upset about my room. I'll try to do better." For a child, this response produces an additional problem; it creates an obstacle to the child's fulfillment of the commandment to honor his parents.

Besides failing to produce progress, nagging erodes a relationship. People avoid nags. If they cannot escape the nagging person, then they train their ears to stop hearing the complaint. It begins to sound like unpleasant background noise, no more meaningful than the rumble of the neighbor's lawn mower.

Often, the subject of a person's nagging is relatively trivial. If it were serious, the person would most likely take a more serious approach. In the above example, that might mean a quiet talk in which the mother and daughter express their views and come up with a way to improve the situation. Under such circumstances, the daughter would be more likely to take her mother's words seriously and not see the conflict as a power struggle.

Being a thorn in someone's side rarely gains their cooperation. It causes the other person pain and frustration while achieving nothing positive. The squeaky wheel may occasionally get the oil, but in the long term, it loses, for it has consigned itself to a life as a squeaky wheel.

In Other Words:

"
I will consider what my typical topics for nagging or haranguing are, choose one and work on a real, productive approach to the problem.
"

ז כסלו
7 KISLEV / CYCLE 1

ז ניסן
7 NISSAN / CYCLE 2

ח אב
8 AV / CYCLE 3

❧ *Unreasonable Cause*

*Y*aakov's well-known temper was beginning to boil over. It was the day of his son's wedding, and he had arrived at the hall with his family to find that the photographer had yet to show up. The caterer was also running late. Guests were beginning to arrive and the hot dishes had yet to be brought out from the kitchen. He did his best to keep his cool, realizing that his own tension could quickly spread to the rest of his family and spoil the simchah for them.

But then, as he passed through the lobby to find the caterer, a strange man in a floppy hat and baggy coat stopped him. 'Tzedakah (charity)?" he asked.

"Are you here every night?" Yaakov asked the man. Indeed, the man was one of a group of beggars who were permitted to sit in the lobby and try their luck with the waves of well-dressed guests passing through on their way to or from the grand wedding banquets that took place on most nights.

"Sure, I am," answered the man, sounding proud of his consistency.

"Do you know," said Yaakov coldly, "that if you spent the same amount of time at a job, you wouldn't have to beg?"

The man turned away quickly, scanning the crowd for a more sympathetic face.

In this scenario, Yaakov was in a state of high anxiety. He had no patience for a beggar, but even so, he did not want to admit to himself or the man, "I don't feel like helping you right now. I'm in a bad mood."

Instead, he belittled the beggar. By making the man and his needs small in his own eyes, he was able to justify to himself his withholding of charity. This is a common form of *ona'as devarim* which people use to exempt themselves from helping a person or a cause. For example, one might tell a collector for a charity that there are other, more effective charities doing what his organization does. To make such a statement to someone who has undertaken the difficult task of raising funds for the organization is hurtful.

This does not mean that every person must give to everyone who asks. Nor does it mean that one cannot check into the efficiency and validity of a particular solicitation. If these are one's real goals, they can easily be accomplished without *ona'as devarim*. A refusal, if one must give one, should come in words that respect the dignity of the collector.

A harsh refusal is often the product of guilt: the person doesn't want to give. To justify his feeling, he thinks of a reason why the would-be recipient is unworthy, and then treats him as unworthy. The result is a completely unjustified attack on someone who is doing nothing more sinister than asking for another person's help.

In Other Words:

"*Today I will practice a few non-confrontational ways to say 'no' to people when I must refuse their request for a contribution.*"

7 Kislev — 'לזכות בתיה פסיה, אברהם לייב, ורחל דבורה שיחיו
Dedicated by Cory and Jonathan Glaubach

7 Nissan — In memory of our parents
אליה-ו יעקב ורחל לאה ז"ל Blumenthal

8 Av — Lieba Kizelnik לע"נ ליבא בת ר' ישראל ניסן ע"ה נלב"ע י"א אב
Dedicated by Sarah Leah Landa and family

DAY
68

ח כסלו
8 KISLEV / CYCLE 1

ח ניסן
8 NISSAN / CYCLE 2

ט אב
9 AV / CYCLE 3

☙ Or Else

If you don't pass the math test, you'll have to repeat sixth grade," the teacher told his lackluster student.

"If you miss your bus, I'll have to drive you to school and I'll be late for work and I'll lose my job. We'll be broke!" the mother told her son dramatically.

"If you don't grab this opportunity, you'll be struggling along your whole life while everyone else is rolling in cash," the businessman told his associate.

"If you don't help me with the dishes, I won't buy you that new outfit," the mother told her teenage daughter.

There are people who communicate most often in threats. Their idea of motivation is to paint a negative consequence distasteful enough that the other person sees no alternative but to cooperate. This becomes a habitual way of dealing with certain people or certain relationships. Sometimes it becomes a way of dealing with life.

Using threats to get one's way has many negative aspects to it. The first is that it is often ineffective. Once someone becomes accustomed to another person's constant threats, they cease to have meaning.

It may also be that the other person does not care if the threatened result happens. For instance, the teenage daughter in the example may not care whether or not her mother buys her the outfit. Instead of imparting the message of "if you don't do what I say, this dire consequence will happen," the threat might convey the idea that "if you're willing to accept this consequence, you don't have to do what I say." Then the threatened person is not motivated to do the requested act; he is merely called upon to weigh two options and choose the less distasteful of them.

On the other hand, threats that are believable can be a constant source of *ona'as devarim*. Those who are "motivated" in this manner must live in a state of fear, ever aware of all the terrible things that will happen if they do not perform as expected.

The better method of gaining cooperation is to turn the threat on its head and create an incentive instead: "If you help me with the dishes, we'll have some time to go out shopping for that outfit you wanted." "If you grab this opportunity, you can make an excellent return on your investment." "If you study hard for this math test, you'll be way ahead in seventh grade." Rather than giving another person something to worry about, give him something toward which to strive.

In Other Words:

"*When I find myself about to issue a threat, I will think first about the possibility of using positive language instead.*"

ט כסלו
9 KISLEV / CYCLE 1

ט ניסן
9 NISSAN / CYCLE 2

י אב
10 AV / CYCLE 3

✐ *While You're At It …*

*M*rs. Lewenstein was a highly experienced biology teacher. When her husband retired and the couple moved to a new community, she wanted to resume her career teaching Bais Yaakov girls about the wonders of nature. She quickly obtained a job in a prestigious school.

The week before the new school year opened, the secular studies teachers met with their bright young principal. She introduced a new format she wanted them to use for their lesson plans. Mrs. Lewenstein listened in despair. She had 20 years' worth of lesson plans in her file at home, all written in a format that had always worked well for her. Rewriting them in the new format would waste a tremendous amount of time.

She felt sure the principal would respect her professional judgment and leave her to her old trusty lesson plans. "It just doesn't make sense for me to do them over again," she explained. "They work just fine."

"I'm sorry, but that is part of the job and you'll have to do what all the other teachers have to do," the principal said tartly. It was clear that she felt threatened by the older, more experienced educator.

Mrs. Lewenstein took a deep breath, stopped her tongue from releasing the retort that was right on its tip, and said instead, "That's fine, then. I'll redo them."

"And make sure you follow the format exactly and submit them on time," the principal added, once again feeling secure in her position.

If the first round of the argument was a wound to Mrs. Lewenstein, the last, superfluous comments were salt in the wound. She had said she would abide by the principal's wishes. It was clear that this was not what she really wanted to do. Why, then, does the principal have to reassert herself a second time when there is no further purpose to be served?

In this case, it was clear that those last few words were meant to show Mrs. Lewenstein who was in charge. Their only real accomplishment, however, was to irritate a sore spot. Saying more than is necessary, especially after someone has given in on a disagreement or is already performing a task they were not eager to do, is simply *ona'as devarim*. No new information is added by those superfluous words.

Any time one must say something that will be unwelcome to someone else's ears, the rule is to say as little as possible to get the message across. If a person embellishes his unwanted message, it appears that he is enjoying the role. By keeping his words to a minimum, he shows that his real interest is not in aggrandizing his ego, but rather, in getting the job done.

In Other Words:

"*From now on, I will take it upon myself, bli neder, to say only what is necessary in conveying instructions to others.*"

CHAPTER 7:

HURTFUL SPEECH CATEGORY V:

Counterproductive Comments Or Nonconstructive Questions

S ometimes, simply to make conversation or add one's "two cents' worth," people tread upon sensitive personal territory in another person's life.

י כסלו
10 KISLEV / CYCLE 1

י ניסן
10 NISSAN / CYCLE 2

י"א אב
11 AV / CYCLE 3

❧ *How Dare You!*

*A*t 3 a.m., Shaul woke up from a fitful sleep. He got out of bed and wandered down the hall to his son Michael's room. "Good," Shaul thought. "He's home and asleep." The troubled 16-year-old looked so peaceful with his face nestled into his pillow.

The next day, Shaul questioned his son. "I waited up until 2 o'clock for you," he said. "Where were you that you couldn't call?"

"I was with my friends. We didn't realize how late it was. I didn't want to call because I figured you'd be sleeping."

"That's nice of you, but I couldn't sleep knowing you were out so late. You have to let me know where you are. Better still, you have to get home at a reasonable time."

"I don't believe it! You really don't trust me! What do you think I was doing out there, stealing cars? I can't take it here anymore. I have to get out of this house. You'd all be happier if I weren't even here!" Michael ranted, tears forming in his wounded eyes.

"Hold on!" his father replied. "I'm just asking for some consideration, that you shouldn't leave us to worry. What are you talking about?"

But by now, Shaul was talking to himself because his son had stalked off and slammed the door behind him. His friend was waiting outside in a car. Shaul watched out the window as Michael greeted his friend with a big smile, hopped into the car and rode off.

Michael had learned a lesson in life, and that was that the louder and more dramatic his reaction, the quicker everyone backed off. He knew his parents dreaded the idea of hurting his already critically wounded self-esteem. Therefore, he used his sensitivity to criticism to manipulate everyone in his household. No one dared insult Michael, because they feared that his fragile ego would crack.

To some extent, it was true that Michael was sensitive, but not nearly as much as he represented to others. His calculated overreactions caused everyone else pain and guilt as they excoriated themselves for having hurt him yet again.

People who utilize this kind of overreaction do so knowing that through it, they can exert control over others. However, it becomes their habitual way of dealing with adversity. One who falls into this habit will be the cause of much *ona'as devarim* throughout his life as he pulls the strings of guilt and pain in other people's hearts. To avoid making this kind of *ona'as devarim* one's way of life, one must find the strength to face criticism and disappointment head-on, without resorting to theatrics. Not only will this prevent one from inflicting pain on others, but ultimately, it will enable the person to reap the benefits of true give-and-take with the people in his life.

In Other Words:

" Am I really as hurt as I say I am, or am I trying to get my way? This is the question I will ask myself whenever I claim wounded feelings. "

י"א כסלו
11 KISLEV / CYCLE 1

י"א ניסן
11 NISSAN / CYCLE 2

י"ב אב
12 AV / CYCLE 3

❧ *Seeing the Future*

*S*hmuel avoided taking business calls at home, but tonight he had no choice. The client, living in South Africa, could not be reached during regular business hours. When Shmuel's 5-year-old son, Hillel, began yanking on his father's pants' leg for attention, Shmuel tried every hand-signal and facial expression he could muster to make the child understand that this was not a good time. Hillel was undeterred, and soon added a chorus of whining to his campaign. At last, Shmuel hung up.

"Now wanna hear my joke?" Hillel asked.

"Hillel! I certainly don't want to hear your joke now. I don't even want to talk to you now. You behaved so badly! Worse than a baby!"

If Shmuel could have conducted an on-the-spot emotional CAT scan of Hillel's heart, he would have seen utter devastation. Hillel's bubbling enthusiasm went instantly flat. His vision of a laugh shared with his father turned into a harsh rejection. He felt that his father was disappointed in him, disgusted with him.

Twenty minutes later, Shmuel was eating his late dinner, discussing his day with his wife, happy to be home. Hillel was sitting on his bed, playing with matchbox cars and trying hard to ignore the heaviness in his heart. It lasted all night and into the next day, resurfacing whenever there was a lull in the activity at school. Only that night, when Shmuel came home and gave Hillel his usual bear hug did the pain finally wash away, leaving just a trace.

If Shmuel would have considered beforehand that his irritable outburst would pack such firepower, he would never have pulled the trigger. His son would have gone to bed that night secure in his father's love.

Foresight is a crucial key to avoiding *ona'as devarim*. If a person takes a moment before speaking to consider the impact of his words, infinite damage can be prevented. One must restrain the impulse to speak long enough to think: Will these words cause the other person to feel discouraged, anxious, depressed or wounded? Will they plant an idea that will trouble the person, possibly for days or weeks to come? If one of these outcomes seems likely, or even possible, then the words about to be spoken are *ona'as devarim*.

How, then, can a person communicate unwelcome information to another? Did Shmuel have to ignore Hillel's bad behavior? Shmuel could have taken Hillel by the shoulders, looked him squarely in the eye and told him, "A big boy like you has to be patient and not interrupt! Next time, I hope you'll do better." Hillel might have felt chastened, but his trust in his father would have remained whole and untainted.

In Other Words:

"
The next time I am about to speak out of irritation — even if it's justified — I will try to imagine the aftermath of my words. How will the recipient's face look? What will he or she think and feel?
"

---

11 Kislev — Gitel Rabin לזכות גיטל בת נחום שתחי׳
Dedicated by Vadim and Svetlana Bakaev

11 Nissan — May today's learning be a z'chus for K. Fleming and daughters.
Dedicated by S. Norman and family

12 Av — לזכות שמואל ישראל בן אברהם נ״י

י״ב כסלו
12 KISLEV / CYCLE 1

י״ב ניסן
12 NISSAN / CYCLE 2

י״ג אב
13 AV / CYCLE 3

❧ *No Harm Intended*

*F*inally, Moshe had found some time to repair the hole in the kitchen ceiling. His brother Zev, who lived right across the street and believed himself to be quite handy, came over to help.

"What are you doing, Moish?" he asked as his brother began scraping away the stained portions of the ceiling. "I think you need to cut that whole piece out."

"Nah, I'll just scrape it. It's O.K. underneath."

"Maybe check it for mold first," Zev replied.

"I can handle this, Zev. It's not brain surgery," Moshe said emphatically.

"I'm just trying to help."

"Leave me alone already! You're driving me crazy!" Moshe exploded. "Help like this is not what I need. Go cut up your own ceiling."

Zev shook his head in dismay. "I was only trying to help," he muttered as he turned and walked out.

People have very varied tolerance for letting others into their lives. Some seek out advice and help, some accept it when it comes along, and others become confused and distracted by the input, or feel that it indicates a lack of confidence in their abilities. Those who dislike input may find themselves acting as Moshe in the story did, hurling hurtful statements of rejection at those who are simply trying to help.

There are many occasions when unwanted help may play a role in one's life. A parent often finds himself slowed down by the well-intentioned help of his small children, who are eager to get involved in adult tasks like washing the dishes, mowing the lawn or folding the laundry. Elderly parents, too, want to be useful and may insist on helping out, even though the slower motion and forgetfulness of age can try the patience of someone just trying to get a task finished. In these and so many other cases, it is essential for a person to avoid showing impatience and speaking words that can only wound.

It would not seem possible that someone could be "too nice," but indeed there is such a personality. There are people who insist on injecting themselves into situations, even when they are not wanted. Some people fail to pick up the social signals coming from the other person. Some know they are being bothersome, but believe, "He'll thank me in the end."

Most often, when people "insist" on offering their help or advice, their motive is love for the person they are trying to help. They feel they are offering a gift. A harsh response is like throwing the gift back in the giver's face. This is hardly a justifiable response to someone who is really just demonstrating concern. Even when someone is "killing us with kindness," there's no need for self-defense.

In Other Words:

" If I tend to explode with words like, 'Leave me alone!' or 'Mind your own business,' I will think about strategies to better tolerate others' input, or to moderate my response. "

12 Kislev — Beatrice Furst ע״ה לע״נ רבקה בת עוזר אשר ע״ה
Dedicated by Lisa and Marty Furst and family

12 Nissan — Josef Friedman ז״ל לע״נ יוסף מאיר בן משה ז״ל
Dedicated by the Friedman family

13 Av — Farha Cohen ע״ה לע״נ פרחה בת דינה ע״ה
By her children, Marc Cohen, Dina Mizrahi and Abraham Cohen

י"ג כסלו
13 KISLEV / CYCLE 1

י"ג ניסן
13 NISSAN / CYCLE 2

י"ד אב
14 AV / CYCLE 3

ᕫ *The Eggshell Skull Rule*

*W*hat happens if Reuven, carelessly wielding a cutting tool, lightly wounds Shimon, and Shimon turns out to be a hemophiliac? Is Reuven responsible for the serious consequences Shimon suffers?

A concept in American law says that a person who wrongs another is responsible for the full extent of the damage, even if it's unforeseeable and unusual. The rule is named for a hypothetical scenario in which a person hits someone on the head, and the victim has an unusually thin skull that cracks under the blow. The assailant is responsible for the broken skull, even though he could not have foreseen that his light blow would have caused that degree of damage. Once a person wrongfully harms someone, the results — whatever they are — are his responsibility.

This legal concept mirrors an important concept in *ona'as devarim*. One never knows where another person's sensitivities lie. Once someone strikes at his victim, he is responsible for the damage, even if he didn't know the victim would react so strongly. He can't say, "My words should not have affected him like that."

The person's weak spot might be intelligence, appearance, family background, economic status or standing in the community. In sensitive areas, even a half-joking comment can hurt. Since it is not always possible to know where another person's sensitivities lie, the only way to avoid doing unintentional harm is to avoid doing any harm at all. In the case of the eggshell skull, had the blow not been delivered in the first place, no damage would have been done.

Once the blow is delivered, the repercussions can echo on and on. If the victim takes the painful words to heart, every time he encounters this individual or thinks of his words, he will suffer anew; the speaker bears responsibility for this pain.

People sometimes justify their insults as humor, claiming that even the object of the joke thinks it's funny. But this astute observation from a fifth-grade boy reveals what is often underlying the victim's laughter: "If you look in his eyes, you see that he wants to cry, even though his mouth is laughing."

Even when someone acknowledges his own flaws and jokes about them in public, he can suffer humiliation when others make similar jokes:

A woman whose budget was always stretched beyond its limits often joked with her friends about her cacophonous old car. One day, she picked up her friend to go to a *shiur*. The woman said to her passenger, "Wow, you're prompt. You were waiting at the curb." Her friend replied, "Sure. I could hear you coming from two blocks away!" The driver laughed, but inside she cringed. To her, the comment meant that everyone noticed her car. What had been self-deprecating humor was now a neighborhood-wide embarrassment.

In the final analysis, no one possesses the meter that can measure another person's reaction to sharp words. Given the fact that the potential for damage is immense, yet unknowable, there is only one solution. Speak wisely.

In Other Words:

"*Before I make a joke or comment at someone else's expense, I will stop to consider the fact that they might actually be wounded by it.*"

13 Kislev — In honor of my dear husband, Anshel Davis and our family

13 Nissan — לע״נ יעקב בן לונה ז״ל

הונצח על ידי משפחת בן-טאטא תנצב״ה

14 Av — Cantor Jack Schartenberg לע״נ החבר יעקב בן חיים ז״ל
Dedicated by his daughter, Harriet (Hadassa) Zitter and family

י״ד כסלו
14 KISLEV / CYCLE 1

י״ד ניסן
14 NISSAN / CYCLE 2

ט״ו אב
15 AV / CYCLE 3

❧ *In His Shoes*

*T*he Mishnah (*Pirkei Avos* 2:5) teaches that a person should not judge another until he has stood in his place. That means that the person has essentially lived the other person's life: seen what he's seen, known who he's known and experienced what he has experienced. Only with that perspective can one person truly judge what another person says or does.

This standard is obviously impossible to meet. No one can understand what it feels like to be someone else. This means that a person's words may evoke a response from someone that is completely unexpected. A subject that seems benign may be loaded with emotional meaning to someone else because of his particular experience and personality. If a person discovers that someone is sensitive to a specific subject, mentioning that subject is *ona'as devarim*.

For instance, if someone lost a loved one in an auto accident, it would be *ona'as devarim* to tell him, "I passed by a huge car crash on my way over here. It looked like one of the cars was totaled. There were ambulances all over the place."

Such an account might be perfectly acceptable conversation to the average listener, but for this particular person, the story would very likely unleash painful emotions. Therefore, for this person, an account of a car crash is *ona'as devarim*.

There are many areas of subjective sensitivity that render certain discussions *ona'as devarim* for certain people. It is not always possible to know what those areas are. However, once one discovers that he has hit upon a painful topic, he should be sure not to bring it up again.

Furthermore, some words bring up negative associations in a person's mind. This, too, is to be avoided. For example, if someone experienced a terrible or embarrassing incident in a particular location, one should try not to mention that location. If someone has suffered bankruptcy, one should not bring up the subject of bankruptcy with him, even in an impersonal way, for instance, by stating, "I read that the bankruptcy rate is way up this year."

These precautions may seem to demand catering to every individual's peculiarity. The impulse to say or think that the person should "just get over it" may be great. However, the simple fact is that one is not allowed to cause pain to others.

Obviously, there are times when difficult subjects must be raised. If, for instance, a person has advice to offer someone regarding his bankruptcy, and the other person is open to hearing it, it would not be *ona'as devarim* to bring it up. The insensitivity arises in situations in which the difficult subject is simply tossed into the conversation for no constructive reason. Rather than speaking out in such situations, there is nothing to lose and much to gain by standing, for just a moment, in the other person's shoes.

In Other Words:

"*I will make an effort to take heed of the person to whom I am talking and avoid topics that I know he or she might find painful.*"

ט"ו כסלו
15 KISLEV / CYCLE 1

ט"ו ניסן
15 NISSAN / CYCLE 2

ט"ז אב
16 AV / CYCLE 3

❧ *Spilled Milk*

*I*n her old age, Bubbi had developed a trem-
or in her hands. Nevertheless, she insisted
upon feeding herself, feeling that it was far beneath
her dignity to be spoon-fed by another member of
the family.

"Mommy, why don't you tell Bubbi that she has
to let someone help her?" Brocha asked Simi Klein.
"It's always such a mess and she only gets to eat
about half of her food!"

"Because Bubbi is my mother," said Simi. "It
makes her feel like a little baby when people feed
her, and I would never want to hurt her feelings
like that. It's no big deal to clean up her place when
she's finished and gone home. I'm sure she used to
do the same for me when I was little and just learning to eat. I did it for you, too."

In this scenario, no one would expect Mrs. Klein to
rail against her mother's clumsiness, shouting, "There
you go again, Mom, spilling everything all over the
place." First of all, it would violate the commandment
to honor one's parents. But even if Bubbi were not
Mrs. Klein's mother, it is clear that the anger would
be misplaced. The elderly woman cannot control her
hand movements well enough to eat neatly. She is
not spilling out of carelessness or spite, but out of
simple physical limitations.

In truth, however, most people who spill or drop
things do so out of their own physical limitations.
Some people are more confident and others are more
uncertain. Some are more coordinated and some

are less so. If a person tends to drop things out of nervousness, bringing negative attention to his failing will only cause greater nervousness, making the situation worse.

Some people, especially children, drop items because they are distracted and careless. Even in this case, however, berating the person for the accident will serve no purpose. Certainly it won't clean up the spill. A better response would be to offer to help clean up the spill and then — when dealing with a child — calmly remind him to be more careful.

Often parents do not notice that a child is playing with an item until the item falls and breaks. A more productive approach is to speak to the child when he begins mishandling the item. This teaches him to treat things with care. Yelling when it finally breaks merely teaches him that his parent is angry over having lost something, or over extra work to do.

In fact, it is this frustration that usually gives rise to the loss of temper and the insults when a person's belongings are broken or something is spilled. By taking the perspective that such an occurrence is almost always an accident, and the perpetrator usually regrets the accident, one can approach the situation more calmly. Rather than exacerbating the other person's regret, one can ease his mind and show, through his attitude, words and actions, that he does not value objects and convenience above other people's feelings.

In Other Words:

"The next time someone breaks or spills something, I will stop a moment before reacting and try to tune into the person's embarrassment over causing the damage."

ט"ז כסלו
16 KISLEV / CYCLE 1

ט"ז ניסן
16 NISSAN / CYCLE 2

י"ז אב
17 AV / CYCLE 3

❧ *Amazing Praise*

*W*hen the kiruv organization asked Rena if she'd like to teach alef-beis to Joyce, Rena was a little skeptical. Joyce was a middle-aged woman, a retired doctor with a Ph.D. in Eastern Religion. Joyce spoke and wrote Chinese and she had published eight books, as well.

"I'll try," Rena agreed. "But I hope I have the brain power to keep up with her. At least we can assume that, if she understands Chinese, Hebrew shouldn't present much of a challenge."

The learning partnership began, and both Rena and Joyce found that they enjoyed their time together tremendously. Surprisingly, Joyce had to work a lot harder than Rena had expected. Whenever Joyce read a line with fluency, or corrected a mistake she had been making, Rena felt a surge of pride. "Fantastic!" she'd say. "That was perfect!"

As soon as the words escaped her mouth, she'd feel a bit silly. After all, Joyce was a highly educated, lifelong learner. Rena felt her praises were more befitting a 4-year-old who had succeeded in tying his shoe. But a few weeks after the learning partnership began, Rena found out otherwise.

"I spoke to Joyce to see how things were going," reported Rena's contact at the kiruv organization. "She's very happy. She says she really appreciates your encouragement."

As Rena discovered, no one is too old, too smart or too sophisticated to appreciate appropriate praise. But the benefit extends equally to the one who is doing the praising. That is because a person who develops the habit of sincerely praising others must, in tandem, develop an eye for the good in others.

Nevertheless, praise can also become a vehicle for *ona'as devarim*. This occurs when one praises another person too lavishly for the recipient's comfort. Often, a teenager will reject overblown praise, feeling it is babyish or insincere. However, subtle, sincere praise does wonders.

Ona'as devarim also results when one's praise actually implies an insult. "Great job! You managed to get through the day without losing anything" is an example of such a statement. Damage can also be done by praising one person in comparison to another person who is present: "It's good that at least one of you knows how to follow instructions." And finally, praise can result in *ona'as devarim* when it is gratuitously hitched to an insult: "You're very smart when it comes to bargain-hunting. It's a shame you're not as smart in dealing with people."

The best defense against falling into any of these types of hurtful "praise" is to make a practice of verbally recognizing others' good deeds and qualities. Once a person makes praise a regular part of his daily discourse, and sees how it lights up another person's face, he will have no desire to sully the praise with hidden negativity.

In Other Words:

"*Imagine someone you love hearing praise from you, only to be deflated by a negative 'tag line' added to the compliment. Think of that disappointed image before you add anything negative to your praise.*"

DAY 77

י"ז כסלו
17 KISLEV / CYCLE 1

י"ז ניסן
17 NISSAN / CYCLE 2

י"ח אב
18 AV / CYCLE 3

❧ *Just Like You*

luma, Mr. Hoffman's new secretary, offered many attributes that her prede- cessor lacked. While the former secretary would arrive five or ten minutes late each day, Bluma was consistently at her desk, starting on the day's tasks, promptly at 9 o'clock. While the former secretary would get distracted by personal phone calls, Bluma saved all her private calls for home. In addition, she handled customers with aplomb and had a remark- able memory for details.

She was not, however, technologically inclined. To Mr. Hoffman, who loved his Blackberry, his com- plex office-computer programs and high-tech phone system, this was a cause of frustration. His other secretary was extremely savvy and caught onto new technology even before he did.

One afternoon, Mr. Hoffman asked Bluma to cre- ate a mailing list using a program in her computer.

"I'll have to have someone show me how to do it again," she admitted.

"What's your problem?" Mr. Hoffman blurted. "Mrs. Kleigman learned it in two minutes! Where's your head?"

As a general rule of life, comparing two people unfavorably is almost never warranted, never accu- rate and never helpful. Part of the reason for this is that making an unfavorable comparison requires one to engage in selective blindness. Since every person is made up of a plethora of positive and negative traits, the critic has to ignore all his victim's positive traits and zero in only on the negative to conclude that the victim is inferior to someone else. If he were looking at the whole person, he would readily see that while one person has certain strengths, the other person has other strengths.

In the above scenario, the boss completely overlooked all the ways in which his new secretary performed better than her predecessor and ranked her as inferior, based on the one area in which she was deficient.

This message does not motivate a person to improve, because it does not seem to leave room for improvement. Bluma may become more skilled, but she will never be the other secretary. On the other hand, if Mr. Hoffman told her instead, "You're an excellent secretary, but I need you to be more comfortable with our systems," she would perceive that there is something she can do to make him satisfied with her work.

Another type of negative comparison is also hurtful. For instance, if a child swipes a toy away from another child, telling him, "You're just like a mugger on the street!" will accomplish nothing more than inflicting pain on the child. The comparison aligns him with a frightening, revolting image rather than causing him to aspire to be better.

The bottom line is that any comparison of people is bound to be painful to one of them. Also, it is bound to be inaccurate, because each person G-d created is a singular combination of traits. Therefore, each is incomparable.

In Other Words:

"*Rather than comparing someone to another person, I will isolate the trait I wish to see improvement in and in a positive manner, convey that message instead.*"

י"ח כסלו
18 KISLEV / CYCLE 1

י"ח ניסן
18 NISSAN / CYCLE 2

י"ט אב
19 AV / CYCLE 3

❧ *Get Over It*

*A*nd then, he told me that it was all my fault and that I was the worst rebbi he had ever encountered. Can you imagine that?" Rabbi Berkowitz told Rabbi Newman, the principal of his yeshivah.

"Listen, his child is having difficulties and it makes some parents very angry and defensive. Don't take it personally," Rabbi Newman advised.

"I'm so upset! Does he have any idea of the effort I've put into his kid? The special tests I make up for him? The million times I hold my tongue when he acts up? I've never seen such ingratitude!"

"Enough, already," Rabbi Newman chided. "If it's going to get to you like this, you're never going to last in chinuch. Just let it go!"

Rabbi Berkowitz left his principal's office feeling more miserable than before. Not only did one of his students' parents think he was incompetent, but his principal seemed to think he was an immature complainer as well. It was only lunchtime, and there were two more hours of teaching ahead before he turned over the classroom to the secular studies teacher. He had no idea how he would survive those hours with the knot of tension now twisting in his stomach.

If one were to take a few steps back from this scenario, one might well agree with the principal's assessment of the situation. In a few days or weeks, the insulted rebbi might agree as well. However, in the present moment, a chance to soothe another person's wound has been lost, and in its place, salt has been rubbed in.

Regardless of whether a person has a right to complain, insulting him for feeling hurt will never help him over his pain. Instead, the great maturity and wisdom one believes he is offering becomes simple *ona'as devarim* that makes the sufferer feel more alone in his misery. Sometimes people inflict this damage on someone by telling them that their troubles are "for the best" or that they should appreciate the fact that it isn't worse.

The first step in dealing with someone in emotional pain is to offer empathy. Show that you care about his suffering, regardless of whether you feel it is justified. Once you have allowed the person to express his pain, he will usually be calmer and more open to suggestions or perspectives you might have to offer. But the first order of business is to refrain from making matters worse.

In Other Words:

" *I will think about some phrases that express empathy and learn about listening skills that will enable me to respond to other people's suffering effectively.* "

י״ט כסלו
19 KISLEV / CYCLE 1

י״ט ניסן
19 NISSAN / CYCLE 2

כ אב
20 AV / CYCLE 3

❧ *My Favorite Things*

*E*veryone knew that Uncle David had an avid interest in astronomy. He knew the names of stars and galaxies. He knew the dates, missions and astronauts involved in each of America's space launches. And Uncle David loved to share his knowledge.

Unfortunately, not everyone in the family shared his enthusiasm. As his nieces and nephews got older, they began to find his long, detail-laden expositions to be tiresome, and sometimes even comical.

One summer evening when Uncle David was having dinner with his brother's family, he introduced his favorite topic. "Did you hear about the space walk NASA is planning to repair the Hubble telescope?" he asked excitedly. "It's an incredible mission. The longest space walk ever. I heard that they're going to have to ...."

"Not more outer space!" cried Sara, a 17-year-old niece. "I can't take a whole meal of astronauts and light-years and space dust and all that stuff!"

"Sara!" her mother interrupted. "Go ahead, David, we're all listening."

"Never mind," Uncle David said quietly. "She's probably right. I do get carried away."

Many people have their "topic," whether it's politics, the state of Jewish community, science, war, health or any of the thousands of other areas that occupy people's minds. Some people can supply very interesting information or offer thought-provoking opinions. Some people, however, appear to be obsessed with their topic.

To prevent such a person from monopolizing conversation whenever he or she is around, it is sometimes necessary to find a way to derail the topic. If this is the case, words can be chosen that get the message across without making the speaker feel like a boorish fool. No one wants to feel that his conversation, which he thought was informative and interesting, or perhaps amusing, was instead the cause of silent suffering all around.

Therefore, to say something blunt such as, "Is that all you ever think about?" is certain to cause the speaker embarrassment and is *ona'as devarim.* Other examples of unkind responses include: "What a depressing (boring, unpleasant, etc.) topic!" "Who thinks about things like that?" "Are you just about finished?"

Nevertheless, sometimes it is necessary to get the speaker to change topics or stop speaking. This can be done in many ways that are gentler than an outright reproach. One can simply interject something interesting: "If you don't mind my changing the subject, did you hear anything about (some timely topic)?"

If one must say something direct, it should be as absolutely gentle and polite as possible, taking into account that the message itself — "You're boring," or "You're inappropriate" — is one that stings.

In some cases, the better route is to patiently hear the person out. This is especially so if the speaker is lonely and in need of attention. Once the listener has decided to tune in, he might surprise himself and find that he learns something new after all.

In Other Words:

" If I know someone who tends to ramble on about a pet topic, I will make an effort not to interrupt or stop him in a way that would cause him embarrassment. "

כ כסלו
20 KISLEV / CYCLE 1

כ ניסן
20 NISSAN / CYCLE 2

כ"א אב
21 AV / CYCLE 3

◈ *To Whom You Speak*

ow was I supposed to know the vase was cracked?" Eli defended himself. "All I did was pick it up and it fell apart in my hands!"

"But Eli, you know you're not allowed to just pick up other people's things without permission," his mother answered. "If you hadn't touched it in the first place, nothing would have happened. Now we have to pay for it."

It was an antique vase, painted lavishly in an Oriental style; it had been glued back together along a barely visible fault line right down the middle. Now it lay in two pieces, a casualty of Eli's habit of touching what should be left alone.

Like Eli, many people go where they shouldn't and touch upon that which they shouldn't, with the words they speak. Like the vase, many of the recipients of this unwarranted input are more vulnerable than one could know at first glance. The cracks and fissures in a person's psyche come from many sources: character traits, past experiences and insecurities.

Often, this type of *ona'as devarim* is committed not out of malice, but out of sheer ignorance of the listener's personal situation:

One day, a man noticed a 13-year-old boy standing outside the shul smoking a cigarette. The man felt he could not observe this behavior without doing something to try to discourage it, and so he approached the boy.

"Does your father smoke?" he asked him pointedly.

"No, he doesn't," the boy answered.

A moment later, there was an announcement that Minchah was about to begin. The man followed the boy inside and was astounded — and ashamed — to discover that the boy was approaching the bimah to lead the services. It was this boy's obligation to do so, for he had recently lost his father.

The man could not have known unless he had made the effort to inquire about the boy before he spoke to him. Even one who has learned to refrain from speaking words that are patently hurtful can stumble into *ona'as devarim* by touching, with his words, that which is not his to touch. If one knows another person well, then he must think about this person's sensitivities before he makes a personal comment to him. Does this man have children? Grandchildren? A livelihood?

If, however, he does not know the other person, how can he assess the propriety of his words? He cannot. Therefore, unless one is dealing with a life-and-death emergency, one should not make forays into other people's lives without taking the time to get to know them.

Awareness goes far in building new habits of speech. For those who take a good look at the person to whom they are speaking, and put a few moments' thought into the words they are about to speak, the rewards can be immense. Instead of being the person someone else associates with pain and distress, one's name can come to mean encouragement and friendship.

20 Kislev — May today's learning be a z'chus for our family.
Dedicated by אברהם ישראל ונעמי

20 Nissan — Joseph Chroman לע״נ יוסף לב בן שמואל זאב הכהן ז״ל
Dedicated by his wife, Esther and his children

21 Av — Samuel H. Sasson לע״נ שמואל בן רחל ז״ל
Dedicated by his wife, children and grandchildren

✎ *The Nitpicker*

*E*veryone loved when Hillel told stories about his youth on the Lower East Side of New York. His family often lingered at the Shabbos table on Friday night just to hear his tales. The truth was, however, that the storytelling was much more enjoyable when it took place out of the hearing range of Hillel's wife, whose passion for detail always ended up stopping her husband's narrative dead in its tracks.

"Right across the street from us was this little shul," started Hillel one Friday night.

"It wasn't exactly across the street," his wife interjected. "You showed it to me once. It was more diagonally across the street, closer to the corner."

"Yes, that's right, but anyway," he continued, "the gabbai of that shul was an old, old Jew from some small village in Russia. "He used to give all the kids who came to shul these delicious cherry drops ...."

"Cherry drops? But you said last time it was lemon drops," his wife corrected.

With his wife's "helpful" input after every few sentences, Hillel quickly lost interest in telling his story. "It's late, kids," he apologized. "I'll tell you the rest tomorrow."

Sometimes, detail is vital. One who wants to properly observe a mitzvah must know the details. A doctor prescribing medication or reading test results must attune himself to the finest details, because in these situations, details count.

But sometimes, people use their memory for details to constantly correct and revise meaningless things.

Sometimes, the motivation is their desire to display their superior memory or knowledge. Sometimes, they might be motivated by the little prickle of distress it gives them to hear the facts inaccurately stated. This unease can be compared to the feeling some people get when they see a "missed spot" on a recently cleaned window or blackboard. They will claim that "it drives me crazy" and that they have an overwhelming urge to fix it.

However, in that situation, they would refrain from fixing it if doing so required insulting or distressing someone. For instance, a person would not rise up out of his chair and erase a smudge on the blackboard while his rebbi was delivering a lecture to a full classroom. Even if it "drove him crazy," he would hold himself back.

For the person who is bothered by the details, it is important to weigh the value of offering a correction against the distress that might be caused. The proper balance can only be reached when a person fully respects the feelings of the speaker and considers whether the accuracy of this particular detail is important enough to be raised at that moment, or at all.

As with almost all forms of *ona'as devarim,* the key is to refrain from speaking on impulse. The momentary thought one gives to the words he is about to say can, and will, save him from this sin many times every day.

In Other Words:

"*Before I correct someone, I will ask myself, 'Does this make any material difference?' If not, I will hold back my input.*"

21 Kislev — Morris Ickowits לעי"נ משה בן יום טוב ליפמן ז"ל נלב"ע כ"ב כסלו
By his daughter and son-in-law, Ruth and Yitzchak Vidomlanski

21 Nissan — לכבוד עקרת ביתנו רנה פיגא בת חיים זאב למשפחת פרענקל תליט"א

22 Av — Dedicated to my dear children
May they be shomrei Torah umitzvos with great joy all their life

כ"ב כסלו
22 KISLEV / CYCLE 1

כ"ב ניסן
22 NISSAN / CYCLE 2

כ"ג אב
23 AV / CYCLE 3

✒ *Just Testing*

*W*hat are you going to do this summer?"
Elisheva asked her friend Leah.

"I'm going to be a counselor at Camp Sleepaway,"
she responded.

"That's such a dumb idea!" Elisheva countered.
"Why do you want to be stuck in a bunkhouse with
a bunch of little kids for a month?"

"I did it last year and it worked out fine. I like
camp," Leah answered mildly.

"Loser," Elisheva mumbled out loud.

At that moment, another classmate, Rina, walked
by. "Oh, there's Rina!" Elisheva exulted. "I know she
wanted to talk to me about our plans for the summer."

Elisheva turned her back on Leah and ran after
Rina, calling, "Rina, Rina, wait up!"

Leah shrugged her shoulders and wondered, "Is
Elisheva my friend, or isn't she? Sometimes she is
the best friend a person could have, and sometimes,
she's just awful."

Leah would be less confused if she could read the
subscript running beneath Elisheva's hurtful words.
They say, "How do I know Leah really likes me?
Maybe she's just pretending to be my friend because
I help her with her math. Or maybe she just feels bad
for me. Let me see if she'll still be my friend if I insult
her."

A person who is lacking in healthy self-esteem is
faced with a dilemma when it comes to friendships.
How can he believe that others like him when he does

not even like himself? How can he trust that they really see value in him when he does not see it? He cannot imagine what he has to offer that is sufficient to earn him the friendships he has.

With this as a perspective, such people may respond by testing their friendships. Each abusive word or act is followed by a silent, "Now, do you still like me? Are you still my friend?"

This behavior has everything going against it. First of all, it will always result in *ona'as devarim*. The friend who is being tested is being hurt and insulted in the course of the other person's "experiment" to discover the limits of his friend's affections. Second of all, the behavior will almost certainly act as a self-fulfilling prophesy, for eventually the victim will tire of the abuse and drop the friendship.

If a person recognizes this behavior in himself, his immediate goal must be to stop, even before he manages to repair the self-esteem issues that are causing him to speak hurtfully. *Ahavas Yisrael* is the tool that accomplishes the repair. No matter what a Jew feels about himself or others, his duty is to focus on loving his neighbor: helping him, encouraging him and treating him with respect. When one stops gazing inward and constantly assessing how he feels, and instead, turns his focus outward to the needs of others, "testing" friendships becomes a thing of the past, and real friendship has a chance to blossom.

In Other Words:

"*If I have a friend who I tend to mistreat, I will try to analyze my motives and begin a campaign today to act in ways that strengthen, rather than test, our relationship.*"

22 **Kislev** — לע״נ משה זאב בן דוד לעבאוויטש ז״ל
Dedicated by his children and grandchildren

22 **Nissan** — L'Ilui Nishmas Yoel Dovid ben Noach z"l

23 **Av** — As a z'chus for the family
Dedicated by Ephraim & Raizy Barkai

CHAPTER 8:

HURTFUL SPEECH CATEGORY VI:

Negative Imitation

Exaggerating another person's speech, looks or habits in an effort to ridicule him is equally as powerful as cruel words in its ability to induce shame and embarrassment.

כ״ג כסלו
23 KISLEV / CYCLE 1

כ״ג ניסן
23 NISSAN / CYCLE 2

כ״ד אב
24 AV / CYCLE 3

~ *Inimitable*

*W*hen the Kellerman family moved into their new neighborhood, they were quite the novelty. Born and bred in a small Jewish community in North Carolina, they spoke with a thick Southern accent. Most people found it quaint and charming, but the Kellermans' next-door neighbors, the Adlers, found it — as well as everything else about the Kellermans — annoying.

The Adlers were a wealthy family with a landscaped garden in the front of their grand, brick-and-wrought-iron home. The Kellermans had purchased a "fixer-upper," but were without funds for the fix-up. The Adlers cringed at their neighbor's weedy yard and peeling front door. The Kellerman children were outgoing and casual, while the Adler clan was quiet and more refined. The Kellermans left their windows open in the spring, letting the lively music on their CD player waft up and down the block. The Adlers called their new neighbors "hillbillies" behind their backs.

One day, Mr. Adler knocked on his neighbor's door to register a complaint. "One of your children dropped a gum wrapper on my front lawn," he told Mr. Kellerman curtly. "You have to teach them how to live in a civilized place."

"Why, Mr. Adler, there's no need to get offensive," Mr. Kellerman replied. "We may not be from around here, but we're civilized."

"Whaah, Mistuh Adluh! We're civilaaahzed! Are you kidding?" Mr. Adler responded in a thick, mock-Southern accent. "Just make sure it doesn't happen *again!" And off he stalked to his home, muttering, "hillbillies" under his breath.*

Hearing his accent mocked in front of his face was a rude shock to Mr. Kellerman. There is little as personally insulting as maliciously mimicking and mocking someone's habits or other personal traits. People have many idiosyncrasies; no one is immune. One person stutters, another has an odd laugh, another speaks with an accent, another has a facial tic, another dresses in a style that appears to be out dated.

Some people can barely resist picking up on these trademark characteristics and using them against the person who has them. This propensity turns into a weapon when there's a conflict and tempers are rising. In that context, mimicking someone seems to be the ultimate means of rubbing his face in disdain.

The harm a person does when he succumbs to this temptation is incalculable. With children, such treatment can destroy their self-confidence and make them fear social interaction. If they are made fun of by classmates, or worse yet, by adults in their lives, they completely lose their self-esteem. "I'm weird, and everyone knows it," is the message they absorb, and it can take them decades to shake it.

But even adults, whose self-image should be set on firmer ground, are stung by mockery. It is not only painful in the way that insults are painful; it is humiliating as well. Mimicry is generally a childish way of expressing one's irritation. So much more can be gained by speaking to someone directly, addressing the issues at hand and respectfully trying to resolve them.

In Other Words:

" *If I am the type of person who tunes into people's idiosyncrasies and mimics them, I will be more alert for the potential ona'as devarim in this behavior.* "

CHAPTER 9:

HURTFUL SPEECH CATEGORY VII:

Revealing Private Information

*W*hen someone trusts another person with his confidential information, he leaves himself tremendously vulnerable to that person's good faith. Discovering that the information has been passed along creates a devastating sense of betrayal.

כ״ד כסלו
24 KISLEV / CYCLE 1

כ״ד ניסן
24 NISSAN / CYCLE 2

כ״ה אב
25 AV / CYCLE 3

✍ *Betrayed*

*T*he three yeshivah boys stayed up far past curfew, talking quietly in the dormitory room they shared.

"It was the weirdest thing," one boy, Aaron, told Benny and Shmuel, his roommates. "I never did anything like this before. But there it was, this really cool, expensive watch, sitting right on my cousin's kitchen table. I don't know, maybe I was jealous because his family is so rich and he has everything in the world. I figured his parents could always get him a new watch. But I would never be able to have a watch like this.

"So I took it. I didn't stop to think that I'd never be able to wear it, because anyone who knew me would know it wasn't mine. After a couple of days, I couldn't stand the guilt, so I sneaked back to their house and put it right back on the table where I had found it. I've never told anyone in the world about this except you guys."

A few weeks later, Aaron borrowed Benny's notes and left them in the Beis Medrash.

"Where are my notes?" Benny asked him that night.

"I'm sorry, I forgot them in the Beis Medrash. I'll get them back to you tomorrow."

"Well that's not good enough. I wanted to study tonight."

"I'm sorry, but there's nothing I can do now. The Beis Medrash is locked, you know."

"Figures. That's what happens when you lend stuff to a thief. Here, you want my watch, too?"

Nothing stings as much as a betrayal of confidence. Here, Aaron poured out his heart to his friends, believing he could trust them with this story that obviously weighed heavily upon his conscience. Both roommates then had a responsibility to guard his confidence and refrain from ever using the information he entrusted to them in order to degrade or humiliate him.

By taking this confidential information and turning it against Aaron, Benny betrayed his friendship and trust in a major way. Aaron had essentially handed a knife to someone who he thought would guard it, but instead used it to stab him. This left Aaron feeling foolish for having trusted the wrong person, and terribly vulnerable, for who knew what Benny might do with the information next.

Once a person knows confidential information about another, he is obligated to treat that information with the greatest sensitivity. He must never use it against the person who trusted him, even if he becomes angry or annoyed at that person. It is not the listener's secret to do with as he pleases. It is not an appropriate topic for a joke or even a cryptic reference that others won't understand.

Someone who is a trusted friend can, just through listening and acting responsibly with what is told to him, provide others with an invaluable benefit. He can be a source of comfort and understanding: the person to go to when there's nowhere else to turn.

In Other Words:

"*I will commit myself to never being the one to bring up any embarrassing information another person has told me in confidence.*"

כ"ה כסלו
25 KISLEV / CYCLE 1

כ"ה ניסן
25 NISSAN / CYCLE 2

כ"ו אב
26 AV / CYCLE 3

❧ *The Word's Out*

*A*fter much deliberation, Zev Goldberg decided to leave the medical practice with which he had been associated for the past 10 years and strike out on his own. He informed the other doctors of his decision, and everyone agreed to keep the matter quiet until Zev had settled on a location and opening date for his new office.

Soon after the decision was made, Zev's friend Avi came for an office visit. As he signed in at the reception desk, he overheard a doctor tell the receptionist, "Don't make appointments for Dr. Goldberg after November."

"That's when he's leaving?" the receptionist inquired.

"Probably. But he's not announcing it yet," he said in an audible whisper.

A few minutes later, Avi was called to the examining room. "So, Avi, what's up? What are you here for?" Zev asked.

"Never mind what's up with me," he answered wryly. "What's up with you? I hear you're leaving the practice!"

With so many details still unsettled, Zev had not wanted anyone but his wife and his associates to know about the move. He dreaded being the topic of conversation, and if anything should cause a delay or cancellation of his plans, he dreaded having to explain.

"No one is supposed to know yet," Zev answered. "Please keep it to yourself. It's still in the planning stages."

"Oh, really? I heard November."

While it might be a difficult concept to accept in our media-saturated age, people's lives are their own business. Sometimes it is good news, sometimes it is bad, that a person wants to keep to himself. For instance, he may not want others to know he is ill, or that he lost his job. On the other hand, one may not wish to announce his engagement yet, or to spread news of his great new job.

To such a person, the realization that the word has gotten out is a painful one. Therefore, if one happens to accidentally find out something that has not yet been made public, he should not repeat it to anyone and certainly should not discuss it with the person whose secret it is, unless there is some constructive purpose for doing so.

Still more painful is for someone to have his private information disclosed to someone else, right in front of him. For instance, in the above scenario, rather than Avi making the discovery, a fellow-doctor might have told Avi, in front of Zev, "You heard, I'm sure, that Dr. Goldberg is leaving us."

This strikes at Zev from two directions. First, he doesn't want the information spread. Secondly, he is now face-to-face with someone to whom he is going to have to explain his desire for secrecy. Avi is apt to wonder, *Why didn't Zev tell me?* Both of these outcomes spell distress and embarrassment for Zev.

A good guideline for avoiding these situations is to keep other people's personal information off one's agenda, unless there is a constructive reason to do otherwise. Then you won't trip on the unseen wires that could be right in front of you.

In Other Words:

"*I will wait for others to tell me news about their personal lives rather than questioning them or repeating to others information that is not meant to be revealed.*"

25 Kislev — Dedicated in honor of our children on our anniversary
Mr. and Mrs. Mordechai Dovid Levine Spring Valley, NY

25 Nissan — לזכר ולע״נ מורנו הגה״צ רב אביגדור הכהן מיללער זצ״ל נלב״ע כ״ז ניסן
Chaim Elya and Dassy Gross

26 Av — לע״נ אסתר בת פנחס ע״ה
Dedicated by her children and grandchildren

CHAPTER 10:

HURTFUL SPEECH CATEGORY VIII:

Misinforming And Misleading People

*W*hen one raises another person's expectations, one puts that person at a risk for disappointment. Sometimes disappointment is unavoidable, but a person must be careful to avoid doing unnecessary harm.

כ"ו כסלו
26 KISLEV / CYCLE 1

כ"ו ניסן
26 NISSAN / CYCLE 2

כ"ז אב
27 AV / CYCLE 3

✒ *False Hope*

*W*hen Nachum heard of his neighbor's financial troubles, his heart ached. The family had been quietly enduring unemployment for the past six months. Their reserves were gone, their debts were mounting and the family breadwinner, Moshe, was rapidly descending into depression.

Nachum wanted to help. "Listen, I have lots of friends in accounting," he told Moshe. "I'm sure someone knows of an opening. In fact, my sister's brother-in-law just opened his own accounting firm. I'll bet he still has some positions."

This was the first spark of hope Moshe had allowed himself for months. Someone with a live connection — a close connection — really might be able to help him surface above the piles of resumes and be seriously considered for a job.

A week went by and Moshe hazarded a call.

"Any word from your sister's brother-in-law?"

"Oh, I have to get ahold of my sister and get his number. She's so hard to pin down. I left her a message a couple of days ago. I guess I'll try her again today."

And so it went. Every week, Moshe checked in with Nachum, whose good intentions were now lost in a sea of poor excuses. The spark of hope had been little more than an illusion, and Moshe was more disappointed than ever.

When a person is in need of a job or a *shidduch*, networks and connections are vital. Many people feel that they would love to be the Heavenly messenger that makes the match, and they may offer to help out of their sincere desire to do so.

However, they may not see that their noncommittal "I'll try" is being taken by the other person as a golden strand of hope. Therefore, they may not realize the hurt they inflict when they do not follow through.

Obviously, when someone suggests a *shidduch* or a job he believes to be a good possibility, he cannot guarantee the results. However, once a person raises hopes, he is obligated to see the matter through in a timely and sensitive way. If he builds the other person's hopes up and then carelessly lets him down, he has made the situation worse.

To avoid inflicting this kind of pain, one must realistically assess the help he can offer before offering it. He should understand how seriously the other person takes his offer; how he trusts that every effort is being made on his behalf and eagerly waits for good news. To do less than one's best under these circumstances transforms the original comforting words of concern into *ona'as devarim*. To come through, however, even if one cannot produce the solution to the problem, is a precious act of lovingkindness. It's the follow-through that makes the difference.

In Other Words:

" *If I offer to help someone, I will take my words as a firm commitment and do everything I can to follow through on what I have offered.* "

---

26 Kislev — May today's learning be a z'chus for our family.
Dedicated by Simcha and Miriam Chamberg

26 Nissan — Annette Rabinowitz לע״נ חנה בת זאב וואלף ע״ה נלב״ע כ״ז ניסן
Dedicated by Andrew R. Meyers

27 Av — Esther Segal לע״נ אסתר בת צבי אלימלך הכהן ע״ה
Dedicated by Alvin Segal and family

**DAY
87**

כ"ז כסלו
27 KISLEV / CYCLE 1

כ"ז ניסן
27 NISSAN / CYCLE 2

כ"ח אב
28 AV / CYCLE 3

✑ Chain Reaction

*E*sther was new to the city. She needed to have her vacuum cleaner repaired.

"Where should I go to have this fixed?" she asked her next-door neighbor, a cranky woman who had already grown tired of her new neighbor's questions.

"I don't know, I don't know. Why don't you try the supermarket?" the neighbor replied brusquely.

It didn't seem like a likely spot for a vacuum cleaner-repair operation, but then again, Esther thought, they rented carpet steamers and sold small appliances at this massive supermarket. Maybe they fixed vacuum cleaners too.

She walked in with her vacuum cleaner, attracting some amused stares from the other customers. Unable to locate the repair desk, she went to the courtesy booth to ask for directions.

"WHAT?" the clerk asked her. "Did you say vacuum-cleaner repair? Here?"

"Never mind," Esther replied, searching for the least conspicuous exit.

The *Shulchan Aruch* (*Choshen Mishpat* 228:4) describes a situation in which someone asks another person where he can purchase a certain item. The person sends him to a store at which this kind of merchandise is not sold. This is forbidden because the person would certainly feel embarrassed when he realized that he had been sent to the wrong place.

But were the words directing him to the wrong store actually *ona'as devarim*? Does it cause pain to a person if someone tells him he can have his vacuum cleaner repaired at a supermarket? Certainly at the moment the words are being spoken, they inflict no harm. Obviously, however, the end result of those words is pain. Therefore, the situation outlined in the *Shulchan Aruch* teaches us that we are not only responsible for the impact of our words when we speak them, but also for the chain reaction they set in motion.

This concept carries over into many areas of life. When one brushes someone else off with unclear directions or misleading explanations, the speaker is responsible for the difficulties his words later cause. When the person, attempting to follow the unclear directions, gets lost and misses an important appointment, his difficulties are the fault of the person who carelessly gave him those directions. The words are *ona'as devarim,* even if they were spoken days before the actual harm occurred.

On the other side of the coin is the ability to achieve long-term good with the words we speak. If Esther's neighbor would have taken the time to give her a list of stores or useful phone numbers, or even taken the time to drive her around town, the words she imparted would help Esther for months or years to come. The point is that once one's words emerge, they have a continuing ripple effect in the world. That thought must be taken into account every time we speak.

In Other Words:

" *If someone asks me for directions or advice, I will take the time to be accurate and clear and to make sure the person understands me.* "

27 Kislev — Beryl Bisco לע״נ ביילא בת משה ע״ה
Dedicated by Michael and Diane Kaplan and family

27 Nissan — לע״נ משה בן יודל ז״ל
Dedicated by Chana Chaya Klein

28 Av — לזכות דוד פסח בן אברהם ואשתו פרומה אסתר בת יעקב ע״ה
אברהם יהושע העשל

כ"ח כסלו
28 KISLEV / CYCLE 1

כ"ח ניסן
28 NISSAN / CYCLE 2

כ"ט אב
29 AV / CYCLE 3

Just Browsing

*W*ouldn't *you love to try on some of those bracelets?" Kaila asked Ariella as the two girls pressed their faces against the enticing window of Levy's Fine Jewelry Shop. It was midwinter vacation, and the two high-school girls were on a shopping trip in the city.*

"Yeah, but how are we going to do that?" Ariella asked.

"We'll just walk in and ask to see the bracelet," Kaila said confidently. "I'm sure plenty of people try things on and then don't end up buying. Anyway, we're not taking up the salesman's time. I see him standing there dusting the showcase."

"Are you sure it's all right?" Ariella replied doubtfully. "It seems kind of mean."

Ariella's assessment was 100 percent correct. According to the *Choshen Mishpat* (228:4), asking for a price when one has no intention of making a purchase is not only mean, but prohibited. The reason is that by inquiring about the item, the person raises the salesman's hopes and then, when the inevitable happens and the "customer" walks out empty-handed, the salesman suffers disappointment.

Why is this worse than when a legitimate customer inquires about an item and then decides against buying it? It would seem that the salesman would be disappointed in that case as well. The difference is that in a case like the one above, other people created his disappointment unnecessarily. If one is truly shopping for an item, asking prices and comparing the offerings of various sellers is part of the process, without which no business would be done.

Similarly, a salesman would not mind if a person is asking about an item that is closer to his price range; although the person may not think of himself as a customer, the salesman knows that he may be tempted to buy it one day, and is more than willing to help him. However, the Torah does not allow a person to play the shopper when it will clearly serve no purpose at any time.

One might wonder why someone would ask for prices when he has no intention of purchasing an item. Curiosity is the primary answer. A person sees a gracious mansion for sale and wonders what it looks like inside. He calls the real-estate agent pretending to be an interested buyer, and thus wins himself a free tour. Another scenario is the desire to test-drive an expensive car one could not afford to buy. (This may also entail *geneivah* as the car dealer would never have allowed him to test-drive the car had the dealer known that the customer had absolutely no intention of buying it.) Nothing — except a person's conscience — stops him from presenting himself to the dealer as a potential buyer.

Even where there is no verbal deception, one can stumble on this prohibition. In the opening scenario, the girls are not actively pretending to be buyers. They are just curious to see the bracelets and try them on. They need not say a word to the salesman about their intentions; they are still implying that they are prospective buyers just by expressing their interest in the merchandise.

In truth, displaying his merchandise to a noncustomer might not take much time from the salesman's day. He may never even become aware that his disappointment was for naught. Yet, just because these

In Other Words:

"*If I have the temptation to inquire about merchandise I have no intention of buying, I will imagine the salesman's disappointment as I walk away empty-handed.*"

Cont. on pg. 196

actions inflict unnecessary pain, the Torah says, "No, do not do this to a fellow human being."

A simple way to avoid this problem is to inform the salesman that one is "just browsing." He may still be quite willing to spend time with the customer, realizing that a browser who admires a certain item may some day return to the store with the resources to buy it, or might recommend it to someone else who is in the market for the item.

CHAPTER 11:

HURTFUL SPEECH CATEGORY IX:

Subtle Negative Statements

*I*n an effort to avoid outright confrontation, people sometimes employ vague, indirect statements. Nevertheless, the negative message comes through.

כ״ט כסלו♦
·29 KISLEV / CYCLE 1

כ״ט ניסן
29 NISSAN / CYCLE 2

ל אב
30 AV / CYCLE 3

❧ *Beware*
the Undertone

ev and Miriam were facing one of the most difficult situations that had arisen in their 20 years of marriage. They had lived in Israel since they were wed, and had been raising their children in an environment they truly loved. However, Zev's company had closed down six months earlier, and all his efforts to find new employment had thus far proved futile. The couple was beginning to despair when suddenly, seemingly out of nowhere, Zev received a lucrative job offer ... in America.

Zev wanted to go. Miriam felt it would be devastating to their children and inconsistent with their vision for their family. Zev felt reality came before vision. They tried to keep their discussions of the matter calm and productive, but Miriam, the more outspoken of the two, tended to dominate the discussions. Zev would walk away shaking his head and muttering softly under his breath.

"What are you saying?" his wife would demand. "Say it to me! Whatever you're saying, say it to me so we can have a discussion."

"It's nothing, nothing, I'm just talking to myself," he finally replied. Throughout their arguments and debates on their family's next move, the muttering continued, serving as a release valve for Zev, but a detonator for Miriam.

Well aware of the impact of angry words, Zev used his muttering to say what was on his mind but avoid

♦ When this month has only 29 days, the lesson for 30 Kislev should also be studied today.

direct accusations and conflict. He thought he was taking the high road, restricting his volume to an inaudible level even though he was not capable of restraining the words themselves, or better yet, working through his anger with his wife.

From Miriam's point of view, however, the muttering itself was *ona'as devarim*, regardless of what words were actually being muttered. She clearly perceived that it represented anger, or at the very least, sharp disagreement. She also understood that her husband obviously felt the words were too hurtful to say to her face. Knowing that he thought these angry thoughts was discomforting, and all the more so because she was not being allowed to hear and respond to them.

This of course does not mean that it is preferable for one to shout his hurtful statements. It simply means that one should not fool oneself into thinking that just because the other person doesn't hear what's being said, he or she is not hurt by it. In fact, the other person may be more deeply upset by the muttering, because he might assume that the muttered comments are far worse than they actually are.

The real solution is to learn basic assertiveness: how to present one's own point of view with clarity, calm and firmness, even in the face of opposition. In this way, disagreements can be productive. Each side can present his perspective and respond to the other person's comments without having to suffer a stealth attack of words that he cannot hear, and that do nothing to move the discussion forward.

In Other Words:

" If I have the habit of muttering under my breath when I am upset, I will take notice of this habit and try to channel my frustration more productively. "

ל כסלו*
*30 KISLEV / CYCLE 1

ל ניסן
30 NISSAN / CYCLE 2

א אלול
1 ELUL / CYCLE 3

☙ *Get the Hint?*

*E*leven-year-old Shimon and 9-year-old Reuven labored together in the backyard of their house, raking up the masses of crunchy brown leaves that carpeted the lawn. There were many places Reuven would rather have been at that moment, and therefore, he worked without much enthusiasm. It seemed clear to Shimon that his younger brother hoped to get away with doing as little as possible.

"I once heard of a kid who was so lazy, he hired his little brother to carry his books to school for him," Shimon informed Reuven.

"I am not lazy. I'm tired!" Reuven protested. "And you better not say one more word to me or I'm not helping at all!"

"I didn't say you were lazy," Shimon responded with what seemed like disbelief that his brother could have judged him so harshly. "I just said I heard about a boy who was lazy. But you know what they say ... 'If the shoe fits, wear it.'"

"What's that supposed to mean?" Reuven accused.

"It means whatever you think it means," Shimon answered. His younger brother seemed ready to burst with frustration. He knew he was being criticized, but he couldn't pinpoint the insult well enough to fight back.

When a person criticizes another person by hint, insinuation, allegedly unrelated quotes of other people or of well-known sayings, he delivers a stealth attack that is not only damaging, but also, difficult to

* When this month has only 29 days, the lessons for 30 Kislev should be learned together with 29 Kislev.

counter. Telling a child "I'm sure I've seen people take longer to do their homework, but I can't remember when," is not any less insulting than saying, "You're so slow!"

Using "wise sayings" to put another person down is especially insidious, because the victim's sense is that his actions not only run counter to what his critic desires, but they run against common wisdom as well. Furthermore, the victim cannot argue with the statement.

For instance, a person who is embroiled in a dispute with another person, even if he contributed to the development of the dispute, does not benefit by hearing, "You know what they say ... we reap what we sow." Such a statement only makes him feel that he is a negative person who generates negative energy. Using quotes to hint at one's displeasure or even one's constructive criticism of another person is rarely perceived as an effort to help the person make positive changes. Rather it is seen as what it often is: the desire to assert one's sense of superiority at another person's expense.

In Other Words:

"

If I am about to hint a negative message, I will instead phrase my opinion in an informative, positive way.

"

30 Kislev — Florence Adler לע״נ צפורה יענטעל בת דוד מאיר ע״ה נלב״ע ב׳ טבת
Dedicated by her grandchildren

30 Nissan — לע״נ אברהם בן יחיאל מאיר ז״ל

1 Elul — לע״נ יעקב נטע בן משולם זוסיא ז״ל
In loving memory of Edward Klamen

DAY 91

א טבת
1 TEVES / CYCLE 1

א אייר
1 IYAR / CYCLE 2

ב אלול
2 ELUL / CYCLE 3

❧ *The Cutting Edge*

*W*ow, you're a ball of sunshine this morning," the mother said to her sullen teenage daughter, who was eating her breakfast cereal in hostile silence.

"Oh, you're just a genius, aren't you," the boss said acidly to his assistant, who had made a costly mistake.

"Nice job cleaning the playroom," the mother told her children. "Soon it might be possible to see the floor."

"You get an A plus for customer service," the irate customer told the clerk who refused to accept her returned merchandise.

"How gentlemanly," said the middle-aged woman to the young man who preceded her into the bank and let the door close in her face.

"You want me to treat you with the respect you deserve? Well, I do!" the man told his next-door neighbor.

All of these comments have two things in common. First, their meaning is the opposite of what it seems to be. Secondly, the people on the receiving end of these comments will end up feeling either foolish or angry. What they will *not* feel is repentant.

Sarcasm is a form of *ona'as devarim* that comes in a thin disguise, for the words used in a sarcastic comment are often, taken at face value, either neutral or positive. However, the circumstances and tone of voice supply what the simple meaning of the words does not. In addition, most sarcasm conveys a level of disdain that would be absent from the same criticism stated directly.

For instance, the mother could tell her children, "Look, there are still lots of toys on the floor. It isn't clean until everything is put away." They might not like hearing the criticism, but they would not feel demeaned by it. They would simply understand that they had not performed up to par, and were expected to do better.

In some cases, people use sarcasm as a way of veiling their displeasure, imagining that a bit of ironic humor will convey the message less painfully. For instance, a teacher might think it preferable to ask an unfocused child, "How are things in outer space?" than to say, "Shimon, pay attention to the work!" In reality, however, the latter comment gives the child direct instructions that he can implement, while the former simply ridicules his personality.

A person who uses sarcasm often does so because he fears the consequences of direct communication. The problem with this approach, however, is that it projects tremendous negativity toward the recipient of the comment. If someone cannot accept criticism, it is usually preferable to say nothing or wait for an opportune time to speak sincerely.

Another motivation for sarcasm is the humor many people find in ironic comments. Clearly, however, the prohibition of *ona'as devarim* precludes us from causing others pain for our own or others' amusement.

With rare exception, the sharp comment is a dangerous weapon. It cuts and wounds, but is nowhere near as powerful as a direct, softly and carefully stated comment, in conveying the message one really wishes to convey.

In Other Words:

" *I will choose one person with whom I tend to be sarcastic and work on communicating directly and sincerely instead.* "

ב טבת
2 TEVES / CYCLE 1

ב אייר
2 IYAR / CYCLE 2

ג אלול
3 ELUL / CYCLE 3

❧ *A Day at the Zoo*

*Y*ou snake!" the man said to his business competitor. "You lied to me."

"You eat like a pig!" the boy told his older brother. "Save some food for the rest of us."

"You're a bunch of wild animals!" the baby-sitter scolded the rowdy children.

"You have a mouth like a sewer," the man told his neighbor.

"Your friends are garbage," the mother complained to her teenage son.

When a person wants to make a strong point, he sometimes chooses a strong, jarring word to convey his message unequivocally. He deploys his big guns, just to make sure that the shot is heard. Comparisons to unsavory animals or objects accomplish this goal. In one word, these comparisons paint an ugly image of subhuman behavior that immediately conveys total disgust with the other person.

A person who is subject to such a comparison gets the message: "I am beneath contempt in his eyes. I am like an animal to him. A mindless, loathsome creature."

Such a message may succeed in shocking someone momentarily, but it will be very unlikely to inspire him to change. Rather, his self-image will have been brought so low that change will appear impossible. A "pig" will never be able to control his appetite. A "sewer" mouth can never be purified of its stench. Someone who has the poor judgment to befriend "garbage" is too tainted to attempt to find better friends.

This is labeling of a most drastic kind. Here, one is not just labeling the individual as a deficient type of person; he is labeling him as a nonperson. One is identifying him with the most animalistic part of his being, and denying recognition to the person's *neshamah*. Rather than giving the person an opening through which he can rectify his flaws or mistakes, one is closing the window tightly.

In all instances, the Torah teaches that one should speak in as mild a form as possible to accomplish one's goals. Harsh, ugly words and images should not be used where softer words will do the job. Comparisons to animals or vile objects violate this principle, for there are always softer ways to make the point.

The bottom line is that the Torah prohibits us from afflicting each other with the words we use. However, given the fact that negative messages must sometimes be conveyed, a person is required to express the message in the least hurtful and most effective way possible. Ugly comparisons can be extremely hurtful, and are definitely not effective. Therefore, there is no justification for using this type of language.

The question one should ask himself is, "What do I really want to accomplish?" If the answer is, "To get the other person to realize his error," then the way is not paved with harsh, ugly metaphors, but rather, with words that open the other person's heart and help him see the potential that is there.

In Other Words:

"*Rather than trying to make a point with harsh comparisons, I will try to approach the other person with a positive image that can stir him to improve.*"

ג טבת
3 TEVES / CYCLE 1

ג אייר
3 IYAR / CYCLE 2

ד אלול
4 ELUL / CYCLE 3

❧ *Music to Their Ears*

*I*n a recent article in a Jewish women's magazine, the author wrote, half-humorously, about her husband's willing obedience to the voice on their car's GPS system. She noted that the same directions, coming from her, would not be so readily received. In fact, her husband very much disliked when she interfered with his driving.

What was the difference between the mechanical voice and that of his own loving wife? The author analyzed: When the driver (her husband) took a wrong turn, the GPS voice simply noted the mistake and suggested a corrective action. Her tone never carried accusations of inattention, a poor sense of direction or worse.

Everything the GPS "lady" said was in an even, pleasant tone. It was all productive and informative and goal oriented.

The writer concluded that she could take some lessons on interpersonal communications from the GPS "lady." If she could keep impatience and frustration out of her tone of voice, she opined, she would most likely find that her words would be heeded. Perhaps it wasn't what she said, but how she said it, that caused her husband to react to her driving instructions with annoyance.

Most people have friends with whom they particularly enjoy sharing good news, because those friends show in their voices true excitement for the other's good fortune. Most likely, these are the same friends whose tone conveys real concern and empathy when the news is sad. The succor comes not so much from the words the speaker chooses, but from the sincere empathy his voice conveys.

On the other side of the coin, a hostile or cold tone of voice can completely reverse the impact of even positive words. Imagine a conversation in which an employee tells his boss that, due to a death in the family, he will have to miss an important meeting. Perhaps the boss will respond, "Oh, no problem. I'm sorry for your loss." Those words, said with warmth and eye contact, are comforting. Said in a perfunctory monotone, they convey no concern for the loss, but rather, a simmering anger over the inconvenience the loss is causing him.

One cannot mask negative emotions behind neutral or positive words if his tone of voice quickly reveals what lies beneath the surface. A mother who snarls at her child, "What you did was wrong!" cannot disguise her message with parenting-class phrasing, in which she carefully criticizes the action and not the child. The child hears anger in the tone, and it conveys rejection despite the wording.

Tone of voice has a profound impact on people. Obviously, detatched and hostile tones make people feel uncomfortable, disliked and distant. People who tend to become shrill also evoke a reaction, adding fuel to whatever fire is burning. When people feel they are being attacked, they fight back.

When they feel they are being addressed, they listen. But they're not just listening to the lyrics; they're listening closely to the tune.

In Other Words:

" I will try to listen to my tone of voice as I speak to people, perhaps using a tape recorder as an aid. If necessary, I will work on modifying my tone. "

CHAPTER 12

HURTFUL SPEECH CATEGORY X:

Nonverbal Forms Of Ona'as Devarim

A person can send a destructive message to another person without using one word. Facial expressions, body language and even silence can speak volumes.

ד טבת
4 TEVES / CYCLE 1

ד אייר
4 IYAR / CYCLE 2

ה אלול
5 ELUL / CYCLE 3

❧ *In Your Face*

*O*nce a person learns how to read, a world
opens up to him. The written word becomes
a major means of gathering the information he
needs in order to function at his maximum capacity.
Road signs, newspaper articles, textbooks, instruction manuals — all of these words convey important
information the reader can use to navigate his life.

One of the most important messages a person
must decode, however, does not come from the written word. Rather, it comes from the expression on a
human face. Without uttering one word, a person's
expression can tell someone, "I think you're wonderful," "I'm happy to see you," "I understand what you
are telling me," "I'm interested in your story," or thousands of other messages.

By the same means, a person can convey negative messages as well: "You bore me," "I dislike you,"
"I'm angry at you," "You're strange." Literacy in this
area of communication is a vital tool for responding
appropriately and understanding the feelings of others. It is vital for a person — both for survival and for
social success — to know if he is facing a friend or an
enemy.

So vital is this skill that human beings are born
with an understanding of nonverbal cues. Even
infants have been shown to respond to facial expressions, becoming upset when their mothers gaze at
them with a frown and becoming relaxed when their
mothers smile.

Clearly, facial expression can cause others much

pain. If even a tiny infant can pick up the negative message of an angry face, certainly older children and adults can just as instantaneously read what is written there.

Because faces express so much, a person has to take control of the messages his face is sending. The simplest method for doing this is to adopt a pleasant expression as one's "default mode." In other words, endeavor to not look like something is wrong when everything is fine. Even when things are going wrong, it is not necessary to advertise one's misery on one's face.

Sometimes a negative expression arises from a nonstop negative monologue running through a person's mind. He may be thinking about his problems or his grievances against others, even when those issues are not on his present agenda. His "self-talk" is full of negativity, and that is what shows on his face.

This habit not only inflicts the person's pain on others who see him, but forces him to carry his problems around with him everywhere he goes, increasing his sense of stress and fatigue. He can do himself and all those around him the greatest service by living in the present, seeing the good around him as he goes about his daily business and isolating his problems in their own time and place.

By mastering this approach, we fulfill the Mishnah's directive (*Pirkei Avos* 1:15) to greet each person with a pleasant expression. In doing so, we lighten others' moods and make others feel welcome, loved and appreciated, without saying a word.

In Other Words:

"*I will monitor the internal monologue that goes on inside my head and replace negative thoughts with those that are infused with happiness and gratitude.*"

4 Teves — לע"נ יואל אהרן בן יעקב יצחק הכהן ז"ל
Dedicated by the Montal, Banash and Dresner families

4 Iyar — May today's learning be a z'chus for our family.
Dedicated by Mr. and Mrs. Mendy Elefant

5 Elul — In honor of our parents, Leon & Renee Hazan and Leon & Linda Betesh
Dedicated by Ralph & Sharon Hazan

DAY 95

ה טבת
5 TEVES / CYCLE 1

ה אייר
5 IYAR / CYCLE 2

ו אלול
6 ELUL / CYCLE 3

✥ The Poison Pen

*A*ryeh had always wanted to tell Dan exactly what he thought of him. However, in the interest of peaceful neighborhood relations, he had held himself back. The condescending comments, snubs and insults of eight years living side by side, attending the same shul, community and school events, had created a powder keg of anger. But now, Dan had gone too far. He had made a Bar Mitzvah for his oldest son and omitted just one neighbor — Aryeh — from the guest list. To Aryeh, there was no more need to protect the veneer of goodwill.

But Aryeh didn't want a face-to-face confrontation. He simply wanted to let Dan know what he thought of him, and then never speak to him again. He pulled out a blank sheet of paper and began writing. Three pages later, he was done. His venom was expelled into the bitterly critical letter he had written. Now, all that was left was to sign it, seal it, stamp it and send it on its way, via the central post office, to the house next door.

If Aryeh sends this letter, he will have engaged in *ona'as devarim* no less than if he had knocked on his neighbor's door and spewed the same biting words verbally to his face. In some ways, the harm could be worse, because the written words can be read over and over again, delivering their sting anew each time.

In some cases, people resort to written *ona'as devarim* because they are afraid to face the person with whom they are angry. They feel that the distance provided by the written word will somehow protect them from the other person's reaction. Nevertheless, if the words are hurtful and insulting, they are not permitted. One would be wise to heed the inner voice that says, "I can't say this to his face," and realize that this means the words are probably ones that should not be said at all.

In the age of e-mail, the challenge of restraining one's written words has become enormous. The spontaneous nature of the medium makes people far looser in their verbiage and far quicker to respond. At the click of a mouse, their diatribe can travel through cyberspace and assault another person's dignity within a few seconds.

The time needed for composing a "snail-mail" letter — time devoted to the process of writing, printing, addressing and mailing — can serve as a cooling-off period, at the end of which people often decide that the better choice is to throw the letter away. With e-mail and text messaging this barrier is gone. There is no time for second thoughts.

When used properly, however, writing can offer tremendous help in avoiding *ona'as devarim*. Even e-mail is less spontaneous than verbal communication. The writer can take his time in framing his statements. He can review his words and think about how they will be received. He can erase and rewrite. Someone whose goal is to address a problematic situation while avoiding insult to the other party has every opportunity to do so when the written word is the medium.

In Other Words:

"*I will institute a 24-hour waiting period between writing any negative correspondence — whether on paper or by e-mail — and deciding whether to send it.*"

5 Teves — In loving memory of our dear mother and grandmother, Bracha Gross
Cheryl & Duvy Gross, Tzvi & Gila, Burry, Moshe, Debra, Kobe and Chani

5 Iyar — As a z'chus for Idit Noah and Matisyahu Avraham Stein
Dedicated by Dr. Steven & Julie Stein

6 Elul — Dr. Rhoda Golden Freeman לע״נ רחל לאה בת יצחק יעקב ע״ה נלב״ע ח׳ אלול
Dedicated in loving memory by Shayna and Craig Prupis

ו טבת
6 TEVES / CYCLE 1

ו אייר
6 IYAR / CYCLE 2

ז אלול
7 ELUL / CYCLE 3

🌿 *In Your Hands*

*T*he mischievous little boy points with his left hand to his classmate sitting in front of him, and points to his temple with his right hand. A few back and forth twists of the right pointer finger gets the message across to the boy sitting next to him. They giggle together at this witty "comment," which they both understand to mean that the other boy is crazy.

"You said I was crazy!" the victim accuses his classmate at recess.

"I didn't say one single word," the perpetrator responds. "Did I say he was crazy?" he asks his accomplice.

"Uh-uh. You didn't say one word," the boy concurs.

"Well, half the class is telling me that you said I'm crazy," the victim tried again.

"Maybe they're all crazy," the perpetrator suggests triumphantly. "Because I didn't say anything."

Until the victim clarifies with his classmates that the boy's insult was a gesture, not a word, the victim will probably remain confused. But the boy who insulted him knows just what he did. He knows that his gesture was the exact equivalent of the word, understood by him, the boy to whom he communicated his "comment" and the many classmates who had apparently witnessed it.

Insulting gestures cause pain to those at whom they are aimed, and are therefore included within the prohibition of *ona'as devarim*. They may not seem to be *devarim* — words — however, they do what words do, which is to communicate an idea. Therefore, whether one uses actual sign language or informal gestures that convey some message, his hands can speak *ona'as devarim* just as surely as his mouth can.

Hand motions can also cause distress when they don't have an actual verbal meaning, but rather, impart a negative feeling to others. For instance, a person who stands close to someone and points a finger at him, even if he is speaking in a relatively calm manner, makes the listener feel assaulted and uneasy.

The same is true of one who punctuates his comments with loud thumping on the table or other emphatic gestures. These motions are intended to create an effect — to manipulate others' emotions without having to verbally voice the threat that is inherent in the gesture. Nevertheless, the threat is communicated. Therefore, a person who wants his message to be caring and sincere must measure not only that which he says with his mouth, but that which he says with his hands as well.

In Other Words:

"If I tend to use my hands to impart negative messages to or about others, I will refrain from doing so and make an effort to speak directly and sincerely instead."

לע״נ הרב מאיר בן הרב איתמר ז״ל — **6 Teves**
Dedicated by Yossi and Bella Greenfield and family

לזכות חי׳ עטקא בת גיטל שתחי׳ — **6 Iyar**

לע״נ מרדכי ז״ל בן אברהם יבלח״ט — **7 Elul**
Dedicated by his siblings: Gerson, Teichman and Reisman families

ז טבת
7 TEVES / CYCLE 1

ז אייר
7 IYAR / CYCLE 2

ח אלול
8 ELUL / CYCLE 3

❧ *Not a Word*

*E*very morning, 11-year-old Sarah refused to get up for school. Her mother coaxed, nagged, warned, bribed and often ended up driving her daughter to school in a frantic rush. One day, her mother decided to delve a bit deeper into the problem.

"Sarah, I know you're not a lazy girl," she began. "Why is it that after a perfectly good night's sleep, you just can't get up and make the bus?"

Reluctantly, her daughter revealed the problem. "There's a really popular girl who sits right at the front of the bus, and whenever I get on, she stares at me. I can tell she thinks I'm weird. Then one time I got on the bus and my knapsack strap got caught on something and this girl and all her friends had these big smiles on their faces. I can't ride that bus."

Sarah's mother might have thought that her daughter should be able to simply ignore the looks that greeted her as she boarded the bus. After all, no one was physically hurting her or even saying anything offensive to her. However, Sarah's sense of humiliation was no less painful than that which aggressive words or acts might have produced. The popular girls in the front seat had mastered the art of the wordless attack.

Condescending looks and smiles, disapproving stares and grimaces are as powerful an expression of disdain as the words they silently express. In fact, most people read these expressions even more clearly, for they cut straight to the heart without traveling first through the intellect.

One need not be an 11-year-old to be sensitive to this type of *ona'as devarim*. Most people can think of someone in their lives who makes them feel distinctly uncomfortable without saying one negative word. The discomfort comes from the way the person looks at him, as if he were a specimen of some lower life-form.

Disdain is so powerful that it can actually impede a person's spiritual life. The *Shulchan Aruch* takes this phenomenon very seriously. In the very first *halachah* it recognizes this as one of the most likely causes for someone to abandon his effort to stand up for a mitzvah and move forward in his service to Hashem. By opening the entire code of Jewish law with a warning to the Jewish people not to allow themselves to be dissuaded by derision, the *Shulchan Aruch* illustrates how overpoweringly negative this force can be.

Once a person recognizes the pain that derisive expressions cause in his own life, there is but one short step to understanding that one can inflict this pain on others as well, with no more than a wry smile or a hard stare. The effect of this behavior is to drive others away, for one's expressions can easily belie kind words and even helpful deeds.

On the other hand, sincere warmth can shine through one's eyes equally powerfully. The person who wears this expression opens his life to a world of *chesed,* as he becomes a trusted friend others can confide in, knowing that whatever they tell him, he will never respond with derision.

In Other Words:

"*If I feel myself starting to laugh at someone or look at someone with a disdainful expression, I will change my mode by telling myself, 'I care about this person.'*"

7 Teves — לע״נ יצחק בן נתן יהודה ז״ל
Dedicated by Shlomie & Miriam Kaufman and family

7 Iyar Gertrude Hochberg לע״נ ברכה גאלדע בת ר׳ שלמה הכהן ע״ה
In loving memory by her children, Moshe and Susan Gartenberg

8 Elul — May today's learning be a z'chus for Klal Yisroel.
Dedicated by Tzvi and Emily Schwartz

ח טבת
8 TEVES / CYCLE 1

ח אייר
8 IYAR / CYCLE 2

ט אלול
9 ELUL / CYCLE 3

❧ *The Silent Treatment*

*W*hen Yossi returned home from his three-day business trip, he had an unwelcome surprise awaiting him. Dina, his wife, had stopped speaking to him.

"What's wrong?" he asked her, although he was pretty sure he knew. His return trip had been delayed by one day, causing him to miss a ceremony conferring siddurim upon their son's first-grade class. It was an important day to their enthusiastic little boy, Yitzy, but the delay could not have been prevented.

Yossi's overtures to open a conversation with his wife fell flat. She marched around the house in stony silence, making herself busy with household chores.

"At least you could talk to me and say what's on your mind," he persisted. "Look, I bought a special present just for Yitzy to try to make up for not being there, at least a little bit. It's a siddur for him to use at home. Look, I got his name engraved on it."

But Dina would not relent. Her campaign continued into the evening and the next morning as well. Yossi left for work under her silent storm cloud. By the time he came home, Dina had softened. "How was your day?" she asked nonchalantly. But now, her husband was angry; the fight would clearly have to go at least one more round.

Silence can be a powerful, painful weapon. It tells a person, "Not only am I angry, but I don't even care enough about you to try to talk it out."

Sometimes, people resort to silence because they

are so angry that they fear they will say something they will regret. This is sometimes, under the right circumstances, a good temporary strategy for handling a volatile situation. Although the silence is painful, it may be, in this instance, less painful than the words that would emerge in its place.

However, even under these circumstances, a person must work on calming his negative emotions and framing the situation in a way that it can be dealt with productively. Perhaps he should use the period of silence to try to see things from the other person's side or to see the *"gam zu l'tovah"* — Hashem's inherent goodness — in whatever occurrence has upset him.

In most instances, however, angry silence is simply another weapon, another means of hurting someone without having to take responsibility for uttering cruel words. One should not try to deceive oneself into thinking that offensive silence is better than offensive speech, for both cause pain. Sometimes, the words left unsaid are more frightening to ponder than words that have actually been voiced.

Most often the same restraint being exercised to maintain stony silence can be used to tamp down one's anger and speak to the other person in words that address the issue with directness, calmness and respect.

In Other Words:

" *If I am the type of person who falls silent when I am angry, I will think of a sentence or two I can use to break the silence before it becomes an affront.* "

CHAPTER 13:

Identifying Personal Pitfalls

ach person has his own unique challenges in the realm of ona'as devarim. By identifying these challenges, a person can channel his efforts in the direction which will yield the greatest positive changes in his relationships and his life.

ט טבת
9 TEVES / CYCLE 1

ט אייר
9 IYAR / CYCLE 2

י אלול
10 ELUL / CYCLE 3

✦ *A Gentle Awakening*

*T*he top of Moshe's head was just barely visible at the edge of his quilt. The rest of him was buried deeply in the down. The soft rise and fall of his breathing let his father know that the young man was lost in the far provinces of Dreamland.

His father's heart sank with a sense of dread. "This is not going to be pleasant," he said to himself in preparation for what was surely to come.

He tousled his son's hair affectionately and said, "Moshe, Moshe. Hello, hello. It's morning. Time for minyan. Moshe!"

"Awww. Nawww," the boy replied as he buried his head deeper.

"It's late! Come on! You're 15 years old. You have to go to minyan! Look, I'm going out of the room and I'm trusting you to get up and get dressed. I'll check in another 10 minutes."

Ten minutes later, Moshe was exactly where his father had left him. "I've had it with this nonsense!" his father shouted. He ripped the quilt off Moshe, hoping the cold air would complete the job of waking him. "Every morning we have to go through this. You are the laziest person I have ever known. What kind of a Jew shows up for minyan 40 minutes late?"

Moshe now took the offensive, shouting back at his father with words he knew could only arouse further anger. Finally, the father gave up. He had to get to minyan himself and did not want to be as late as his son would undoubtedly be. Both father and son were completely exhausted, and the son had his poor self-image confirmed yet again.

The subject of waking the sleeping child — especially when that child hits his or her teenage years — is one that has confounded parents and experts alike. It is a situation ripe for *ona'as devarim* as the rush of meeting morning obligations crashes up against the rocklike obstinacy of a tired child. If this is an area of contention in a person's life, that means that every day will likely start with an onslaught of *ona'as devarim*. Certainly, no one really wants this as a daily diet.

Therefore, it is worthwhile to think of alternative strategies for this, or any part of one's daily routine that often results in harsh words. Homework time, bedtime, cleanup and other chores are all potential areas of repeated conflict. Rather than simply accepting that these battles must be fought to the death, one can consult experts, parenting books, other parents or their own better instincts and find ways to manage the situations. If one approaches these power struggles using *ona'as devarim*, the impact of the words that are spoken may remain long after the child has outgrown his uncooperative ways.

In Other Words:

"*I will choose one area of my daily routine that often engenders ona'as devarim and seek an alternative strategy.*"

9 Teves — Mrs. Ettil Spiegel לע״נ עטיל בת שמואל ע״ה
Dedicated in loving memory by her grandchildren

9 Iyar — Rabbi Nahum Moshe Ben-Natan לע״נ הרב נחום משה בן מיכאל בן ציון ז״ל
Dedicated by Families Ben-Natan, Fleischmann, Jager, Pelberg, Carmen

10 Elul — Jack Lewis Geller לע״נ יעקב לייב בן שאול ז״ל
Miriam Zuckerman לע״נ מרים בת גרשון ע״ה

י טבת
10 TEVES / CYCLE 1

י אייר
10 IYAR / CYCLE 2

י"א אלול
11 ELUL / CYCLE 3

✑ *Hello, Goodbye*

*W*ith three full plastic grocery bags hanging on one arm and two on the other, somehow Leah manages to reach into her pocket and answer her cell phone's rendition of Tchaikovsky's Nutcracker Suite.

On the other end was Rochel, her dearest friend from her old neighborhood. Rochel is excited to hear Leah's voice; they hadn't spoken for several months.

"Hello?" Leah speaks breathlessly, trying not to drop the cell phone, which was now squeezed between her ear and her shoulder.

"Hi, Leah! It's me, Rochel! How ARE you?"

"Oh my goodness, Rochel. I can't talk now. I'm loaded down with bundles. I gotta go."

To Rochel, it feels as if her friend opened the front door, saw her face, said hello and then slammed the door shut. She thinks it through and understands that there was no insult meant, but still, is this how you greet a friend?

Because a person's cell phone is usually wherever he is, a whole new set of telephone etiquette questions have been created, along with a whole new category of potential *ona'as devarim*. Anyone may call at any time, and not all of those times are appropriate, or even plausible, times to speak.

The tone of voice that people often use in these situations implies that the caller should somehow know what an inappropriate moment this is for a phone call. When someone says, "I can't talk right now. They're taking my mother into surgery!" the caller feels as if he is an insensitive fool. When a person picks up and says, "I'm in the middle of a meeting," the caller feels like a nuisance.

What can be done in a situation where a conversation is out of the question, but the cell phone is beckoning?

The simplest strategy is to let the caller leave a message and be sure to return the call at the earliest possible time. Most people would rather get a voice mail message than a harried, pre-occupied answer.

If one does pick up the call, he should be extremely careful of the words and tone he uses. He should try to make the caller feel that his contact is welcome, even if it cannot be pursued at that moment. It doesn't take much longer to say a few calm, explanatory sentences than it does to grumble a distracted hello and end the call abruptly.

It may seem extreme, but it is even worthwhile to rehearse the words one will say before the situation arises. There was once a Torah scholar who spent time in front of his mirror practicing his smile. Because smiling at others is a way of showing them respect, he wanted to give the mitzvah his best effort by giving others his best smile. Today, the tone with which we answer the phone serves the same purpose. It is a way of showing respect to others: a goal that is surely worth our best efforts.

In Other Words:

"*I will pay attention to how I answer the phone when I am unable to carry on a conversation and make sure that my tone does not convey irritation.*"

CHAPTER 14:
Strategies

A person speaks tens of thousands of words a day. There are perhaps no more frequently repeated habits than those of speech. Thus, changing the way one speaks can seem to be an impossible task, too overwhelming to even approach. The key is to find strategies that provide a means to succeed, step by step, until new, positive habits replace the old.

DAY 101

י"א טבת
11 TEVES / CYCLE 1

י"א אייר
11 IYAR / CYCLE 2

י"ב אלול
12 ELUL / CYCLE 3

 ## *The Big Payoff*

*N*othing could keep Toby on a diet. Not the looming threat of high blood pressure, nor the closet full of elegant clothing she could no longer wear. Not even her own disgust with the person she saw in the mirror.

Every morning, she would awaken with fresh resolve, thinking about the fruits and vegetables and eight glasses of water that she would consume that day. But by noon, she would be looking for something to satisfy her craving for a sweet, and by 12:05, the diet would be doomed for another day as a snippet of cake turned into a slice, another slice, and so on.

Most people have as much difficulty controlling what comes out of their mouths as Toby had controlling what went in. In both cases, the urge of the moment overcomes the truer, long-term desire. Toby wants to lose weight, but when she is faced with a more instinctual desire, her higher self instantly wilts. In the same way, a person may truly want to be kind and gentle, but when his more immediate goals are frustrated, he reacts instinctively with anger, which instantly overtakes the loftier goals.

But imagine for a moment that Toby found a benefactor who promised: "Every time you resist a fattening temptation, I will put $10,000 into your bank account." With this offer, which promises her immense reward and leads her in the direction in which she really wants to go, she would find it easier to ignore the cookie jar.

228   ☐   STRATEGIES

In the case of *ona'as devarim*, this strategy would work just as well. Imagine that a person's brain emitted a signal every time he derailed a thought that would lead to a hurtful word. For each signal, the person would receive $10,000. In no time at all, he would be eagerly batting down every harsh thought and critical comment that arose in his head.

This fantasy scenario is not really a fantasy at all, except that the reward for refraining from hurtful words is really far greater. In describing this reward, the Vilna Gaon sites the Midrash, *"Kol hachosem piv zocheh l'or haganuz"* — 'Those who close their mouths (rather than insult another Jew) are worthy of the hidden light (the light of Creation which Hashem reserves as a reward for the holiest *neshamos*)." With this incentive of eternal riches, someone with an inner desire to improve in this area can find ample motivation.

To ensure his share of this reward, a person can identify an area of life in which he is apt to lose control, and prepare a way to remain in control for that period. For instance, if the last half-hour before Shabbos is a frequent battleground, he can prepare a strategy to prevent falling into anger during that time.

It's not within our power of perception to understand the exquisite treasure we amass when we hold our tongues to preserve another person's honor. Yet, knowing that it is there for us can help us do that which, in our deepest hearts, we really wish to do.

In Other Words:

"*I will think of one situation in which I commonly find myself speaking thoughtlessly and formulate a strategy for handling the situation without ona'as devarim.*"

י"ב טבת
12 TEVES / CYCLE 1

י"ב אייר
12 IYAR / CYCLE 2

י"ג אלול
13 ELUL / CYCLE 3

❧ *Prepared for Landing*

*A*s he flew over New York City, the pilot glanced out the window of his propeller plane and realized that one of his engines had gone dead. He wasn't worried, though; he was excited. What a great learning opportunity this was going to be for the student pilot with whom he shared the cockpit! Like well-trained soldiers, the pilot and his student notified the closest air-traffic control tower and went through a series of maneuvers designed to bring the plane to a safe airport landing. Unfortunately, the procedures did not have their desired result and it became clear that the plane would not make it to the airport. Instead, the pilot and student would have to make an emergency landing in the East River. The pilot was so well prepared for this eventuality that he allowed his student to fly the crippled plane until it was just 300 feet above the river.

The pilot then took over and steered the plane to a perfect landing. As soon as the plane came to rest in the river, the pilot and student shot off a flare, jumped into the river and swam away. When they were rescued a few minutes later, they were calm and cool, as if nothing unusual had happened.

At the crucial turning points of life, preparation can be the difference between a safe landing and disaster. This is the Ramban's message when he advises us, through his famous *Iggerres HaRamban*, on how to avoid falling into sin: "Accustom yourself *always* to speak *all* your words gently to *all* people at *all* times."

"Tisnaheig tamid — accustom yourself" implies practice. When one plays out a potential scenario in his mind and plans an accepting, calm response based on the concept of *"gam zu l'tovah* — this too is for the good," he creates a flight plan for a soft landing. The more he practices this response, the more likely he will be to follow it instinctively when the situation arises.

If you prepare to respond in the manner prescribed by the Ramban, you will be able to deal with the possible disappointment with a peaceful heart. You will be focused on productive, forward-thinking responses rather than wallowing in bitterness or engaging in unproductive "payback."

The Ramban advises us to recognize an angry response as a real risk, equal to crash landing in the East River. When one comes to this recognition, one naturally puts time and effort into preparing for potentially risky situations, until he becomes the kind of person who can remain positive, calm and focused no matter what life throws his way. From this wellspring of true trust in Hashem, only good can flow.

In Other Words:

"*Before I am faced with a situation that may or may not go my way (whether simple or complex) I will rehearse the possible outcomes in my mind and practice a gam zu l'tovah response.*"

י"ג טבת
13 TEVES / CYCLE 1

י"ג אייר
13 IYAR / CYCLE 2

י"ד אלול
14 ELUL / CYCLE 3

❧ *Defusing the Bomb*

*I*t seems to me that you're getting lazy with this job," the boss told his assistant.

"Nothing is done on time, and you're forgetting things right and left. It's as if this is the last thing on your mind."

The employee couldn't even reply. He felt as though the air had been sucked out of him. How could someone be so blind? Didn't the boss see that he had 10 times more work to do than he could possibly manage? Forgetting things? Missing deadlines? What about the 10 hours a day he was working, the crushing deadlines he did manage to meet, the swarms of details he did keep track of?

The meeting ended with the employee feeling like a complete failure. Someone else — someone more talented — surely could do this job to the boss's satisfaction. He had no doubt that he had just witnessed the beginning of the end of this job. He crept through the rest of the day like an old cat looking for a quiet place to die.

Insults are often referred to as "a bombshell" and a situation that spins out of control is said to have "blown up in his face." These are apt comparisons, because insulting words really do have a destructive impact that can rip right through a person's confidence and cripple his sense of self.

In Israel, where terrorist bombs unfortunately are ruthlessly planted in random locations to harm innocent civilians, there are highly trained soldiers whose specialty is defusing these bombs. This image is a perfect metaphor for defending oneself against *ona'as devarim*. If one can understand the mechanism that enables the verbal bombshell to do its destructive work, one can disassemble it and render the words harmless.

One factor that gives insults their explosive power is the victim's suspicion that the words carry a grain of truth. Because a person may already be dealing with this weakness, either by trying to hide it or by trying to improve it, having someone else notice it and drag it into the open is especially painful. On the other hand, if the insult is a total misconception, one can be stunned by the sense of injustice.

To defuse the explosive ingredient, a person must quickly seek to rebalance himself. He may have weaknesses, but so does everyone else. The fact that someone has noticed his weakness does not make him less of a person than he was moments before the words were spoken. If the insult is based on nothing at all, then the victim should take stock of himself and realize that the words were essentially meaningless.

This doesn't mean that words do not matter or that the fault lies with the victim's oversensitivity. It means that even if others do wrong, even if they speak without thinking and drop a "bombshell," there need not be total war. To stop the course of destruction, it is worthwhile to examine an insult, take it apart and lay it to rest.

[**Note:** At times another person's hostility can be excessive or destructive. If this seems to be the case, it is worthwhile to seek a knowledgeable, objective opinion.]

In Other Words:

"When someone speaks insensitively to me, I will try to defuse the situation rather than absorbing the full impact."

13 Teves — May today's learning be a z'chus for my children.

13 Iyar — Sylvan Garfunkal לע״נ פנחס בן כלב ז״ל
Dedicated by David and Debbie Popper

14 Elul — Samuel Bentolila לע״נ שמואל בן לונה ז״ל
Dedicated by his wife, children and grandchildren

י״ד טבת
14 TEVES / CYCLE 1

י״ד אייר
14 IYAR / CYCLE 2

ט״ו אלול
15 ELUL / CYCLE 3

❧ *Image Transplant*

*T*here is a saying that "love is blind," meaning that a person who loves someone cannot see that person's flaws. On the other hand, dislike tends to endow people with microscopic vision, enabling them to detect the smallest indications of fault in the object of their dislike. When that happens, one's mind switches into critic-mode the moment the person comes into view. "There he is, talking too loudly." "There she is, bragging about her children." "He's crude, stingy, dishonest, unfriendly ...."

All of this might be based on unpleasant interactions with the person, or it might be based on nothing more than superficial impressions. In either case, the probable result of your negative view of this other person is that he will end up being the target of your *ona'as devarim*. Unless he is someone you would not dare insult, there is bound to come a time when your negative thoughts will turn into hurtful words.

The Torah provides no special dispensation for insulting those we dislike. On the contrary, it demands that we try to love them. When the person seems to be so very unlikable, the commandment to love him can seem to be impossible to fulfill. However, with an open mind and an open heart, there is an effective strategy you can use.

The first step is to realize that with rare exception, every person has people in his life who love him and think well of him. They see attributes in him that you may not see, or may see but choose to overlook. If you would sincerely like to avoid carrying around a dislike of this person, now is the time to think about his good attributes.

The second step is to think about the fact that everyone has flaws. Just as you have been focusing on this other person's flaws, others could do the same to you. They could see your hard work as workaholism, your reserve as unfriendliness, your enthusiasm as loudness, your spiritual striving as fanaticism and so forth. But that is not what you want others to see; rather, you want them to accept you as you are and validate your vision of yourself.

The other person — the one you can't stand — wants that too. He has a vision of himself, not as a scoundrel but as a good person doing his best to live a good life. Choose some positive aspect of this person's character and vividly imagine it. If he's friendly, imagine him smiling and laughing with someone. If he gives a lot of charity, picture him writing out a check to a worthy cause and handing it to a grateful recipient. Give him a new identity: Mr. Friendly, Mr. Helpful, Mr. Tzedakah. Now, whenever you see this person, call that picture to mind. When you think about this person, think of him by his "new name." Gradually, you will be able to remove your old negative image of the person and transplant a new positive image in its place.

In Other Words:

"*Right now, I will think of someone in my life who arouses a negative response in me and begin the process of an 'image transplant.'*"

14 Teves — In memory of my aunt Rebitzen Shirley Rosner לע״נ שרה בת ר׳ משה ע״ה
Dedicated by Shaindi Hirsch

14 Iyar — לע״נ משה בן יששכר ז״ל
Dedicated by Rabbi Avigdor and Rochel Slatus

15 Elul — לע״נ יצחק בן דוב בער שכטר ז״ל נלב״ע י״ד אלול
מאת משפחת פרנקל

ט"ו טבת
15 TEVES / CYCLE 1

ט"ו אייר
15 IYAR / CYCLE 2

ט"ז אלול
16 ELUL / CYCLE 3

❧ Human Like Me

*Y*osef glanced at his dashboard clock. It was 6:38 p.m. His class started at 7 and he was 10 minutes away. He would be on time, but just barely. It seemed that he was getting every red light on the road, and there up ahead was another. He slowed down to stop, when suddenly he heard a loud thud and felt his car jolt forward.

He shut off his engine and got out of the car. Smashed up against his now-crumpled trunk was a small red Honda. The driver got out of his car and began to approach Yosef apologetically.

"I don't know what to say ... I'm so sorry ... I guess I was just overtired, you know, I'm sorry ..."

"You idiot!" Yosef exploded. "It's my first week in school, I've got to get to this class if I'm ever going to get my accounting degree and get a job. Now you've wrecked my car! What am I supposed to do? What do you care? You're just driving around with your eyes closed."

The other driver's face collapsed. "I'm so sorry. I really am. I'm working two shifts these days and I guess I'm just too tired and now I've made a mess for you, too ..."

Suddenly Yosef saw in the other driver someone much like himself. Struggling to support a family, working too hard, and now, stuck in the middle of the road with his disabled car, getting an earful of abuse.

"Look, it's O.K. I'm sorry I exploded," Yosef apologized. "I've got insurance and I can get a rental meanwhile. I hope things will be all right for you too."

When we lose ourselves in anger, we immediately forget one salient fact: It's another human being on the receiving end of the diatribe. It's a person with a heart, with feelings, hopes and struggles. It's a person like ourselves. Finding the moment to connect to this reality is one of the most effective means available to curtail *ona'as devarim* in our lives.

Effective as it is, this strategy is difficult to enact when one's temper has been lost and he is in the middle of an angry tirade. It helps to plan the strategy now, when one is not being pulled by the undertow of powerful emotions. What will you do the next time you feel the urge to launch a verbal attack? Look into the other person's eyes as you speak to him. See that there is a separate person there, with his own thoughts, his own problems. Will your words disturb his sleep? Arouse anger in him that he will take out on someone else? Cause him to lose confidence in himself?

We don't have to inflict pain on each other. If we can feel the other person's suffering, rather than blocking it out of our consciousness, we will be motivated to find another way: a gentler, more sensitive and respectful way. The way we, ourselves, would like to be treated.

In Other Words:

"*When I am angry at someone, I will try to put myself in his place before I express my grievance.*"

---

15 Teves — In memory of Jonas Fenakel לע״נ יונה בן שמואל דוב ז״ל
Dedicated by his grandchildren and great-grandchildren

15 Iyar — As a z'chus for Efraim and Shoshana Gordon
Dedicated by Vivian & Michael Gordon

16 Elul — Paul Mouldovan לע״נ פסח לייב בן אהרן ז״ל נלב״ע כ״ח אלול
Dedicated by the Mouldovan family

ט"ז טבת
16 TEVES / CYCLE 1

ט"ז אייר
16 IYAR / CYCLE 2

י"ז אלול
17 ELUL / CYCLE 3

≈ *Positively Powerful*

I just want you to know how much we enjoy having your son around," Leah told her friend Tova. Leah lived in Israel, where Tova's son was learning in yeshivah. He spent many a Shabbos with Leah and her family, eager as he was to enjoy a family atmosphere and home cooking. Tova sometimes wondered if he wasn't perhaps overusing his welcome.

"He's so helpful and such a terrific addition to the table," Leah enthused.

Later on, when Tova spoke to her son, she was happy to relate her friend's warm words. Her son was happy to hear that his presence was welcome. He felt valued and good that he was seen as someone with something to offer. Thereafter, each time he visited Leah's family for Shabbos, he aimed to enhance his reputation further. He made sure to bring an especially interesting d'var Torah. He brought puzzles and games for the family's children, and delicious cake from the local bakery for the family to enjoy. He wanted to maintain and enhance his status as a "terrific addition," and he did.

Everyone is well aware of the negative impact of hearing unkind words passed along about oneself. People do not often consider, however, the ripple effects of good words being passed along. Everyone loves to hear that something nice was said about them. It enhances their self-esteem, and more importantly, it builds their desire to continue doing the good thing for which they were praised. The child who is told, "Your teacher says you always have interesting ideas to add to the class discussion," will look forward to the next opportunity to raise her hand in class. The husband who is told, "Your wife always quotes your opinion," will feel honored and admired by his wife, thereby encouraging him to continue earning her respect. The wife who hears, "You husband says he couldn't manage anything without you," will be happy to dig in and provide the support her husband counts on.

People long to feel acknowledged and appreciated. Praising someone to his face is one way to convey this recognition, yet there is always the lingering thought that perhaps the praise is meant "just to be nice." When a person hears that he was praised to another, the praise rings that much truer, for there can be no ulterior motive.

Aaron HaKohen employed this method to foster peace and friendship among the Jewish people. He would tell each person how much the other person valued him, thereby building friendship and warmth.

Often, we hear good things about someone, but fail to pass it on. It just takes a little awareness to tuck that compliment away and bring it out when it counts. Doing so takes the positive power of the comment itself and amplifies it a thousand times over, giving someone the encouragement to keep on doing what they do well, and the blessing of knowing they are appreciated.

In Other Words:

"*When I hear a compliment or positive statement about someone, I will try to pass it on to the subject of the comment.*"

י"ז טבת
17 TEVES / CYCLE 1

י"ז אייר
17 IYAR / CYCLE 2

י"ח אלול
18 ELUL / CYCLE 3

❧ *Take 15*

*A*s Chava Lerman walked up the pathway to her house, she could already smell the acrid odor of burnt challah.

"I told Michoel to watch the challas," she thought to herself. "I asked him to do one simple thing, and he forgot all about it. How can a 14-year-old boy be so completely irresponsible?"

As she opened the door, a thin fog of smoke irritated her eyes. The exhaust fan was on and the kitchen door was open in an effort to air out the house. The challahs sat on top of the oven, two large lumps of coal. Now Chava would have to go back out into the Friday-afternoon traffic and buy challah from the supermarket.

Michael came running down the stairs into the kitchen.

"Ma, I'm sorry," he said sincerely. "I just completely forgot about ....."

"No kidding, you forgot!" Chava interjected. "When are you ever going to learn to think about someone besides yourself!"

She saw her son's crestfallen expression, but that didn't stop her tirade. He needed to hear how angry she was, she believed. This was the only way to impress upon him the consequences of being irresponsible. She had to make sure he would not forget.

"I can't count on you for anything!" Chava continued. "Your little sister is more reliable than you are."

Michoel saw that there was nothing he could say to allay his mother's anger. But Chava did not see.

She was blind to the fact that her anger and the hurtful words were not instructive; they were merely an expression of her disappointment over the ruined challahs and annoyance at having to run out on another errand. Ten minutes later, as she drove to the market, she began to regret her words, but they had already been spoken and were roiling miserably in Michoel's heart.

When one is disappointed by another person, the first reaction is often anger, followed immediately by justifications for the anger. "I've been wronged." "He deserves it." "She should know better." Thus justified, a person convinces himself that letting his anger out on the perpetrator is the fair and right thing to do.

Often, however, with the passage of just a short period of time, the burning anger subsides and one is able to address the perceived "wrong" without resorting to *ona'as devarim*. The ego that is screaming "How dare you do this to me!" has a chance to settle down, and the wrong is able to appear in its true form, as a mistake or an inconvenience, rather than as an assault to one's dignity.

Waiting before responding has pragmatic value as well. In the course of those 15 minutes, a person gives himself the chance to realize that the harsh words which might have sprung to mind will do nothing to rectify the wrong that gave rise to the anger. They cannot repair what was broken, restore what was lost or undo what was done. Trying to repair a situation with hurtful words is like trying to repair a broken item with a sledgehammer. The Torah urges us not to make this mistake, but rather, to choose words that build and strengthen each other.

In Other Words:

" The next time I feel someone has wronged me, I will wait 15 minutes before I respond. "

17 Teves — Joseph Pinhas לע"נ יוסף פנחס בן שמחה ז"ל
Dedicated by Dr. and Mrs. David Pinhas and family

לע"נ שלמה זלמן בן חיים דוד ז"ל ואשתו חנה בת קלונימוס ע"ה — **17 Iyar**
Dedicated by the Rotbard family

18 Elul — May today's learning be a z'chus for Klal Yisroel.

י"ח טבת
18 TEVES / CYCLE 1

י"ח אייר
18 IYAR / CYCLE 2

י"ט אלול
19 ELUL / CYCLE 3

❧ No Offense

A long line of rowdy teens waited for their chance on the go-cart course. As they watched the lucky drivers who were already out on the track, an excited buzz began circulating up and down the line. One boy was racing with no hands on the steering wheel! He was shouting with delight as he flew off the track and flipped over onto the grass. Then the whooping was replaced by a low groan as he gripped his broken, bleeding leg.

A person whose emotions have overwhelmed his good sense is like a person who lets go of the steering wheel as he speeds down the road. He has so vastly increased his likelihood of doing damage that it is almost inevitable.

There is one strategy, however, that can go very far to keep one's emotions under control and thereby reduce the chances that a person will speak words that will inflict damage on others. That is to learn to overlook insults. Insult is one of the most powerful forces that wrest a person's hands from the emotional steering wheel. An insult "flips the switch" almost before the victim has fully absorbed what's been said. He meets insult with insult, and soon, the situation, and the hurt inherent in it, is escalating beyond all bounds.

Learning to shrug off insults is a skill that provides tremendous protection against the verbal "accidents" that occur when one loses control of his emotions. In fact, the *Sefer Hachinuch* (§338) teaches that by responding calmly or with humor to insults, one gradually diminishes the amount of insult that comes into one's life.

Eventually, the *Sefer Hachinuch* explains, a person who is careful in how he speaks to others will find that the only people who insult him are fools. Since their opinions carry no weight, their words certainly need not be heeded or answered.

This does not mean, however, that a person must stand by and allow his dignity to be assaulted by others. Even while promoting a calm, cool response to insult, the *Sefer Hachinuch* maintains that if someone begins harassing another person without provocation, he is entitled to defend himself just as he would protect himself from physical assault. This is an important rule to keep in mind in cases where there is verbal abuse. How to identify the point at which words fall into this category, however, is a question that should be discussed with a *rav* or mental health professional.

Under the normal circumstances of personal interaction, however, tremendous conflict, hurt and even long-lasting feuds can be avoided altogether by learning to step back from an insult and realizing that taking offense is a choice a person makes. In fact, *Sefer Hachinuch* states that one who is insulted and does not respond in kind merits tremendous blessing in his life. These blessings can belong to all of us if we let someone else's thoughtless words or careless comment dissipate into the air and disappear without leaving a nick, scratch or dent.

In Other Words:

"*If there is someone who tends to leave me feeling insulted, I will imagine a scenario in which he/she speaks as usual, but I respond without taking insult. I will use this response when I interact with this person.*"

18 Teves — In honor of our children: Zoey, Pauline, Elijah Abraham and Nili Rose for continued success.   Dedicated by Mom and Dad

לז״נ רבי שמעון בר יוחאי זצוק״ל זי״ע — **18 Iyar**

19 Elul — Pearl Nussbaum ע״ה לע״נ פערל בת ר׳ שמואל ע״ה
Dedicated by the Nussbaum family

י"ט טבת
19 TEVES / CYCLE 1

י"ט אייר
19 IYAR / CYCLE 2

כ אלול
20 ELUL / CYCLE 3

✑ *Fork in the Road*

*A*t 11:15 pm, Yaakov still had a long trip ahead of him. Fortunately, the traffic was light and he sped along the highway unimpeded. Soon, he reached a spot on the road where a choice had to be made. If he took the exit coming up and proceeded to the toll road, he would be home sooner. If he took the longer route, he would avoid the toll. Because the hour was late, Yaakov opted for the quicker, more expensive route.

Everything went along smoothly until he reached the approach to the George Washington Bridge. There, the traffic suddenly coagulated into a slow-moving mass. Instead of arriving home at 12:30 as he had expected, he arrived at 1:30 a.m. His choice of route had resulted in an hour of lost time.

Most people take no time at all to decide whether or not to say something to another person. In fact, there is often no pre-thinking process at all; the words just rush out of people's mouths like water from a bathtub faucet. Yet just as Yaakov's decision on the road had implications that lasted far longer, the fleeting decisions one makes with the words he speaks can have implications that last not just an hour, but a lifetime.

Four-year-old Rivky comes down the stairs clothed in an outfit she chose. Her brightly flowered cotton shirt may be a bit unusual for a January day, but at least the black wool jumper she is wearing over it fits the season. Sandals and orange kneesocks, procured for Purim, complete the outfit.

"Go back upstairs and put on the clothes I picked for you," her mother orders. "You can't go shopping with me unless you put on something normal."

"Normal," Rivky ponders. "I chose something that's not normal. I'm not normal."

The mother spent no time pondering how to best convey her displeasure. She just said what came naturally. But what might have happened had she take that one second to think? Which road would she have chosen? One that hurts her child's self-esteem, or one that offers instruction and direction, in a tone that conveys loving concern?

"Remember how hard you worked on planning that fantastic Chanukah party?" the teacher asks her student. "I know you've got it in you to accomplish. You can't fool me. Use that energy on your studies and you'll see, your Cs will turn to As."

The girl thinks about those words all year, whenever she feels that she doesn't have what it takes to tackle a job. Planted firmly in her mind, those words sprout new plans, goals and achievements every day.

Hundreds of times a day, we come to a fork in the road. Our words can take us on a route that leads to pain and tears, or the route that leads to joy and friendship. In the split second between thought and word, we must choose.

In Other Words:

"
I will try to remember as I am speaking that my casual words can have long-term impact.
"

לע״נ יענטא בת ר׳ צבי אלימלך ע״ה — **19 Teves**
Dedicated by Sid and Esther Borenstein

19 Iyar — In loving memory of Ethel Goldstein לע״נ עטל בת פרץ ע״ה
By her children, Lynn & Elliot Neustadter

לע״נ יונה בן דוד ז״ל נלב״ע ח׳ חשון — **20 Elul**
Dedicated by his grandson Avraham Gershkovich

DAY
110

כ טבת
20 TEVES / CYCLE 1

כ אייר
20 IYAR / CYCLE 2

כ"א אלול
21 ELUL / CYCLE 3

❧ *Under Examination*

*M*rs. Levin walks into her son's room to put away some laundry and is dismayed to see empty Coke cans on the dresser, piles of papers on the bed and dirty laundry on the floor. She hears the inner voice that is about to call Yossi upstairs and scold him. "You always leave your room a mess!" she wants to say.

Imagine if instead, she wrote those words on a piece of paper and studied them, word by word.

"You": It's an accusation. Better to start with "I."

"Always": Not true. Sometimes he keeps the room clean.

"Mess": Negative. Why not instead evoke a positive image with the word "neat."

"Yossi, come here for a minute, please," Mrs. Levin calls.

Yossi sees his mother standing at his bedroom door.

"I was noticing that lately, your room's been nice and neat. Isn't it nicer to walk into a neat room?"

"I know where everything is, Ma. I like my room this way," Yossi says, simply to avoid the outcome of having to spend a half-hour cleaning up.

"I'll bet you'll like it even better when it's all cleaned up."

How does the story end? The imaginary scene stops here. However, it is clear that Mrs. Levin managed to convey a positive image of her son, and to impart to him that there's value in a clean room. Today or tomorrow, hopefully sometime before Shabbos, the room will get cleaned.

The *Medrash* in *Vayikra Rabbah* (33:1) tells of a feast Rabbi Yehudah HaNasi hosted for his students. The main course of the meal was tongue. As the students ate, Rabbi Yehudah observed that each of them chose the softest parts of the tongue. The tougher parts they left on their plates.

Addressing his students, he drew their attention to the way they had eaten the tongue. Just as they had preferred the softest part of the tongue, he explained, others prefer that we give them the softest part of our tongues, that we speak to them gently.

Sometimes parents, teachers and others in positions of authority feel that it is their duty to "lay down the law" when those under their rule do not perform up to expectations. However, the Torah teaches that authority does not exempt a person from sensitivity. When Hashem addresses Miriam and Aaron to rebuke them for speaking *loshon hora* about their brother Moshe (*Bamidbar* 12:6), Rashi explains that Hashem used a gentle request. *Sifsei Chachamim,* in explaining Rashi, offers the surprising explanation that Hashem employed this soft approach because Aaron and Miriam may not have accepted a harsh rebuke. Thus, even Hashem, the Ultimate Authority, softens His rebuke, even to speak to two righteous individuals who would be expected to accept His words without question.

The responsibility of correcting and rebuking others is part of almost every adult's life. Spoken without forethought, the words used can become the root of strife and pain. By exchanging each harsh word for a softer one, our rebuke will be received not as a blow, but as a helping hand.

In Other Words:

"*When I know I must rebuke someone, I will take time to examine the words I plan to use, and choose the softest possible language.*"

כ"א טבת
21 TEVES / CYCLE 1

כ"א אייר
21 IYAR / CYCLE 2

כ"ב אלול
22 ELUL / CYCLE 3

✑ *The Cure*

*M*oshe struggled mightily to keep his sub-urban lawn green and clean. Every two weeks a lawn service came to spray it with whatever insecticides or fertilizers it needed. Another crew came to mow. His sprinkler system lavished the lawn with generous showers of water at 5 a.m. each day. Indeed, it looked beautiful.

When Moshe's children asked if they could take a pile of discarded wood from their neighbor's yard and build a clubhouse on the lawn, his answer was an unequivocal "no." Such an idea would never even enter into his realm of possibility.

Why would Moshe never allow the children's clubhouse on his lawn? The reason is that he cared for it scrupulously. He invested tremendous money and effort into nurturing it, and would therefore never incline himself to do something toward damaging it.

Likewise, when someone lavishes great care upon another person, damaging that person runs deeply against his grain. It makes no sense to hurt that which one tenderly, carefully nurtures. Therefore, one powerful preventive measure against speaking *ona'as devarim* is to use one's words for the opposite purpose. A person who trains himself to speak words that bring comfort, confidence and happiness to others simultaneously loses his urge to speak words that damage.

Building this capacity in oneself enables one to offer true comfort to people facing difficult times.

While a person may not have the answer for the one who is suffering — he may not have the cure for the illness or the antidote to grief or worry — he can help the person recognize that Hashem is there with him in his time of darkness. The person may be in pain, but he need not feel alone if he has a friend who can gently reconnect him to the Source of all comfort.

It is not as difficult as one may think to become this kind of person. One can arrive at that level by developing an *ayin tov* — an eye that looks for the good in others — and *lashon tov* — a manner of speech that expresses the good. Often one sees something he admires or appreciates, but doesn't mention it. He notices that his son is waking up on time for *minyan* more frequently, or his wife has been serving a dish he particularly likes, but the recognition of these small gift packages does not make it all the way from his mind to his mouth.

By learning to notice the good and then articulate it, one can reconstruct his entire way of interfacing with others in his life. Surrounded by a world filled with good people whose lives he himself has helped to nurture, the last thing he would wish to do is mar this beautiful landscape with words that would damage it.

In Other Words:

"*At the same time as I work on restraining myself from speaking hurtfully, I will look for opportunities to say positive, encouraging words to others.*"

21 Teves — Dedicated by Mrs. Laurie Rovehzadeh

21 Iyar — לע״נ חיים פנחס בן לייב ז״ל נלב״ע כ״ב אייר
Dedicated by the Goren family

22 Elul — Samuel Riesel לע״נ שמואל אליעזר בן נחום צבי ז״ל
Dedicated by the Schwarzmer and Riesel families

כ"ב טבת
22 TEVES / CYCLE 1

כ"ב אייר
22 IYAR / CYCLE 2

כ"ג אלול
23 ELUL / CYCLE 3

✒ *Soft Spot*

*W*hen Yonason hung up the phone from Eli, his former business partner, he felt as though he had been kicked in the chest. "There's something seriously wrong with you," Eli had said coldly. "You've got no more sense of responsibility than my 5-year-old son. It's no wonder that everything you touch ends up failing."

It had been a difficult breakup with much negotiation and arguing on both sides, but until just a few moments ago, Yonason had thought there were no personal grievances. Now he discovered that his former partner blamed him for the demise of their business. But why did it matter what Eli thought? Yonason knew that there were many factors involved, most of them outside of his control. Why were Eli's words so very painful?

A quick analysis of this situation offers one important answer to the question of why Eli was able to wound Yonason with nothing more than a string of words: Somewhere in Yonason's heart, he feared the words might be true. For an insult to deliver its sting, it has to strike in a place where the recipient is vulnerable. Otherwise, the comment seems ludicrous and the speaker blind and misguided.

For instance, had Yonason been a fabulously successful tycoon, Eli's claim that all his endeavors ended in failure would have not even warranted a response. They would have been seen as the obvious ranting of someone overcome with anger or jealousy.

Another factor that makes an insult hurtful is that it attacks an area that is important to a person's self-image. For instance, if Yonason had been told he would never make it as a race-car driver, it is highly doubtful that the verdict would have hurt him. He had no pretensions of knowing how to drive a race car, nor any ambitions to do so.

Once one acknowledges the reasons why he finds an insult hurtful, it is sometimes easier to take the sting out of the words. Is there some underlying truth to the statement? Is this an area in which one fears he is deficient? If so, he can work toward shifting gears, going from defensiveness and anger to receptiveness of the message, even if the messenger seriously erred in his method of delivery. The comment could be seen as bad-tasting medicine that performs a positive function. [**Note**: At times another person's hostility can be excessive or destructive. If this seems to be the case, it is worthwhile to seek a knowledgeable, objective opinion.]

If, in the final analysis, it seems that there is no truth to the message, then one can dismiss the words as irrelevant, just as Yonason in the above example could easily dismiss the comment that he would never be a race-car driver.

An angry retort, on the other hand, will almost always lead to an escalation of hostilities. More insults will fly back and forth, making both parties guilty of *ona'as devarim*. The opportunity to grow from the experience will be lost. By understanding why we find certain words insulting, we help to defuse them, and thereby ensure that the situation will not eventually blow up in our own face.

In Other Words:

"The next time someone says something I find insulting, instead of answering the insult, I will stop to analyze why I am aggrieved."

כ"ג טבת
23 TEVES / CYCLE 1

כ"ג אייר
23 IYAR / CYCLE 2

כ"ד אלול
24 ELUL / CYCLE 3

✑ *Reading the Signs*

*T*he world abounds with signs: "Stop," "Danger," "Welcome," "Go Slow." The wise person pays attention to the signs and proceeds accordingly. One would walk into a store marked "Welcome" with an entirely different posture and demeanor than that which one would bear entering a store marked "Beware of Dog."

People's facial expressions, too, bear signs. "I'm tired," "I'm annoyed," "I'm relaxed," "I'm interested." Those signs serve as warnings to others, letting them know where danger may lie and advising them to take proper precautions. A face that says, "I'm exhausted," is telling others not to choose this moment to barrage the person with demands or questions. A face that says, "I'm angry," tells others not to push the issue further at this moment.

But what good does a sign do if one doesn't read it or, worse yet, if one intentionally defies the warning? A person who pays no attention to the cues others provide is someone who often finds himself on the receiving end of angry responses. In his mind, he's done nothing wrong: "I just asked a simple question and she exploded!" But in reality, he ignored the person's unspoken request — signified by the look on her face, her posture and perhaps the circumstances all around her — to stand clear.

Why would a person place himself in peril? Perhaps he is so preoccupied with his own agenda that he fails to notice the other person. The husband comes home and habitually asks, "What's for supper?" without stopping to notice that his wife looks as though she hasn't slept in days. A wife greets her husband, who has come home late from work, with the words, *"Baruch Hashem*, you're home! The boys all need help with their homework ..." She does not notice that her husband's face says, "I need to relax for awhile."

If the person who posts the "sign" then releases a barrage of *ona'as devarim* at the person who ignored the warning, it is still *ona'as devarim*. The person certainly has choices other than a verbal attack. He could calmly say, "I'm sorry, but I need a little time before I deal with this." But by "reading the signs," one can avoid setting the drama into motion in the first place. In addition, one avoids the possibility that, insulted by the person's brusque response, he will respond with *ona'as devarim* of his own.

The need to be sensitive to others' expressions and posture does not, however, mean that people should feel they have to "walk on eggshells" around others in their lives who are unduly moody. Such situations warrant special consideration and professional advice may be needed. But within the realm of normal human relationships, sensitivity to others' ups and downs goes a long way toward maintaining peace, showing empathy and, ultimately, finding the opportunity to express oneself in a way and at a time that one's words will be heard.

In Other Words:

"I will look at people when I speak to them, and try to recognize the expression on their face."

**DAY
114**

כ"ד טבת
24 TEVES / CYCLE 1

כ"ד אייר
24 IYAR / CYCLE 2

כ"ה אלול
25 ELUL / CYCLE 3

❧ *Be a Seer*

*W*hen Rabbi Yochanan met the bandit, Reish Lakish, he formulated in one instant a mind-boggling proposal for the bandit's remediation: If Reish Lakish would agree to learn Torah, he could marry Rabbi Yochanan's sister. How does one dare to propose a match between one's sister and a robber? Rabbi Yochanan did so with confidence, because at his high spiritual level, he was able to perceive the neshamah of Reish Lakish. He knew that he had greatness within him.

Even without such elevated perception, however, one can be sure that every person put into this world was put here for a reason, that there are tasks that are his alone to perform. Hashem makes no mistakes. He creates nothing without a reason. Therefore, even if a person encounters someone in his life whose sole purpose seems to be vexing other people, he cannot go wrong by assuming that this person, too, is worthy of respect by virtue of the potential within him.

A frequent obstacle to perceiving others this way is the bias most people have toward their own way of behaving, dressing, speaking and acting. "Normal" and "good" are often defined as "just like me." Yet the Talmud teaches (*Yerushalmi Brachos* 9:1) that just as no two faces are alike, neither are two minds alike. Each person sees things through the lens of his own upbringing, nature and experiences. When one expects others to think and act as he does, he invites frustration, which soon evolves into disapproving thoughts, which in turn express themselves in insensitive, disapproving words.

When a person's mind focuses on the differences or the flaws or limitations of another person, the raw material for *ona'as devarim* is manufactured in abundance. It is only a matter of time before those thoughts turn into hurtful spoken words, even if they are modified somehow in the belief that they will thereby deliver less of a sting.

The higher and more productive road is that taken by Rabbi Yochanan. Once a person makes the effort to acknowledge the essential worth of another person, he will see that person's strengths. He will realize that even the person's apparent flaws are signposts that mark the road to his greatness. The shy person needs his shyness and the aggressive person needs his aggression. The soft-hearted person needs his softness and the tough guy needs his toughness. They all have before them the opportunity to accomplish something unique with their specific collection of traits and abilities.

By validating the person's value, rather than deriding him for his flaws, one can help the person channel all his traits — those that are positive and even those that appear negative — into hope, growth and achievement.

In Other Words:

"*The next time I notice someone who is different from me and begin to make prejudicial assumptions in my mind, I will stop myself and think, 'He is who he is supposed to be. He is the man for his job.'*"

לע"נ ר' יהודה בן ר' ברוך ז"ל נלב"ע כד' טבת תש"נ — **24 Teves**
ואשתו שרה בת ר' צבי ע"ה קאטץ נלב"ע כו' טבת תשמ"ח
24 Iyar — Dedicated as a z'chus by Mr Isak Boruchin
25 Elul — Morris David Rosenholtz ז"ל לע"נ מנחם דוד בן חיים צבי ז"ל
Dedicated by his granddaughter Shira Seidenwar

כ"ה טבת
25 TEVES / CYCLE 1

כ"ה אייר
25 IYAR / CYCLE 2

כ"ו אלול
26 ELUL / CYCLE 3

❦ *Just Like Me*

*I*magine meeting someone new. Perhaps the person is sitting next to you at a wedding, and you begin to talk. You find out that he is from your old neighborhood. He knows many of the same people you know. In fact, he favors the pizza shop in the neighborhood that you used to love when you lived there — and for the same reason. You both like the spicy tomato sauce! The more you talk, the more you find what you have in common. You share your opinions on politics, education, the challenges of raising children and much more. By the end of the evening, you both feel that you've made a new friend.

Why? You feel connected because you are so much alike. You hear your own perspectives validated by this like-minded companion and see in him someone who really understands you. Very little is as comfortable and comforting as being with someone similar to oneself.

Perhaps this explains why people have so difficult a time accepting differences in other people. Differences challenge our assumptions and force us to defend our point of view. Since, as the saying goes, "the best defense is a good offense," there are some people who deal with differences by going on the offensive and rejecting or attacking the other person.

This mind-set has caused untold misery for the Jewish people. Divisiveness, defensiveness and belittling of the "other" are all elements of our age-old nemesis, *sinas chinam* — baseless hatred — which our Sages teach (*Yoma* 9b) is the root cause of our exile. Our desire to be surrounded by people just like ourselves will never be satisfied, for "just as no two people look exactly alike, no two people think alike," (*Yerushalmi Brachos* 9:1).

This comparison provides the proper perspective for viewing the differences among people. We accept the idea that Hashem created each person with physical differences. By the same token, the realization that a person does not think as we do should arouse no animosity, for this is also the result of Hashem's design.

A person who cannot accept differences is someone who will constantly be finding fault with others, and, most likely, expressing his disapproval using *ona'as devarim*. At work, he will resist other people's ideas if they are at variance with his own. At home, he will become angry when family members do things differently than he would. In the community, he will reject people whose customs or background are different from his. His world will be a narrow one, mostly populated by adversaries.

By opening his eyes to the value of others and acknowledging that Hashem put them, too, into this world for a positive purpose, he can live a completely different kind of life. He can learn from others, expand his horizons and enjoy that which may not be "his cup of tea," but is worthy nonetheless.

In Other Words:

"*If I find myself judging someone critically, I will ask myself if the other person is really wrong and bad, or just different from me.*"

DAY 116

כ"ו טבת
26 TEVES / CYCLE 1

כ"ו אייר
26 YIAR / CYCLE 2

כ"ז אלול
27 ELUL / CYCLE 3

~ *Going Another Round*

*B*ehind their backs, Reuven and Ruth Bluestein were known by the neighbors as the "Battling Bluesteins." As one old friend jokingly described them, "If he says it's night, she says it's day."

The situation was no joke for the four Bluestein children, however. Money, in-laws, household chores, social plans, major purchases — everything was a potential minefield in their home.

Eventually, the children grew up and went on with their lives. Their parents, stormy as their marriage had been, had always done their best to let the children know that they were not the cause of the fighting, nor were they the enemy. And there had been many happy times as well — family vacations, holidays and normal days as a family living together under one roof — which bound them all together despite the troubles.

One Sunday afternoon, Shmuel Bluestein, the eldest son, brought his 6-month-old son to visit his parents while his wife grabbed a quick nap at home.

"Remember how we used to fight?" Reuven asked his son. "Boy, your mother and I could fight. But you know what? Now we hardly even argue. And do you know why?"

"No. Why?" Shmuel asked, trying not to betray his shock at the casual tone with which his father tore open a painful wound.

"Because it wasn't worth it. We never solved any-

258   ☐   STRATEGIES

thing. And what was so important, anyway? It was just the same fight over and over again for 30 years. Little by little, we just lost interest in it. I guess we grew up. I wish it would have happened long ago, before you kids had to live through all that drama."

There are people with whom one tends to re-enact the same script, with minor variations, over and over again. Nothing ever gets solved. For instance, the parent is always trying to protect and restrain the child; the child is always trying to break free. The details will change: Is he old enough to drive? To travel alone to Israel? To choose her own clothing? To choose his own yeshivah? But the theme of the drama stays the same, as does the conflict and the characters. Yet the "characters" feel impelled to go another round. With each round, they create more hurt feelings and add more resentment to each other's internal bank accounts.

If a conflict can lead to a solution of a worthwhile issue, then it most likely is important to calmly, respectfully play out the conflict. However, many arguments go nowhere but around in circles.

There is but one preventive strategy to avoid the pain and hurt that comes with pointless conflict. Refuse to succumb. Know that, like the couple in the story, you will eventually regret the misappropriation of your time and energy, realizing that none of it, after all, was very important, and nothing was solved.

In Other Words:

"——

If I find myself embroiled in a conflict, I will ask myself, 'Can anything be solved by this, or is it just one battle in an endless war?'

——"

---

26 Teves — In memory of our father, Nathan ben Yosef z"l

26 Iyar — לע"נ זכרי' יצחק בן אברהם ז"ל
Dedicated by his children

27 Elul — לע"נ החכם אברהם מסעוד נחמן בן רחל ז"ל נלב"ע כ"ט אלול
Dedicated by Mrs Rebecca Elbaz and her family

כ"ז טבת
27 TEVES / CYCLE 1

כ"ז אייר
27 YIAR / CYCLE 2

כ"ח אלול
28 ELUL / CYCLE 3

⚜ *Doing the Mending*

*S*uddenly, there was an awakening. A small, quiet thought began irritating the inside of Mordy Levine's mind, like a grain of sand in a pearl-bearing oyster. And like the sand, this grain of doubt began stimulating the release of a precious substance — something called teshuvah — repentance.

The first thought of teshuvah hadn't occurred on its own. Rather, it had been forcefully inserted into Mordy's mind, again like the grain of sand in the oyster. In the midst of a bitter argument, his brother had told him bluntly, "You think you're smart. But do you know what you are? You're a guy who steps on other people. Life is short, Mordy, and you better start cleaning up the mess you're leaving behind."

Since then, Mordy's mind was filled with painful images: faces stained with tears, eyes filled with fear, heads turned to avoid his eyes, the pasted-on smiles of those who needed to stay in his good graces. Indeed, he had made a mess. But could he ever clean it up?

Hashem provides His imperfect creation, man, with a means to move toward perfection through the process of *teshuvah*. A person can never claim, "That's the way I am and I can't change." Change is wired into the universe, available to anyone willing to flip the switch.

The Sages teach (*Yoma* 85b) that sins between G-d and man can be erased by confessing one's sin, sincerely regretting it and making a commitment to refrain from repeating that sin. Those whose sins are against other people have another preliminary step to take before they can enjoy the blessing of a clean slate. They must gain forgiveness from the person they have harmed, which means acquiring the humility to approach the other person, admit one's mistake and ask forgiveness.

A person who hurts another with words must first realize that he has caused someone pain. He must empty himself of justifications: He deserved it ... He's said worse to me ... He didn't mind ... It wasn't really an insult ... etc. Once a person has arrived at true regret for his words, he must ask the victim to forgive him and commit himself to refrain from repeating the offense. If he is rejected once, the Torah teaches, he must try a second and even a third time.

For people with a pattern of verbal abusiveness, forgiveness may eventually become impossible to obtain. To appease a victim, the abusive party will probably have to prove himself, for instance, by saying, "Give me a month and see if I keep my word," after which time he can ask for forgiveness again.

The sooner a person comes to realize that *teshuvah* is necessary, the less painful the process will be. Wounds heal far more easily before they've had time to fester.

Because we have the gift of *teshuvah*, we need not leave behind a list of casualties when we make our inevitable journey into the Next World. We need only find within ourselves the humility and optimism to begin again.

In Other Words:

"*Starting today, I will set a regular time to think back over the past and determine if there is anyone from whom I need to ask forgiveness for ona'as devarim.*"

❧ *The Foolproof Cure*

it outside in the sun for two hours a day and that will cure your condition," the doctor told his patient.

Each day, the patient dutifully sat on a lawn chair on his front porch as the sun blazed in the sky. Several weeks went by, but his condition was not improving. In fact, it appeared to be worsening.

He returned to the doctor. "I don't understand why it's not working, but it isn't. I'm doing exactly what you told me to do, sitting two hours a day in the sun, and I'm only getting worse."

The doctor questioned the patient closely, trying to discover why this well-known remedy was not working. Eventually, he understood. The patient was sitting in the shade. The sun's healing rays were not reaching him, and thus, his condition was not alleviated.

Hashem gave the world a cure for all of its ills, and that is the Torah. One who learns Torah each day exposes himself to its unparalleled curative properties which bring vigor and health to one's soul. With this healthy, wholesome soul, the person finds that negativity and cruelty becomes repugnant to him. He is filled with light, and wants to radiate light — not pain and darkness — into the world.

Thus, a person who attaches himself to Torah and spends his time poring over its holy words should find himself immensely strengthened in the fight against negative, hurtful speech. He should become a person who is not easily angered, and thus, not easily pro-

* On 29 Elul, the lesson for Day 119 should be learned together with today's lesson.

voked into displays of temper. He should develop a sense of appreciation of all Hashem has given him, and is thus spared the jealousy that sometimes motivates a person to insult another.

Most importantly, he builds a love of Hashem's Torah and His people. His desire is to do what is pleasing in Hashem's eyes.

Despite the Torah's tremendous curative potential, however, there are those who learn diligently and yet, seem unable to break free of the habit of *ona'as devarim*. When that is the case, the reason is often that, like the patient in the story, they are not allowing the light to penetrate. The Torah's healing power is being blocked by contrary thoughts or emotions. Therefore, a person must examine his motives and intentions in his Torah learning. When the motive is simply to bask in Hashem's light, the light will certainly penetrate, and eventually come to permeate the person's being. And such a person can only bring light into the world.

In Other Words:

"*I will increase my study of Torah with the intent of coming closer to Hashem, His mitzvos and the Jewish people.*"

לע"נ יצחק בן שלמה ואשתו חנה בת ישמעאל ע"ה — **28 Teves**
Dedicated by Dr. & Mrs. Shomer Israelian
לע"נ ברוך שרגא בן שלמה יהודה ז"ל — **28 Iyar**
29 Elul — May today's learning be a z'chus for our entire family.
Ahron and Estee Schron, Brooklyn, NY

כ"ט טבת
29 TEVES / CYCLE 1

כ"ט אייר
29 IYAR / CYCLE 2

כ"ט אלול
29 ELUL / CYCLE 3

❧ *In Other Words*

*I*n the course of the past 118 days, we have learned to identify *ona'as devarim*, studied how it seeps into our lives, our relationships and the self-image of those around us, and reviewed strategies to help rid our lives of this destructive force. Now, we invite you to test your understanding. Below are thirteen *ona'as devarim* statements. Try to sift out the constructive purpose of each statement and restate it in a way that achieves that purpose without unduly inflicting pain on the object of the comment.

1. Two *beis medrash* boys are discussing where they will be learning in the coming year. "I think I'm going to go to the Mir," says one boy. "Not me," says the other. "I'm not interested in going to Eretz Yisrael yet. I'm going to stay here in the States." His friend gapes at him. "That's not normal! Nobody's staying here!" (DAY 36)

2. The yeshivah's fund-raising dinner was a day away and Meir, the chairman of the journal, opened a carton of journals to see how his pride and joy had come out. The first thing that greeted his eyes as he opened the box was the journal cover, upon which was written "Yeshivd Ben Torah." Frantically, he dialed his friend Shalom. "You idiot!" Meir screamed. "Didn't you proofread the journal? You've made us look like total fools! All our efforts are wasted because of your carelessness! I hope you're happy!" (DAY 44)

3. It's 9:30 a.m. on Shabbos morning. Moshe is davening with one eye on the empty seat where his 13-year-old son Avi should be sitting. Avi has been

having trouble waking up for *minyan* and Moshe is angry that his son, a Bar-Mitzvah boy, could be so lazy. Avi finally arrives and Moshe says, "It's about time! Don't you even have any *yiras shamayim?*" (DAY 49)

4. Esther is going out of town for the day and won't be home in time to greet her children when they arrive from school. She calls her neighbor Chaya for help. "Would you mind if they come to you when they get off the bus?" she asks. "I should be home about an hour later." Chaya agrees. "Please don't be late, though," she says, "Because I can only take so much of your little Moishie!" (DAY 50)

5. Leah lives in a neighborhood full of struggling middle-class families. Her husband, an importer, recently began marketing a product that had been taking the country by storm. Leah's best friend, Rivka, on the other hand, wonders how she will afford camp for her son. "What are you doing this summer?" she asks Leah. "I'm so excited!" Leah responds. "We're renting out a house in Eretz Yisrael and taking the whole family!" (DAY 58)

6. It was a small thing: a burned-out bathroom light-bulb that was too high for Zahava to reach without climbing a ladder. "Please change the bulb before you leave for work today," she asked her husband Nachum. Afraid he would forget, she caught him again as he came home from shul. "Why haven't you changed the bulb yet?" she asked. As he drank his coffee, she offered another reminder. "What about the bulb? Are you going to go off to work and leave me with a dark bathroom?" (DAY 66)

7. "Did you have your cavity filled yet?" Shira asked her friend Chana. "I haven't got time to take care of it right now. I've got to get things ready for Pesach." "Well don't let it slide," Shira warned. "My cousin got blood poisoning from a rotten tooth and almost died! She was in the hospital on an IV for a week!" (DAY 68)

8. Shimmy is 28, unmarried and painfully aware of this void in his life. At the wedding of an old friend, he meets Yossi, a young man from the neighborhood in which he grew up. They haven't seen each other since elementary school. "So tell me everything!" Yossi asks. "How long have you been married? How many kids?" (DAY 80)

9. Michael had spent the past 20 minutes regaling his older brother Moshe with his complaints about his yeshivah. Moshe, tired of the tirade, stomped his foot like a toddler having a tantrum and shouted, "It's just not fair! I can't take it!" His voice was pitched in a squeaky falsetto in imitation of Michael, a 13-year-old who was a bit small for his age. (DAY 83)

10. "Don't feel bad about your son leaving yeshivah," Shmuel said to his friend Dovid kindly. "It happens. I shouldn't tell you this, but Chaim told me that his son is on the verge of being kicked out of his yeshivah, too, and they're looking for a new place for him. That's just between you and me, of course." (DAY 84)

11. Rose's heart went out to her friend Mindy as she related the difficulties she was having finding a much-needed job to help support her family. "Maybe I can help you," Rose offered. "I have a cousin who's the assistant principal at a high school in the city. I'll see if she knows of anything." Mindy felt hopeful for the first time in weeks. The week wore on, however, and Rose forgot to make the call. Meanwhile, Mindy jumped at each ring of her phone, certain it was her friend Rose with a promising lead for her. (DAY 86)

12. Leah should have known better than to leave dinner cooking and head into her home office to catch up on her work. How many times had she completely forgotten about dinner, only to be reminded by the sounding of the smoke alarm? Tonight, her husband Avraham came home, opened the door,

took one sniff of the air and greeted his wife with the words, "Great job, Leah. What a cook I married." (DAY 91)

13. Zev, the owner of a small manufacturing company met with Aaron, his marketing manager. "I think we need a website," Aaron said excitedly. He began laying out his vision of the website and how it would open up new markets for them. As he spoke, he saw Zev's eyebrows draw together and his nose wrinkle quizzically, as if he were viewing a strange insect. Aaron muttered a few more words and stopped, squirming uncomfortably under Zev's gaze. (DAY 94)

29 Teves — לע״נ הרב ישראל איסר בן מנחם ז״ל
Dedicated by the Indich families

29 Iyar — In honor of Warren & Irene Cutler and Marvin & Sonia Emmer
Dedicated by Louis and Stacy Emmer

Don't Shut the Book Yet

❧ *On the Receiving End*

*T*his book shines a stark spotlight on the words a person speaks, revealing the immense impact they can have upon others. To be sure, nothing mitigates our responsibility to measure our words and ensure that they cause no unnecessary harm.

However, human relationships are a two-sided phenomenon. The speaker has his or her obligation to avoid causing pain to others, and the recipient of his words has an obligation as well. That is, to make a sincere effort to overlook and forgive a speaker who has said something hurtful, whether out of anger, ignorance, or misguided good intentions.

Before going any further into this topic, however, we must set out one vital *caveat*. We are talking here about normal interpersonal relations in which a certain amount of insensitivity can be expected. A situation in which one party consistently dominates, insults, and belittles another is one which must be addressed by professionals, for this constitutes abuse which must be curtailed in order to prevent permanent harm to the victim's psyche.

Leaving such situations aside, let us examine interactions between individuals who are generally emotionally healthy and well-meaning. In matters of speech and interpersonal relationships, the pain inflicted upon a person is subjective in nature. One with a strong sense of self-worth or a kindly, forgiving attitude toward other people and their foibles will learn not to take verbal slights and insults personally.

To be sure, this is easier said than done. The natural response is to bristle at any insult to one's dignity. However, our obligation is to be concerned with the propriety of our responses, reactions, and behavior, and not utilize someone else's misdeeds, no matter how egregious, to feel sorry for ourselves and assert our claim as the "victim."

This focus on one's *own* obligations and not on that of the other person, Rav Chaim Shmuelevitz explains, constitutes the basis of inter-personal relationships.

Reb Chaim would cite the statement of Chazal that "one should love his wife like himself and honor her more than himself." On the other hand, our Sages tell us that "a fine wife is one who does her husband's will." If the husband focuses on his responsibility to his wife and the wife on her obligation to her husband, they will have a good marriage. The trouble begins when the husband stresses the wife's obligation to him, and the wife is primarily concerned with the husband's requirement to honor her.

The same applies to every type of human relationship. Although one may not speak hurtful words to another, when one is the target of such words, he should do his best to ignore them. If that is too hard, and sometimes it can be very difficult indeed, one should make every effort to forgive and forget, even if the other person does not ask for forgiveness.

Every night when we recite *Krias Sh'ma* before going to sleep, we declare that we forgive anyone who may have angered or antagonized us in any way, whether willfully, carelessly, or even purposely. It is not always easy to actually feel this forgiveness, especially if one is angry.

We add to this prayer the request that no one be punished on our account. Even when a person is insulted, would he really wish for the perpetrator to suffer Heavenly retribution for the slight? Would he wish to see the person ill, broken, or worse? In the vast majority of cases, the victim would be greatly saddened by such a turn of events. He might be angry for now; he might feel misunderstood, undervalued, or even betrayed, but he realizes that no capital offense has been committed.

This ability to ignore hurtful words is not merely a "nice" character trait. It has very powerful benefits for the one who develops this strength of character. Chazal (*Rosh Hashanah* 17a) stress that Hashem forgives *all* the sins of one who overcomes his nature and overlooks insult and hurt. In addition, the Gemara (*Chullin* 89a) tells us that the world exists in the merit of he who closes his mouth at a time of strife. There have been more than a few authentic accounts of the unusual Heavenly blessings that accrued to people who have managed to do so.

But how does one succeed in fighting the normal human tendency to take offense? A healthy sense of who one is, along with an awareness that no one can really hurt someone if Hashem does not want it to be, are effective mechanisms. In addition, a person must realize that by not responding or even taking the hurt to heart, he can greatly enhance his own spiritual, mental, and emotional welfare. He can develop the emotional strength to ignore hurtful words and insults, real or imagined, and make his journey through life equipped with a peaceful, loving heart.

✄ Afterword
The Life You Save May Be Your Own

By now, you have read many scenarios and life situations that ring true. You've pondered ways in which you might avoid some of the pitfalls illustrated in this book, and thereby enrich your relationships with family, friends, coworkers, students – all of those whose lives are touched by the words you say.

But there is one more vital point to impart. Those hurtful words, whether spoken with an intent to strike back at someone, or said with no malice at all, are in fact a powerful boomerang. Whenever we sow pain, we reap pain. There is no other option. As in all Heavenly calculations, the results may not be immediately evident, but they will eventually make themselves known.

There are many real-life accounts of individuals who have suffered from some trouble in their lives, some difficulty that no amount of prayer or teshuvah seems to alleviate. The trouble might be in the area of shidduchim, health, child-bearing, parnassah, chinuch or spirituality. Only when these people look back on their lives, search for someone upon whom they have inflicted hurt, and then find that person and gain forgiveness, does the solution to their difficulties finally arrive.

Naturally, this does not mean that every person we meet who is dealing with a challenge in his life is to be assumed guilty of hurting someone. There are many reasons for suffering, and very few

---

The author of the afterword is an American-born Rosh Yeshivah in Israel who merits being a *talmid* of HaGaon HaRav Aharon Leib Shteinman, *shlita.*

people are capable of guiding someone to discover the source of his own difficult situation. Nevertheless, as so many eye-witness accounts make clear, it is essential to all of us, to our own happiness and fulfillment in life, to be as careful as possible with other people's feelings.

For most of us, however, it would seem to be impossible to be so very careful that we never accidentally insult someone or mention a topic they find painful. The scenarios presented in this book, so very common in our day-to-day lives, might seem to stand as proof that one need not be a mean-spirited villain to hurt others. It would seem, then, that all of us are destined to trip into the trap of ona'as devarim.

One might then wonder, what is the point in trying? The answer to that question is that our reward comes from our sincere dedication to eradicating this type of speech from our lives, to become more sensitive and to banish the rationalization that our interaction with others is "just words."

Chazal illustrate the vital importance of this effort with accounts of terrible consequences suffered by tzadikim who faltered ever so slightly in their care for others' feelings. We should not be disheartened by these harsh episodes, for it is well known that ordinary people are not judged by the strict standards that are applied to the tzaddik. To our eyes, the righteous may seem to suffer unfairly for sins that appear to be miniscule, leaving us to wonder fearfully what our own, far more egregious transgressions might reap. But, just as a drunken pilot responsible for the lives of 400 passengers should be judged more harshly than a drunken bicycle rider, it stands to reason that a great tzaddik is judged by a stricter standard than an ordinary individual who is striving to improve, but sometimes falls short. Our job is not to evaluate the justice of a given situation faced by a tzaddik, but rather, to understand from it the seriousness with which Heaven views any lack of consideration for another person's dignity, and then to apply that knowledge to our own lives, to the best of our ability. We are judged for who we are, rooted in the lives we've been given and the situations we find ourselves in. How we respond in those situations and how high we grow from those roots is the measure of our success.

HaGaon HaRav Aharon Leib Shteinman, shlita, one of the Gedolei Hador, has been the advisor and comfort to thousands of Jews facing difficult life situations. Time and time again, he has urged people to search their past for episodes, perhaps long forgotten by the individual, in which pain was inflicted on another. Often, the situation was ameliorated after amends were made. To prevent the suffering he has seen as a result of ona'as devarim, the Rosh HaYeshivah urges us not to inflict pain on others through our careless choice of words or explosions of anger. The Rosh HaYeshivah stresses that vigilant avoidance of ona'as devarim is not merely a way to prevent suffering; it is what Hashem demands from us and cares about. Prevention of suffering is just one of the benefits of that vigilance. Rav Shteinman has urged that a great effort be made throughout Klal Yisrael to raise people's awareness of the power of the spoken word and the serious repercussions words can cause.

The following powerful words were written to unequivocally convey Rav Shteinman's message, and each word and phrase bears his personal endorsement. It was meticulously translated into Hebrew and was reviewed from beginning to end by HaRav Shteinman, shlita, who gave his haskamah specifically for its inclusion in this book:

The power of words to hurt others is well known. While it is easy to comprehend man's ability to hurt another through his or her words (ona'as devarim), it is less apparent to us that the individual one hurts most may be him or herself.

What is unique about transgressions *bein adam lachaveiro* is that they demand constant vigilance. Almost every situation in life and almost every interaction with one's fellow is filled with opportunities for good, and *chas v'shalom* the reverse.

It is an axiom of every Jew that each mitzvah brings with it reward, and no *aveirah* goes unnoticed or unpunished by Hashem. One may not realize the gravity of ona'as devarim because it does not carry the severe punishments connected to some *aveiros*, such as *kareis* or *misas beis din*. Nevertheless, the damage it can cause to the perpetrator is incalculable.

In fact, we see from a discussion of Rabbi Shimon ben Gamliel and Rabbi Yishmael, as they were being led to be killed by the Romans, that hurting one's fellow human being, even slightly, can bring disaster. On their way to execution, Rabbi Shimon lamented to Rabbi Yishmael that it pained him greatly that he did not know why he was being killed. Rabbi Yishmael replied, "Did it never happen that someone came to ask you a *din* or a question, and you made him wait until you finished your drink, tied your shoe or finished putting on your jacket? And the Torah (*Shemos* 22:22) states clearly the punishment " *im anei se'aneh oso* — if you [dare to] cause him pain ..." Rabbi Yishmael explained that this verse means hurting someone, whether much or little.

Rabbi Shimon's response was that this awareness put him at peace, for he now understood why he was deserving of death (*Yalkut Shimoni, Shemos* 349).

This is indeed an astounding conversation. The great *Tanna* Rabbi Shimon ben Gamliel was not concerned that he was being put to death. That, he understood, was the will of the Almighty. What bothered him was that he could not fathom, after reviewing his entire life, what he had done to deserve that horrible death. The reminder that he may have hurt someone's feelings by even once in his life making him wait for even a short time was enough to explain to him why he was being put to death.

THE EXTENT OF HASHEM'S PROTECTION

*C*ould it be that hurting any other individual sets this Divine retribution in motion? The Torah (*Shemos* 22:21) tells us that this is indeed so. The starting point of the verse is the protection Hashem affords to widows and orphans: "*Kol almanah veyasom lo se'anun* — You shall not cause pain to any widow or orphan." But this protection extends much farther. The *Yalkut Shimoni* cites Rabbi Akiva's explanation that the Torah is actually referring to any person at all, and mentions the widow and orphan only because they are defenseless and more vulnerable to attack.

The Torah continues (v. 22): "*Im anei se'aneh oso* — If you [dare to] cause him pain ...!" On these words, the *Yalkut* expounds that it makes no difference whether the pain one inflicted is great or small.

It does not even matter if the victim does not cry out for retribution. "*Ki im tzaok yitzak eilai shamoa eshma tzaakaso* — For if he shall cry out to me, I shall surely hear his outcry." The *Yalkut* explains that the double usage of the word "to cry out" means that Hashem will punish the perpetrator even if the victim does not cry out to Hashem.

The Torah then describes the Divine response to hurting a human being: "*Vecharah api v'haragti es'chem becharev v'hayu nisheichem almanos u'beneichem yesomim* — My wrath shall blaze and I shall kill you by the sword, and your wives will be widows and your children orphans." The *Yalkut Shimoni* adds that not only will the perpetrator die as a result, but even his wife will not be able to remarry. Now, this case refers to where the perpetrator was the husband who died. It is frightening to even contemplate what this portends for one who himself hurts another person.

Clearly, we can never know the ways of Heaven, and no person can ever determine the cause for the pain or suffering of another human being on this world. The prophet Yeshayahu makes this clear: *Ki gavhu shamayim me'aretz kein gavhu de'rachai m'darkeichem u'machshevosai mi'machshevoseichem* — As high as the heavens over the earth, so are My ways higher than your ways, and My thoughts than your thoughts (*Yeshayah* 55:9). But only a fool will ignore, at his own risk, the Torah's and Chazal's vivid description of the possible consequences for one who hurts another human being through word or deed.

But what of the people, and there are many, who sail through life hurting others at will with no apparent Divine response? Doesn't that dispel the conviction that there is a reckoning for every hurt one may inflict on another?

The answer to that seeming contradiction is that not all Divine retribution takes place in this world. HaRav Aharon Leib Shteinman, *shlita* cites the statement of Chazal (*Yevamos* 105b) with regard to Avdan. Avdan was punished severely for embarrassing Rabbi Yishmael, the son of Rabbi Yose. After detailing the discussion between them, the Gemara relates: "Avdan became a leper, his two sons drowned, and his two daughters-in-law annulled their marriages."

Upon seeing Avdan's downfall, Rabbi Nachman said, "Blessed is the Merciful One for punishing Avdan in *this* world" (ibid.). As terrible as Avdan's punishment was, Rabbi Nachman considered it mild compared to what it could have been in the World to Come. There is no doubt that there is retribution; the only question is whether it will be the transient pain of this world, or a deeper, soul-searing pain in the World to Come.

THE MOST DIFFICULT TASK IN LIFE

*H*aRav Aharon Leib Shteinman frequently quotes the Chazon Ish, who said that the lifework of every human being on this world is to live the 70, 80, or 90 years that Hashem allots to him *and not to hurt another human being.*

This is indeed a difficult task, Rav Shteinman agrees, and therefore one must put all his energies and efforts into this very challenge. In addition, he says, the overwhelming majority of *nisyonos* — the authentic challenges of life — pertain to issues between man and his fellow. Even in matters that are truly insignificant, man feels the "me," feels the challenge to his ego, self-esteem or position, and as a result, will lash out. Yet when all is said and done, he or she will bear the brunt of the damage.

The *Talmud Yerushalmi (Demai* 1:3) tells the story of Rabbi Pinchas ben Yair who, on the way to perform the mitzvah of *pidyon shevuyim,* was able to order the river to split so that he could pass. He explained to his disciples, also *Tannaim,* that they would be able to do the same *only* if in their entire life they had never hurt another Jew. HaRav Aharon Leib Shteinman points out that Rabbi Pinchas ben Yair did not condition the ability to split the river on never having transgressed Shabbos or never having eaten non-kosher food, whose punishment is clearly greater. He conditioned it, rather, on having never hurt another Jew.

The challenges and struggles to meet this standard constitute the lifework of a human being. Hashem created powerful drives, a powerful evil inclination and human character traits, and overcoming them is clearly hard work. These mitzvos are harder to keep than mitzvos that are between man and His Creator only.

Thus, it is no wonder that Hillel (*Shabbos* 31a) told the prospective proselyte that the first and most basic rule of Judaism is that one is not permitted to do to his fellow that which he would not wish to undergo himself.

GOOD INTENTIONS MAY BE IRRELEVANT

*I*nteractions with others comprise a territory even more treacherous than already discussed, and that is because, through insensitivity or ignorance, one may hurt another person without even intending to do so. The Mirrer Rosh HaYeshivah, HaGaon HaRav Chaim Shmulevitz, *zt'l,* would often warn that one is culpable even for well-intentioned actions that result in harming one's fellow.

The classic example of this is the story of Chanah and Peninah. Chanah, the mother of the prophet Shmuel, was constantly taunted by Peninah about her barrenness. The sages testify that *"Peninah l'shem Shamayim niskavnah* — Peninah's intentions were for the sake of Heaven" (*Bava Basra* 16a), for she hoped that her taunting would inspire Chanah to pray for children, which in fact she did. Yet because of the mental anguish she caused, Peninah suffered the loss of all of her children (*Pesikta Rabbasi* 44)!

Moreover, Rav Chaim Shmulevitz added, even unwittingly being the cause of another's pain is sufficient reason for punishment. This principle is borne out by the following incident:

Rabbi Rachumi would usually return home every Erev Yom Kippur. Once, he became engrossed in his studies [on Erev Yom Kippur and forgot to return home]. His wife was watching anxiously for him [saying to herself], "Now he is coming, now he is coming." Seeing that he didn't come, she became upset, shedding a tear. Her husband was sitting on a roof; the roof caved in and he died (Kesubos 62b).

One may wonder how the death of Rabbi Rachumi could be seen as a just punishment, for it only brought more suffering upon his wife. If she had been hurt by his tardiness, surely his permanent absence would be unbearable.

In explaining the principles behind Rabbi Rachumi's death, Rav Chaim Shmulevitz states that hurting another person results not only in retribution in the sense of reward and punishment; rather, it is part and parcel of the reality of our existence. As surely as one will inevitably be hurt by a collision with another object, so too, one will inevitably be harmed by injuring another person's feelings. When one puts his hand into fire, it will be burned, countless good reasons for doing so notwithstanding!

This insight places interpersonal relationships in a different light altogether. We cannot excuse our actions by rationalizing our intentions, for whenever we cause anguish there will be retribution. It is a cause-and-effect relationship, in which excuses and rationalizations are irrelevant.

THE FORGIVENESS IMPERATIVE

So what is one to do if one hurts or is the cause of hurt to another human being? He or she is required to request and to receive forgiveness (*Shulchan Aruch Orach Chaim* 206:1). Without that forgiveness, one's *teshuvah,* which is equally crucial, is meaningless.

Shlomo HaMelech (*Mishlei* 6:1-4) makes this clear in no uncertain terms: *"My child ... you have been trapped by the words of your mouth ... Do this, therefore ... and be rescued. Go humble yourself [before him], and placate your fellow. Give not sleep to your eyes, nor slumber to your eyelids."*

It is not always easy to ask for forgiveness. If the deed or deeds were egregious, or if many years have passed, it can often be extremely difficult, sometimes nearly impossible, to ask for and receive forgiveness from the one you have wronged.

But experience has shown that those who are able to overcome these obstacles and to receive forgiveness often merit seeing clearly the Hand of G-d alleviating what were theretofore inexplicable difficulties. People who have exerted and even embarrassed themselves to ask for and receive *mechilah* despite the difficulty, have merited to be married when that had been impossible until then, have been blessed with children shortly thereafter, have had dangerous illnesses disappear and wayward children return to the fold. These are not fantasies. They are well-known phenomena and an endless source of inspiration to those who have had the good fortune of watching these sagas unfold.

In truth it should not be surprising. If the Torah and Chazal describe so clearly the damage one inflicts on himself by hurting another human being, then it is self-evident that if one removes the obstacles, i.e., the punishment or retribution brought to bear on the perpetrator, then a person's natural state of *zechus* and favor in Hashem's eyes will help him lead a happy, successful and productive life.

In fact, enduring the often difficult and demeaning process of obtaining *mechilah* is itself a *zechus* of unfathomable magnitude. Rav Chaim Shmulevitz would often quote Rashi (*Megillah* 15b), that one of the reasons Esther invited Haman to the feasts with Achashveirosh was so that Hashem would see how she had to demean herself to invite the scoundrel to a feast with the King. That alone, Esther was convinced, was enough of a merit to save the entire Jewish People.

Despite the humiliation entailed in seeking forgiveness, there really is no choice. For as the Midrash cited above and the Gemara (*Yoma* 85b) make clear, Hashem does not forget, nor forgive the perpetrator, without the forgiveness of the victim, even decades later. Failure to ask for forgiveness for a hurt inflicted and failure to do *teshuvah* for hurting another human being can haunt one for the rest of one's life, in countless ways and in myriad areas where one has no rational explanation for things that happen and that may seem so unfair.

GRANTING FORGIVENESS

So far we have discussed the obligations of the one who caused the hurt.

On the other hand, the one who was hurt is not off the hook, and cannot choose to remain the eternal "victim." The *halachah* is equally clear that one is forbidden to be cruel, but is rather required to be mollified and provide the requested *mechilah* (*Shulchan Aruch* ibid). Rabbi Moshe Feinstein would stress that one should say clearly that he forgives. (It does not suffice to say, "Oh, I forgot about it," or "I put it behind me," or the like.)

This ruling is based on a statement of Rabbeinu Bachya (*Bereishis* 50:17). Our Sages tell us that the Jewish people suffered over millennia because of the sale of Yosef by his brothers (*Yalkut Shimoni, Mishlei I*). The execution of ten of the greatest *Tannaim* (the *asarah harugei malchus*) was a direct result of the sale of Yosef.

In reality, though, Rabbeinu Bachya points out, Yosef's brothers *did* ask him for forgiveness (verse 17). As the Torah states, Yosef even cried when they requested it (ibid.) and even attempted to "comfort them and speak to their heart" (verses 19-21).

However, explains Rabbeinu Bachya, "We do not find the Torah expressing [explicitly] that *mechilah*. And so the brothers of Yosef died without receiving his explicit forgiveness, and they could not be cleansed of their sin without his forgiveness."

The very act of forgiveness, the Chofetz Chaim writes (*Mishnah Berurah* 206:8), is of great benefit to the person who was wronged. One who is *maavir al midosav*, overcomes his natural inclination to be offended or hurt, merits forgiveness for *all* his sins (*Rosh Hashanah* 17a).

Therefore, we see that *mechilah* is a two-way street. Requesting it, even begging for it and providing it are endeavors that abundantly benefit both the perpetrator and the aggrieved party.

TO THE FULLEST EXTENT POSSIBLE

*B*ut what is a person to do if his realization that there is an imperative to seek forgiveness does not occur until many years after the deed was done? What if he or she no longer knows where the wronged party lives? What if he is aware that many years ago, he may have hurt someone but doesn't remember exactly who, or what he did?

There is a clear directive for these situations from the Vilna Gaon. Rav Shteinman and other *Gedolei Yisrael* cite the *sefer Toldos Adam* authored by a disciple of *talmidei haGra*.

When he was 14 years old, R' Zelmeleh Volozhiner (one of the greatest of the Vilna Gaon's disciples and a brother of Rav Chaim Volozhiner) once inadvertently hurt a simple Jew. The hurt resulted from Rav Zelmeleh's Lithuanian-Yiddish accent, which caused the one to whom he was speaking to think he was making fun of him. Despite Rav Zelmeleh's *best* efforts, including looking for the man in every shul in Vilna, he was unable to locate him. His anguish at being unable to ask and receive forgiveness for an unintended slight was ruining Rav Zelmeleh's life.

When the Vilna Gaon was told of Rav Zelmeleh's plight, he explained to him that the statement of Chazal (*Succah* 52b), that Hashem helps one overcome his evil inclination, applies only to situations in which one has done everything possible to rectify his misdeed. The Vilna Gaon told his disciple that Hashem knew that he had done everything possible to find the aggrieved party, and therefore, He would help by putting forgiveness into that person's heart.

Shlomo HaMelech, the Vilna Gaon explained, expresses precisely this idea when he writes (*Mishlei* 16:7), "*Beretzos Hashem darkei ish gam oyvav yashlim ito* — When Hashem favors a man's ways, even his enemies will make peace with him." So when one has done all he can to find the wronged party and to receive their forgiveness, Hashem will do the rest for him or her.

It is clear, then, that the study and implementation of the laws and situations of *ona'as devarim*, and the scrupulous care not to hurt another person, will serve as a great merit for every individual.

FINDING BETTER WAYS

So where does all this leave us? Our lifework is to avoid hurting our fellow and we have already shown that this is difficult. Doing teshuvah and asking forgiveness is imperative and makes it more difficult still. Yet, we can break the cycle.

We can make a real change by increasing our awareness of the potential pitfalls, arming ourselves with the necessary "weapons" to fight our own inclinations, developing a sensitive heart and a positive mind-set, and finding the strategies that will make the possibility of hurting another individual repulsive.

You have already taken the first step. You have recognized that one's words are a potent force to be reckoned with, and taken the time to learn how to channel this force productively in your life. Through the daily lessons contained in these pages, you have had the opportunity to examine the full impact of the words you speak, and now you have the opportunity to put these concepts into practice. May your journey into the power of words bring abundant blessing to your life, and the lives of all those blessed to be part of your world.